Blood and Soil

BLOOD AND SOIL

THE MEMOIR OF A THIRD REICH BRANDENBURGER

Sepp de Giampietro

Translated by Eva Burke

Introduction by Lawrence Paterson

Greenhill Books

Blood and Soil: The Memoir of a Third Reich Brandenburger

Greenhill Books

Greenhill Books, c/o Pen & Sword Books Ltd,
47 Church Street, Barnsley, S. Yorkshire, S70 2AS, England
For more information on our books, please visit
www.greenhillbooks.com, email contact@greenhillbooks.com
or write to us at the above address.

PUBLISHING HISTORY
Sepp de Giampietro's memoir was originally published under the title *Das Falsche Opfer?*
by Leopold Stocker Verlag, Austria in 1984. This is the first English-language edition and
includes an introduction by Lawrence Paterson.

CIP data records for this title are available from the British Library

ISBN 978-1-78438-341-1

Typeset and designed by JCS Publishing Services Ltd
Typeset in 11.5pt Minion Pro
Printed and bound in Great Britain by TJ International Ltd

Contents

Introduction

Lawrence Paterson

Of all the special forces that saw action during the Second World War, few are as misunderstood as Germany's Brandenburgers. The years between 1939 and 1945 saw the advent and blooding of many variants on the covert commando theme for which Britain became most famous: Churchill's beloved 'butcher and bolt' troops that began formation in 1940 following the British defeat in France and then developed into a ferociously effective new weapon in the Allied arsenal. However, they were predated by the Abwehr's 'Brandenburger' troops, who had already contributed in no small part to Germany's triumph in the West by employing a combination of deception and ruthless combat skills. Yet, by the very nature of the tactics and methodology which the Brandenburgers employed, they remained an elusive and mysterious organisation of which little was known or celebrated. Though components of this famed unit included paratroopers, marines, light infantry and mountain troops, they frequently operated under cover of other unit designations, or in full disguise as enemy soldiers.

As the war years dragged on and Germany's forces were remorselessly ground into virtual oblivion, the Brandenburger units gradually lost their purpose, until employed as spearhead assault troops with correspondingly severe casualty rates. Though effective light infantry, the specialised covert infiltration techniques with which so much Brandenburger success had been gained previously were subsequently rarely required in a war that had become a defensive struggle on every front. Finally, the original core of the Brandenburgers fractured and men were either relegated to Panzer Grenadier status or absorbed into the Waffen SS, which had been struggling to establish its own mirror unit, illustrating the inter-service rivalries that so bedevilled the Third Reich and its military.

I have always found the Brandenburgers fascinating and was fortunate to be given the opportunity by Michael Leventhal at Greenhill Publishing to write what I hoped would be a thorough account of this most unusual unit. For the contemporary student of the Third Reich's military history, such as myself, untangling the web of misinformation regarding the Brandenburgers was difficult, to say the least. What wartime records remain are often fragmentary or cloaked in cover names, leading to frequent misdirection and confusion. Many operations attributed to the Brandenburgers were either non-existent, or in fact carried out by other units of the Abwehr or SS. In some cases, the Brandenburgers became a 'catch-all' training establishment for agents who were employed by other agencies despite having briefly been identified as belonging to the Brandenburger Regiment. Sifting the fact from fiction is as frustrating as it is fascinating.

Consequently, a personal account such as this written by Sepp de Giampietro is invaluable to increasing our understanding of the Brandenburgers as a whole. It is an enthralling tale that begins in 1938 in the small South Tyrolean town of Sterzing that lay a stone's throw from the Austro-Italian border, within the Alps and near to the Brenner Pass. From there De Giampietro emigrated to Berlin after the anticipated incorporation of South Tyrol into the Greater German Reich failed to materialise. Instead South Tyroleans were granted the choice of emigrating from their homeland to Nazi Germany or remaining part of fascist Italy; De Giampietro arrived in Berlin during 1940 determined to soon be in German mountain trooper uniform.

His and his fellow Tyrolean comrades' enlistment in the Wehrmacht's mountain troops leads unexpectedly to membership of the Lehrregiment 'Brandenburg' zbV 800 of which, at first, he appears alternately perplexed and apprehensive. His commanding officer Siegfried Grabert plays a key role in the settling of this young recruit into his new military career and the book provides an illuminating glimpse inside Grabert's own motivations. The chapters that follow offer an unvarnished account of action as a Brandenburger: De Giampietro's active service as a member of the 8th Company beginning in Romania, guarding the Ploesti oil wells, before being committed to combat during the invasion of Yugoslavia and Greece. From there he became embroiled in the covert bridge seizures at the spearhead of Operation Barbarossa: Hitler's all-out gamble as he ordered the Soviet Union invaded. For the following two years De Giampietro took part in some of the most momentous actions on the Eastern Front before being withdrawn from the front line for promotion to the officer rank of *Leutnant* and a return to the Brandenburgers, now stationed in Greece.

The unit which he rejoined had expanded to divisional size and yet was a shadow of its former self – now committed to action as standard light infantry assault troops. Despite preserving elements of the esprit de corps that had permeated the Brandenburgers since their inception, disillusionment with the war itself had already taken root within De Giampietro. 'The war bore no justification,' he writes. 'I suddenly realised this truth, and all its implications, and I was filled with profound sadness.' Nonetheless, he fulfilled his duties with the professionalism of an experienced veteran until, in December 1943, Sepp de Giampietro was badly wounded during the savage fighting against Tito's partisans in Montenegro as part of Operation Kugelblitz. The end of his war and subsequent attempts to return to his homeland from the ruins of a defeated Germany finish what is surely one of the finest first-person accounts of action as part of the Brandenburgers. Sepp de Giampietro paints detailed portraits of many of the unit's most important luminaries, including his commanding officers Siegfried Grabert and Hans-Wolfram Knaak, both of whose names are synonymous with the height of the Brandenburgers' achievements and both of who were killed in action within the Soviet Union.

Concurrent with the detailed description of pivotal battles fought by him and his comrades, Sepp de Giampietro also provides a captivating insight into the mindset of a Tyrolean member of Hitler's Greater German Reich. The complexities of national identity carried by people born in territory deemed Italian since the end of the First World War, but who had remained steadfastly Austro-German, is extremely interesting. This provides further insight into the complex motivating factors of many citizens of the Third Reich who willingly followed Adolf Hitler into the inferno of total war and eventual destruction. Though clearly not a politically driven man, Sepp de Giampietro nonetheless felt an irresistible connection with Germany that defined his choices in life.

This is an extraordinary book that has not been fictionalised to enhance its readability. Such an extravagance is not required. The pages turn willingly as the author takes us on his journey through the inferno of the Second World War as part of one of the most enigmatic special forces units of that time. During the course of writing my own book on the history of the Brandenburgers I found his descriptive prose of great assistance in filling gaps in our knowledge of the unit's operations, as well as our understanding of the men who carried them out. The rare personal photographs included within his account add the perfect finishing touches, as names become faces and the reality of the action is brought yet more vividly to life.

This book is an important addition to the already extensive quantity of literature related to the Second World War, let alone the Wehrmacht and its specialist Brandenburger commando unit. It is not only action-packed, but accurate in its retelling of incredibly daring exploits undertaken at the tip of the German spearhead within the Balkans and Soviet Union. Furthermore, Sepp de Giampietro's emotional journey from idealistic ethnic-German to veteran Wehrmacht officer provides fresh illumination of a subject frequently written on, but just as frequently misunderstood. Perhaps his own subtitle for the original German version of this book will serve to underline this complex path: 'A South Tyrolean (in the Brandenburg Division) between his Conscience and the Berlin–Rome Axis'.

I dedicate this book to my hometown Sterzing,
a place to which I am inextricably tied through my memories.

Translator's Preface

Eva Burke

If parts of this book, especially the beginning, sound romantic, even elegiac and mournful in tone, it is not due to a fanciful translation. Rather, it very much fits the mindset of the South Tyrolean German-speaking community of that time, and of Sepp de Giampietro in particular. He was a German patriot par excellence, but grew up in a South Tyrol that throughout its history had a deeply divided sense of identity – his name, a composite of German and Italian, exemplifies this split and complex background.

Young South Tyroleans, especially those whose family, like Sepp's, were 'Optanten', grew up enveloped in nineteenth-century German Romanticism. This was a cultural movement whose key components were deep-rooted emotional attachments for German art, literature, music, folklore, history – and their homeland.

This is key to understanding the early lives of Sepp and his compatriots and their nationalism. It is also key to grasping the 'timbre' and style with which they spoke, thought and wrote. This English translation strives to reflect this. Thus, the first part of his book is not narrated in a strictly military or aggressive style, which one might expect a soldier to write in. Rather, the tenor of Sepp's German narration of this early period still harks back to the wistful Romantic genre of that particular school of nineteenth-century writers such as Goethe (Sepp's favourite writer).

Along with Sepp's later deployment in Russia and his engagement in heavy military operations, which constitute the middle section of the book, his writing style moves to a more abrupt tone: shorter sentences, factual accounts, cold and emotionally detached, as if the Russian climate – winter or summer – had erased both the feelings characteristic of the Romantic period and their linguistic expressions.

The third and last part of the book sometimes seems repetitive, with Sepp belabouring the point of how he doubted the meaning of war and how he felt betrayed. Anxious to convince the reader of his realisation that Hitler ultimately deceived his people, that they were victims in this war and not the culprits, Sepp leaves behind the language of the battleground. Short sentences of the previous chapters conveying blind obedience are now replaced by the language of existential questioning and lengthy introspective musings.

Sepp's repetitions suggest a subtext that speaks the unspeakable: actions hard to describe in words, partisan fights with horrifying details, atrocities that Sepp – who may or may not have been part of them – would not have been able to capture with language itself. My task was therefore to reveal these subtexts to the reader, to translate what is hidden. I hope that I managed to deal with this challenge to some degree by offering endnotes intended to direct the reader to what in fact happened in the towns and communities either before, during or after Sepp's unit arrived and who the officers were. What was the fate of the prisoners of war Sepp drove past in his Opel Blitz? What was the fate of German communities in the east, the fate of the Jewish inhabitants, indeed of entire Jewish communities? What was involved in the partisan operations where Sepp got wounded? Such events and operations have only more recently been explored in the historical narrative of the Second World War and are rarely found in military letters, memoirs or reports by eye witnesses.

Some explanation is also offered with respect to the cultural context of the Third Reich, with its unique educational system and social norms reflected in concepts particular to Nazi Germany.

As a Brandenburger, Sepp, as far as we learn, was not at the core of SS operations and thus I translated where possible his military lingo with its English equivalents and did not leave them in the original German. This is to attempt to differentiate Sepp's language from the language used by the Nazis. This notwithstanding, I've tried, where appropriate, to create an authentic dialogue exchange between Sepp and his comrades with their own unique slang, including the military's love of acronyms, and Sepp's local dialect.

Many weapons were manufactured and deployed by the German army for the first time in the Second World War, and these are left in German, whilst explained and expanded on in the endnotes.

Geographic places are referred to as much as possible in English, but the reader might want to remember that the towns' names, and their fortunes, changed frequently throughout the early part of the twentieth century between Russian, Romanian, Hungarian, Polish, Ukrainian or German, depending on who was governing them at the time.

Foreword

When the years of wild youth fade into the past, and the decades of strenuous labour yield a measure of success, the first signs of weariness and age set in, and sooner or later every man longs to sit beneath a chestnut tree, to enjoy the setting sun and indulge in quiet, uninterrupted reflection.

With time running out, when one's inner strength is all but exhausted and motivation is lost, little else remains but memories. We review the years gone by, the times when we were young and once more everything we accomplished in our lives, everything that was meaningful to us at the time and all that we believed in pass before our eyes and trigger memories. What was once a minor event may all of a sudden become significant to us, and without warning comes the moment when one feels virtually obliged to put everything down in writing, to preserve it forever as an image of a tragic, entangled, but nonetheless meaningful period of one's life – one that has left an indelible imprint.

My name has never given rise to headlines; my life, throughout, has remained modest and inconspicuous. I am therefore committing my memories to paper without any ulterior motive. Nor do I wish to influence or lecture anyone. I wish to offer my personal narrative, describe what shaped my youth and which influences affected me, to reflect on what I believed in and what I fought for. I want to depict how I personally lived through the war as an insignificant soldier of the German Wehrmacht. I want to speak about death, the worries, fears and hopes which weighed upon this Landser every single day and every single hour of his life.[1] I simply wish to recount how it really was, and to do so without hatred – hatred I never bore against anyone – and devoid of fanaticism or political opportunism, neither of which was ever part of my character.

Those who read these pages may form their own opinions about a time which changed the world, and about us men who were thrust into the midst of a cyclone.

— ONE —

Sterzing, 1938

On this rainy Sunday morning any observer, even an inattentive one, would have noticed that a surprisingly large number of Sterzing townspeople had decided to take an extended walk. The observer would have been even more surprised to see these men, who had left their homes early in the morning accompanied by their wives, soon take leave of them and head off, while the women went by themselves to attend the Sunday morning services. The observer would have also noticed that these men, leaving town and going in all different directions, did not behave in the carefree manner one tends to associate with a Sunday stroll; averting their eyes, their behaviour invited a degree of suspicion.

They walked with a sense of urgency, carefully choosing remote and rarely used paths and fields in order to avoid meeting acquaintances or out-of-towners, encounters which would inevitably have led to the customary exchange of questions and answers. On this day, however, nobody felt like chatting, nor was anyone keen on being stopped and explaining themselves.

On this wet autumn morning the town had not yet awoken. Lanes and streets were empty, nobody peered out of windows or houses, and no one was there to remark on some of their neighbours being out and about. Thus, nobody noticed when the men – having headed in different directions – shortly thereafter made a detour, converging on the same destination.

Sterzing is a small medieval village nestled at the foot of the Alpine Brenner Pass, where the Pfitschertal in the east and the Jaufental in the west lead to the legendary swampy Sterzing Moss. To the south, the entire Sterzinger basin is enclosed by two hills facing each other, each dominated by a medieval castle erected on its peak. The final destination of these morning travellers was the Reifenstein Castle, situated on the hill on the left, which was not very high but broad.

I too was headed that way.

When I was younger, I had ridden my bicycle countless times along the narrow dam across the Eisack which forces the turbulent river to run in a straight line towards the south. Every single bush, tree and stone was familiar to me. I used to cycle absolutely everywhere, carefree and without a worry in the world. I knew every single house, every meadow and every fence – each one reminding me of an adventure or childish prank.

Today, however, much was going to change in my young life.

I felt an unfamiliar tension take hold of me. All of a sudden, this old and friendly landscape seemed different. No longer was I the happy-go-lucky lad cycling around the area whistling a cheerful tune. Today was different. A new emotion engulfed me, a mixture of agitation and excitement. I sensed that a new part of my life was about to begin, that I was to face tasks and duties which had hitherto been entirely unimaginable to me. This strange and indefinable sensation made everything I had experienced up until now seem bland and insignificant. Something secretive, dangerous and forbidden enveloped everything; it was intoxicating. I was fascinated by the prospect that a small and insignificant young fellow like me would be called on to fight for a great and important purpose. Although I couldn't actually do much with these sensations, a strong desire for adventure attracted and gripped me. The truth was, these feelings were going to determine the rest of my life.

The political events of the previous years, which had given rise to great polarisation and upheaval in Germany, had naturally had an impact on South Tyrol as well. In Germany, Adolf Hitler had come into power with the aim of establishing the Grossdeutsche Reich – the Greater German Reich. This concept of uniting all Germans into one Reich, convincingly conveyed as it was, inevitably filled the South Tyroleans with hope. Citizens of this southern corner of German soil had longed for the moment when they could rid themselves of Italian foreign rule. There was no question in their minds that this could only be achieved with the help of Germany.

After the end of the First World War, Austria had ceased to be a political power. It had withered into a minor state, lacking any international standing. The country's economic situation had deteriorated to such an extent that it too turned towards the newly strengthened Germany, hoping to receive the Reich's help. Indeed, after its annexation by Germany, the country had ceased to exist as an independent state, and even the name 'Austria' had disappeared, making way for 'Ostmark', as it would henceforth be known. Austrians had ceased to be Austrians, and instead had become Germans. Little wonder then that the South Tyrolean population also no longer considered themselves as simply Tyrolean, and thus Austrian. They now saw themselves as German, pure and simple.

It is not difficult to understand why the image of a Greater Germany that was to become a unifying home for all Germanic tribes was attractive to the South Tyroleans; 'Ein Volk, ein Reich' (One People, One Nation) was the leitmotiv which not only greatly excited all German ethnic minorities, but truly enraptured them. The plan that one single Reich would encompass all Germans was crafted on a grandiose scale. These were times when all the nations of the world seemed to express an exaggerated version of nationalism, and so it is easy to understand why the Germans too would wish to see their desire for one nation become a reality, all the more so in view of the fact that other European nations had already achieved national unity.

And so it was that Adolf Hitler set out to create this Reich by bringing home, one by one, those ethnic groups which had been separated from and lost to Germany after the end of the First World War. The time for 'returning home' – *Heim ins Reich* – had come for the South Tyroleans. And why not? South Tyrol had been a German land through and through and its population deeply rooted in prehistoric Germanic ancestry. It was only the miserable Treaty of Saint-Germain that had placed the area into the hands of Italy, which in turn swiftly moved to annex the region.[1] What possible reason could there be to exclude, of all places, South Tyrol from the Greater German Reich? Weren't the words of the national anthem proof that this area was German to the core: '... Von der Etsch bis an den Belt' ('... From the Adige to the Belt')? And weren't these the exact words which erupted from millions of enraptured mouths during those huge rallies declaring German unity?

The light drizzle had stopped. A fresh wind blew down from the Brenner, gradually pushing the clouds up the mountains. I pedalled harder, not so much to warm myself up – indeed I was too excited to even feel the cold – but rather to close the remaining distance to Reifenstein Castle. The closer I got to my final destination, the more my excitement grew.

Finally, I reached the path that ascended to the castle and I got off my bicycle. A young bored-seeming lad was leaning against the fence at the side of the path. I knew him by sight but didn't know him personally. I decided to be cautious. We exchanged a few words; in passing, I mentioned the code word 'Rosengarten' and he let me pass. This turned out to be the first in a chain of security posts in place around the castle. It quickly became obvious to me that all the access roads were discreetly manned and there was no possibility that anyone unwanted or unannounced could approach further than was desirable.

I pushed my bike up the slope and passed through the gate into the empty courtyard. Once again, I was met by a youth but, unlike the previous one, he asked me directly for the code word without skirting the issue. Satisfied with my response, he instructed me to park my bike in a shed. I did as requested and then climbed up a creaking wooden staircase which finally led me to the great hall.

Not many people had gathered there yet. Those who had were clustered together in small groups, deep in discussion. I knew most of them. I spotted the local blacksmith, a short, burly sort of man, middle-aged, with massive hands and sharp features. His forehead and cheeks were covered in countless tiny scars where hot sparks had flown off the iron as he pounded it into shape. To this day I can still see him standing at his dimly lit forge, protected by a heavy leather apron, his shirt unbuttoned, swinging his heavy blacksmith's hammer. There would soon be many times when I would look to him, take his orders and discuss plans or pass on messages and news items. He was one of the leaders of this circle.

Then there was the joiner: a tall, lean man, always friendly and thoughtful, considerate throughout. In spite of having a prosthetic leg he was surprisingly mobile. Not once did he baulk at joining us on strenuous journeys to distant farms where we were lectured and educated by a handful of farmers. He was the central authority who collated the different threads of information to form the content of all the orders. He was the political leader of the circle.

Merchants, as they called themselves, gathered there as well. In reality they were little more than small-scale traders who owned a grocery or corner shop in the old part of town that could barely yield a daily income. That was about the extent of their commercial enterprise. Skilled labourers were also among the crowd, unassuming and honest; you could also find the odd guild master who came with his apprentice. Alongside them stood the farmers. Not the wealthy landowners – there weren't any in the mountains any more – these were lowly peasants, often quite poor, who toiled the meagre and steep fields in order to put food into the mouths of their large families. They had descended to the valley to hear whether the time had come to fight for their country once again.

The intention was to create an illegal political movement. These men could relied upon to help, their leaders were destined to head up the new organisation which the Italian Fascist forces were intent on destroying in any way they could.

I knew practically all of the men gathered there – at least by sight, if not personally. I greeted everyone with a firm handshake and gleaming eyes, hoping to convey my delight at being counted as an equal among this circle of conspirators. It made my heart swell with pride. Among the groups stood some men with whom I was not yet acquainted. The names they gave, usually just a first name, were generally not their real names and only served as a cover. Not even later on would I ever get to find out their real names, even though I frequently met up with them, and even though their assumed identities became well known throughout the country. They were the heads of the illegal national leadership who had arrived from Bozen to carry out, within the framework of the underground movement, the orders meant to ready the Sterzing district for the liberation of South Tyrol.

More and more people were arriving. Soon all the chairs and benches in the hall were occupied. Finally, the head of the county emerged from a group of people that had surrounded him closely. Leaning on his walking stick, he moved slowly towards the front of the room, where a table had been prepared. The hall immediately fell silent and every man lined up and stood to attention. Raising his right arm, he briefly greeted those assembled and asked them to take a seat. Nobody uttered a word. You could tell he had everyone's fullest attention.

He talked about the rise of the Greater German Reich which was to encompass all German tribes and groups. He alluded to us South Tyroleans, reminding everyone that we belonged to this people, and that we formed the southernmost bulwark of the Reich. The Saarland and Austria had already been incorporated. Soon the return home of the Sudeten Germans would become a reality and then – yes, *then* – the hour of our liberation would strike. He said that every single one of us had to muster all our energy to make this goal a reality and rouse our national comrades into action. Much work lay ahead of us and would require our unconditional and total commitment. Without exception, we had to be ready to make any and all sacrifices demanded to prove ourselves worthy of belonging to the Greater German people and the Greater German Reich.

'We send our greetings to our brethren north of the Alps,' he concluded, 'separated from us only by a fragile frontier that too will soon fall, as did the other frontiers separating Germans from Germans. *Kampf Heil! Kampf Heil! Kampf Heil!*'

The entire hall shook with awe and respect. Surely he had never seen such determined men, men who had been prepared to enter battle since the Middle Ages. So thunderous was the acclaim that it resounded outside the hall into the open air, reaching far across the countryside. We had all jumped up from our seats.

It did not take much to ignite national enthusiasm in those times. Germany, defeated, bled dry and humiliated, had been raised up once more by Adolf Hitler. With his firm hand, Hitler had taken the reins, harnessed the people and spurred them on, to the sound of loud fanfares and drum rolls. Nobody cared much where this was leading: surely the future would be better than what they had now and would spell freedom for them all. Their belief in the power of their leader knew no bounds.

Young and old, men and women, everyone wanted to be part of this surge forwards into the Greater German future. No one could help but feel part of it. Many, and we South Tyroleans were among them, wanted almost obsessively to be actively involved. We South Tyroleans wanted to leap straight into the fray. We were the last ones to be called and came running, desperately hoping to grasp an outreached hand that would pull us out of the depths we were in. Our greatest desire was to not be forgotten, to not be left behind while the entire German people was on the brink of greeting the new dawn.

We were even prepared to ignore any misgivings or uneasiness which might have held us back, just to keep up with the accelerating momentum. We did not foresee where this journey was leading us. Only a few realised how it would end, and rare was the voice raised in warning.

Who would even have been capable of halting a raging torrent, an avalanche or a stream of lava by mere conjuring of words or pleas? Those who put themselves in the way of nature's powerful forces will just get swept up by the tornado and disappear.

Apart from a very few men who were insightful but weak, and lacking both in influence and the necessary authority, we South Tyroleans didn't really want to call a halt to anything. On the contrary, we used all our strength and all our power to jump onto this wagon. What we saw in Germany was our ideals, our hopes and our future. Such was our longing for freedom that we put all our expectations into Germany – into a Germany that in the end didn't actually raise a finger to nurture the hopes germinating in the South Tyrolean people. In fact, the opposite was true: the political leaders in Germany perceived the nationalistic feelings of South Tyrol as unwelcome and embarrassing. To them, the Berlin–Rome Axis was far more important than the hopes for liberty expressed by some 250,000 South Tyrolean farmers. The geographical location of South Tyrol, at the very far end of the Reich, was of little strategic importance and therefore did not lie within Hitler's interests. Besides, Mussolini was Germany's only potential ally, and thus supporting

South Tyrol proved much too high a price for Germany to pay as it threatened the alliance with Italy.

It would have required a true genius to untangle this delicate political situation and be able to analyse the circumstances candidly, someone whose intellectual horizons lay far beyond the borders of the South Tyrolean mountains, and whose autonomous stature was such that he could make unpopular decisions and do whatever it took.

Where could such a man be found? Did he even exist? Nobody thought of looking at the situation with the clarity of mind that would have been a precondition for correct and consistent action. Alas, any such considerations were simply pushed aside and not followed to their logical conclusions. Everyone baulked at the merest suspicion that South Tyrol might be nothing but a worthless tool that would be chucked away by the political powers. Indeed, such a thought never arose even once anywhere. The gap between fantasy and political reality was far too wide. Emotions far outweighed the realities; in fact, they were running so high that even when events occurred that entirely contradicted the idealised goals, they were easily excused and wilfully misinterpreted somehow to fit the fantasy.

For me, a young high-school student at the time, this two-day training course was of enormous interest. It was the first time that I had even heard about the Germanic tribes and their customs and traditions, their edifices, their migrations and settlements. It was also the first time I learned about the Baiuvarii, who had come across the Brenner, cleared our land and settled on it.[2] I learned more about Tyrol's history, about Andreas Hofer, the leader of the peasants, about his men and his achievements.[3] The First World War was, on the other hand, quite familiar to me, having listened intently to the stories of my father, who had been a Kaiserjäger and fought on the Italian front.[4] I had grown up during the miserable post-war years and knew about this period of history, albeit only from the Italian perspective, and as taught in the Italian schools.

This was my opportunity to understand the political relationships from the German perspective. It was the start of my seeing things with open eyes and making sense of so much that had been incomprehensible to me until then. It was all buzzing around in my head, and first I simply had to make some order of it all. I had been flooded with too many impressions and in too brief a time span. It was fine to demand and expect enthusiasm from me, that I prove my commitment and willingness to make sacrifices. Yes, I was ready to offer it all, except for one thing: political judgement. I had none. I felt that my enthusiasm to contribute towards the magnificent rise of the German people was sufficient reason to devote myself fully and utterly to this movement.

Dusk was falling and the light filtering through the frosted stained-glass windows had become dim. It was already dark in the great hall where we stood in rows; the end of this unforgettable day was drawing to a close.

We held each other's hands in an unbroken chain as a symbol that we were all united by a single idea. Thus we formed a secret brotherhood determined to fight unconditionally for South Tyrol's freedom. With hushed voices we intoned the German anthem and all of us, firmly gripping the hands of our neighbours, sang the words '... Von der Etsch bis an den Belt', '... From the Adige to the Belt'. Tears ran down our cheeks.

The next months were filled with restless activity. With an enthusiasm typical of a young man, I set to work. I was tasked with putting together a youth group, with organising and training them in different sports that would prepare them for all kinds of assignments. But first, I had to go through my own training. I had no idea how to go about anything.

Our approach, above all, had to be extremely cautious. The Fascist authorities would soon detect that something was afoot, that an organisation was active and becoming increasingly so. Even though we didn't embark on any violent action and tried to minimise provocation – in fact we did everything we could to avoid that – nobody could have ignored the fact that something was brewing in the German people. Wearing a white apron or short lederhosen was much more than just a fashion statement: it was a public statement, an expression of a political stance. As the black corduroy trousers became fashionable, along with the white shirt – as the Hitler Youth wore – there was no longer any doubt that there was a distinct 'uniform'. For the women and girls, the dirndl signified both their ethnic affiliation and their political position.

Pressure from the Fascists became increasingly heavy. Attempts to suppress every expression of German tradition multiplied. The singing of even the most harmless *Gstanzl* was forbidden.[5] Even speaking German was almost considered a crime. The Italian authorities intervened randomly. Arrests were made, endless interrogations and all sorts of harassing and brutal methods of intimidation were employed. People were banished from the area and expelled to southern Italy for many years. Heavy was the yoke of Fascism our land had to endure.

It turned out, however, that all the punitive measures taken against even the slightest expression of German culture or nationalism proved unsuccessful.

In fact, they achieved the exact opposite. These petty Fascist dictators who exercised absolute rule over each city were always left groping in the dark during their indiscriminate attacks. In their fight against the gradual emergence of the South Tyrolean population's self confidence, they were never once able to claim a concrete victory. We would challenge every violent incident, and thus the result was quite the opposite to the intended outcome. South Tyrol never engaged in any violence itself, and not a single noteworthy demonstration to propagate the will of the people was organised. The smouldering fire of the illegal South Tyrolean movement was deliberately kept on a slow burner by right-wing German forces. In fact, Germany did not promote the South Tyrolean desire for freedom; on the contrary, it tried to curb it. For Hitler, there had always been an issue with South Tyrol. It would only have proved an inconvenience had a problem actually arisen. According to Hitler, Austria had betrayed South Tyrol by signing the peace treaty at Saint-Germain, and that rather put an end to the issue in his mind. It even went beyond that: as he wrote in *Mein Kampf*, he believed that the idea that Germans would spill their blood for some 200,000 South Tyroleans was virtually criminal (*Mein Kampf*, p. 711).

All of us knew this – or at least we should have known it. *Mein Kampf* was considered to be something close to the Bible at the time, and everyone had access to it. Nothing that was written in that book bothered us. We refused to take note of what was happening around us and what the facts were on the ground. We simply couldn't comprehend that we were too unimportant, too insignificant a group of people, who didn't even warrant the minimal support we thought we were entitled to from our German brethren. We, on the other hand, were prepared to sacrifice it all, without hesitation, and especially for the German people. The fact that Germany, according to its alliance policy, did not support us in any shape or form, and instead was keen to dampen our legitimate demands, was interpreted by us as a pure stroke of genius on the part of Hitler. We listened to each of his speeches intently, we read each sentence written in the papers, desperately seeking some sign of a covert reference to our problems. It hurt that we couldn't find anything that would have vindicated our deeply felt beliefs, but still we ignored the reality and simply turned the silence on its head, interpreting it as proof that somewhere, something was secretly being organised that would one day suddenly strike us all like a bolt from the blue. Those were the expectations we had of the Führer, that's what we believed he would do. Such was our conviction of the just legitimacy of our demands that we rejected as absurd any argument which attempted to sway us. Any assumption which did not coincided with our fanciful dream of *Heim ins Reich* – back home to the Reich – would have been interpreted by us as hostile enemy propaganda. Indeed, we would have immediately branded such objections as pure manipulation and as proof that the exact opposite was true.

The area was engulfed by an utopian idea. More and more sections of the population came to believe in it. Fertilised by the fervour of this national enthusiasm, South Tyrol ripened like a fruit, waiting to fall into the lap of the German *Volksgemeinschaft*.[6] Here was South Tyrol, offering itself up to the German Reich on a platter; a shining, noble and faithful jewel. Yet the Führer basically saw us as an uninvited and cloying relative who insisted on persevering within the fold of the family.

In my mind, no such political problems even existed. I wasn't interested in more serious politics and, admittedly, I didn't understand much of it anyway. My youthful goals were still set low and only really referred to our own daily lives. The assignments given to me dominated my entire thinking and all my actions. These were years filled with hard work. The starkly contrasting schools of thought with which I was being confronted all the time demanded constant manoeuvring so as not to come crashing down from the precipitous cliffs lurking above me.[7]

In the meantime, I had managed to finish high school and was approaching, whether I liked it or not, the Matura examinations.[8] At my school, the history that was taught was moulded by Fascist ideology and current events, and in order to pass my exams I needed to interpret these in line with the prevailing thinking while adapting my behaviour to the current climate. I thus felt coerced to join the Fascist youth movement known as 'Giovani Fascisti' and participate in their educational programme and events. The training we had to undergo as Giovani Fascisti was paramilitary, and I truly hated it.[9] The demonstrations and marches organised on national holidays – where we had to march through the town dressed in our uniforms and line up in strict battalions – were for me moments of deep depression. Added to this was the humiliation of being ordered to carry the Fascist flag of my school on these parades; I felt I had reached rock bottom. But the second these grotesque demonstrations came to an end, nothing would stop me from immediately changing from the Fascist uniform, identifying me as Italian, into my lederhosen, swapping my black shirt for a white one and rushing off to one of our illegal movement's secret gatherings.

While the Roman salute horrified me, I enthusiastically performed the Nazi salute by raising my right arm. While I had only silently mimed the words of the Fascist song 'Eia-eia-alala', I thunderously shouted out the lyrics of 'Kampf Heil'. When attending the Fascist parade, I deliberately placed myself in the middle of a row, held my head bent low and listlessly traipsed along; but when marching with my youth group along the distant mountain paths, I was a different person, holding myself straight and proud, and leading the others. These contrasting emotions and their associated psychological pressures were enormous.

The political aspects of Fascism and National Socialism, of dictatorship and democracy, never gave rise for contemplation, and certainly not for discussion among us South Tyroleans. We had absolutely no interest in the political or social structure of the state. Our thoughts, feelings and actions were purely shaped by nationalist ideas and expectations. The political, social and economic problems only dawned on us in the course of time.

The colonial dictatorship as practised by Fascist Italy was, as of course is common to every tyrannical power, by its very nature suppressive, often brutal and always humiliating. What the Fascists did – and it was stupid – was to 'italianise' the country and its population by force, as quickly and as thoroughly as possible. The fact that these attempts yielded no fruit, and indeed failed miserably, is hardly surprising. We were too young and too uneducated to understand the core of the Fascist doctrine and the National Socialist ideology. Our whole spiritual education was in the hands of people who held very contrasting viewpoints. On the one side there was the purely German education at the parental home, on the other side was the overwhelming Italian Fascist education provided by the teachers of our schools.

And because young people only manage to deal in extremes, unaware of potential compromises that could be made, and were only capable of taking action based purely on feelings, at the expense of objective and thoughtful reflection, nothing but a radical separation was the only option: you were either going to be a German or an Italian. Thus, the illegal union in South Tyrol was not an actual political party but rather a national movement for freedom. For us, the National Socialist ideology was just as unimportant as the Fascist one; we cared as little about the construct of a dictatorship as about democracy. We were, and felt ourselves to be, totally German, and we wanted to remain so under all circumstances. We accepted anything which was German or came from Germany, and we agreed with everything without giving it further thought. And yet, we were never National Socialists in the party-political manner of speaking – we were simply German. Just as the Fascist indoctrination failed vis-à-vis the South Tyroleans, so did the political instruction attempted by the Germans later on during the resettlement and war period also prove unsuccessful.

There were other secret gatherings which followed on from the one held at Reifenstein Castle, and I attended them all with the same enthusiasm and devotion I had felt the first time. I was utterly consumed by the sports camps held in concealed and remote mountain areas where we were free to compete with our peers, undisturbed, singing German folk songs together to our heart's content and practising our German folk dances. Whatever I learned during these training courses I would later use in my own social circle.

Sterzing had a sawmill. Under it there was a narrow room about twenty metres long where sawdust collected from the timber was stored. You could reach it by climbing through a hatch. Once all the sawdust from that day had been shovelled into a corner, a small empty space was available where some five to six boys could manage to exercise. Depending on how much sawdust there was, we could even do some jogging. Jumping was never possible, however, as the room was far too low. That space was our gymnasium.

We boys would meet there at night. Here, in this forsaken dungeon, we did our physical training and organised games and sports. We couldn't accomplish much in this space other than these exercises. There were never usually more than eight or nine of us, but sometimes maybe a dozen. One of us had to stand guard outside. Although there was hardly any chance that somebody would pass by, since the sawmill lay on the outskirts and the access road was unlit, we didn't want to run the risk and, besides, it turned our nocturnal gathering into an adventure. At the first sign of danger, the guard had to knock briefly on the floorboards. The moment his foot even slightly touched the boards, so much dust fell from the ceiling downstairs that it was virtually impossible to ignore the alarm. We immediately turned off the small lamp which dimly lit the room and remained motionless, listening intently until a fresh downpour of sawdust signalled that we were no longer in danger. But nothing serious ever happened. In any case, our gatherings were much too small to arouse anybody's suspicion. Only in our young and fanciful minds did they feature as important contributions to the fight for our homeland's freedom. To conclude our weekly sports event we sang the national anthem, the 'Deutschlandlied', softly and gently, ending our conspiratorial activity with 'Heil Hitler'. Each on our own, we sneaked back home. Our chests were filled with the proud feeling that we had accomplished something big for our people, for the Greater German Reich, and against the Italians.

During the summer these exercise and sport events took place outdoors. We didn't meet up in that dark dungeon any more, but cycled to concealed spots along the watery meadows of the Mareiter river. In the early hours of the morning, and without drawing any attention, we could practise cross-country running, long jumps in the sandy riverbank and shot-putting with stones we found on the beach, of which there were plenty. We had no equipment, and our only possession was a medicine ball. We had received it from somebody who wanted to entrust it to a person who would look after it. Apparently, he came from Germany – a sign of solidarity of the German people with us South Tyroleans. We were proud of it and knew that we had not been forgotten and written off. If it was true that the medicine ball had actually come to us from Germany, then it was the most important support our freedom movement had ever received from the homeland.

Once or twice 'mass rallies' were organised. There were plenty of pastures in our mountains which allowed gatherings of some 100 to 150 people to take place – there couldn't have been more – without running the risk of unwelcome disturbances. These 'rallies' were modelled after those of the Sturmabteilung (SA) and the Hitler Youth. With his group lined up in an open-ended square, the individual Gruppenführer reported proudly to their commander. Short speeches followed, after which the group immediately dissolved, as it would have alerted any unexpected passer-by that a political gathering was happening. We then sat around casually in groups singing local Tyrolean songs. The cultural 'cells' then performed traditional folk dances and *Schuhplattler*,[10] which they had rehearsed in secret meetings at their private homes, while the youth and sports groups, if not engaged in security, reporting or guard duty, demonstrated their skills in improvised competitions.

These events were hardly ever interrupted. If some hiker chanced by, or if a carabinieri patrol was spotted far away, the boys immediately dispersed. We ran in all directions and returned to our valley in small groups.

Those gatherings on remote pastures, when we would sing together German folk songs, perform traditional folk dances and compete in various sport disciplines – all being organised within a loose paramilitary framework – encapsulated the harmless displays of our Germanness. There was nothing else or nothing different that we really wanted. We were neither revolutionaries nor irredentists. We didn't have any of the practical prerequisites for that. In short, there was nothing our hearts desired other than to be and to remain German. Of course, the German Reich's growing national awareness, which pursued distant goals with hope and blind enthusiasm, and which seemed to make rapid progress, also engulfed us South Tyroleans. There was no chance that the watershed of the Alps could stem the waves of nationalism flooding Germany.

Mussolini's regime was certainly well aware of the fact that South Tyrol had awakened to the drumbeat of National Socialist propaganda, and that a German national movement had begun to spread in the country. Something, they thought, had to happen, and something did happen: any and all signs of Germanness were suppressed while the alliance between Germany and Italy was being consolidated. The Fascists were easily able to translate this policy into action as they had nothing to fear from Germany's side. No protest, no admonition, no wagging finger was to be expected, and certainly no reprisals. Officially, Germany had absolutely no interest in South Tyrol, which for its part was simply yearning for freedom and prepared to offer itself up with the utmost deferential modesty to prove itself the most faithful of all German ethnic minorities.

Germany offered little more than nice words and empty promises – which were only offered by obsequious propagandists and functionaries – to feed the German national consciousness of the South Tyroleans. For Hitler, South Tyrol was neither an ethnic nor a territorial problem. All those nationalistic German demonstrations from this insignificant ethnic group achieved was to cast an embarrassing shadow over the shiny Axis connecting Berlin with Rome. However, the efforts and input made by the Verein für das Deutschtum im Ausland (VDA) and South Tyrol, should not be forgotten (one need only remember Steinacher).[11]

In the meantime, we South Tyroleans enthusiastically dwelt in the land of fantasy. We deliriously embraced our future mission of acting as the southernmost stronghold of the German Reich! We had no space in our minds for any thoughts other than the wondrous and beautiful duty which beckoned us! Our future was based on dreams, not on reality.

— TWO —

The Big Disappointment

Months went by. The German Reich grew bigger every day, as did Hitler's power. Surely our time had come, now that Austria had been annexed? How could Hitler not remember, turn to us and bring our country home? The annexation of South Tyrol would be swift and without complications. Hitler and Mussolini would agree on that between themselves. It would be an internal matter among friends, and we were convinced that this was bound to happen. We believed in it. No other solution was possible.

Finally, at the beginning of May 1938, the moment had come. Hitler wanted to visit his friend Mussolini. Our imaginations ran wild. He was going to visit the Italian capital in order to be presented with South Tyrol by the Duce as a sign of friendship. A gift that would cost Mussolini little. The Berlin–Rome Axis was 'made of steel' and strategic borderlines between the German and Italian people were not needed any longer.[1] The frontier along the Brenner Pass was, at least from a strategic perspective, insignificant. Thanks to their leaders, the two peoples had been brought so close to each other that it was of no interest where a geographic separation was drawn, be it at the Brenner, or 200 kilometres south of it, in Salurn. This was certainly how we thought it was going to be.

Tension grew by the day. Our illegal activities became increasingly less secret, more daring and more intensive. The movement reached ever larger groups, became stronger, and in the end it probably included the majority of South Tyroleans as its members. This was an inevitable development as the concept was really simple – it was understood and experienced by each and everyone: 'We are German and we wish to remain in the German land!' There was surely not a single South Tyrolean who thought differently, nobody who wanted a different outcome, not one who did not long for freedom.

The Italians in the region were growing restless as well. They started behaving towards the German inhabitants with more tolerance and less arrogance. They felt that something was afoot, and the German steel helmets spotted at the Brenner made them nervous. Unlike in previous years, when they had convinced themselves that their claim to the Brenner frontier was legitimate, now they no longer felt so secure. They probably trusted their

Duce, who had just finished building his empire in the face of resistance from the League of Nations, and whose only friend was Germany. But would he be able to overcome all the obstacles? Would the Duce risk testing his strength against Germany just because of South Tyrol? While faith in the future, self-awareness, self-confidence and hope were all steadily on the rise in Germany, doubts, insecurity and resignation took hold among the Italians.

The Brenner railway runs east of Sterzing, along a steep mountain slope referred to as 'the Roaner'.[2] It might have been due to the steep terrain or the lack of water, but the only things that grew naturally there were clover and wild beets. This is where we boys used to head; in the springtime we would dig out fresh roots; in the summer we lured crickets out of their holes; in the autumn we came to steal the juicy turnips. It was no sin to take three turnips from each field, or that's what we once heard someone say. We certainly took advantage of this belief.

Halfway down the hill stood a row of bushes, and in their midst grew a single cherry tree. These cherries never really got to mature properly; the wind coming from the Brenner was much too strong for the fruit to ripen fully. During the spring this tree boasted its full magnificence in blossoms, promising more than it could ever keep. I had dug a small crevice into the steep hill, right under the crown of the tree, and lined it with some flat stones to create a comfortable place for me to sit. This seat, underneath the cherry tree on the hill, became my favourite spot. I had a fantastic view over the whole town, peacefully lying below me. Only once in a while would the scratching sounds of saws from the nearby sawmill reach me, or the noise of a passing train or a roofer's hammer. Those were the sounds of a busy, peaceful and modest small town. I would often sit here for hours, lost in my thoughts as I enjoyed the midday sun. This was my refuge when I was worried about school, or when I had troubles in love. It was this cherry tree in which I confided, and in front of which I would declare the love I didn't dare express to the girl of my dreams, my pain, my joys and hopes and all my desires. And I had lots of them during those years.

This was also the place which allowed me to observe the Führer's train pass by.

The preparations for Adolf Hitler's state visit to Italy were running at full speed. Thousands of swastika flags flew alongside the train track leading from the Brenner to Rome, standing next to the tricolore. At many places banners emblazoned with 'W il Duce' and 'W il Führer' fluttered in the air.[3] Assembled on the platforms of many train stations, even the smallest ones, schoolchildren waving paper flags were assembled to cheer the passing *Sonderzug* and greet Hitler, arms outstretched with the Fascist salute.[4] What a feeling we South Tyroleans had, seeing for the first time the swastika flags blow from church steeples! The Führer was travelling through our country, which soon would become his as well! We were certain that he would stand at the window while crossing the distance between the Brenner and Salurn and wave to us. Maybe one of us would even be so lucky as to actually see him – perhaps even, ever so fleetingly, make eye contact through the glass. We didn't even care that the Führer sped through South Tyrol, and in spite of legions of Fascists waving to him with mixed feelings and a bitter-sweet taste deep inside, we were certain we would bear him aloft and engulf him with thunderous cheers upon his return journey. More than 250,000 would raise their voices to the sky, screaming '*Sieg Heil, Sieg Heil*', '*Ein Volk, ein Reich, ein Führer*', making sure that every single one of our proud mountains, every single peak, would learn of our blazing flame of victory. That was our belief.

Flags with swastikas on them were sewn in secret. There should be one at every window. For now, the Fascists were still able to keep us away from the train track, and there was still time for them to put our fathers into prison just to keep us from making any attempt whatsoever to hand the Führer a petition, a present or even just a greeting card. However, we were convinced that soon the Führer himself would come to us, be with us, take us back home, back into the lap of the Greater German Reich.

However, the reality turned out to be quite different from how I imagined it under the shade of the cherry tree. The Blackshirts and the military drew an impenetrable cordon along the train track. No German was permitted even to come close; in fact, an order was given for all of us to remain in our houses. All demonstrations of support not organised by the Fascist authorities were prohibited. Only Blackshirts and children clad in their Balilla uniforms were permitted to wave to the Führer. Not a single lederhose or dirndl was allowed to be seen from the train window. Nor was a stop-over by the *Sonderzug* on South Tyrolean soil on the schedule. The aim was simply to rush Hitler through the country as fast as possible.

None of the precautions taken by the Italians was actually necessary: when the *Sonderzug* finally did pass through South Tyrol, the Führer could not be seen standing at his window to wave. All the windows remained shut, with their curtains tightly drawn. No South Tyrolean ray of sun could have penetrated. Never would it have occurred to us that the Führer might have specifically asked to travel through South Tyrol with the curtains drawn. How could that be possible, since this man liked nothing more than to see people cheer and glorify him? When we learned later on that the curtains of his train had indeed been drawn at his personal order and that he did not wish to have any contact with the South Tyrolean people, none of us believed it and we simply dismissed the notion as a lie. We were so convinced that our belief in Germany was totally justified that we simply didn't acknowledge anything even faintly negative, or we just suppressed it. We believed only what we wanted to believe.

The minute the Führer was in Rome, I didn't move an inch away from the radio. I followed every single broadcast reporting on the pompous parades, listening to every speech and toast. To me, it all seemed to be empty words and talks about unimportant stuff, but I kept my ears sharply tuned for two words: 'South Tyrol'.

The days passed. Hitler's visit was drawing to an end and there was still no word about our fate.

At long last they announced that a final parade would take place and that Hitler would make a speech. For years we had hoped fervently that this moment would come. All our dreams would come true. Tension grew by the hour. When Hitler took to the microphone, there wasn't a single person on the streets of South Tyrol. Everyone, Italians and Germans alike, was glued to their radios. One side trusted in the Duce, the other in the Führer. Every possibility still seemed to be open. What had the two great men decided? The balance seemed to us to be very much tipped to the German side, even though no concrete signs suggested that this assumption was justified.

Sitting close together, my parents, my sister and a few friends all focused on the Führer's words without making a sound. We didn't want to miss a single syllable. Our hearts beat faster and the tension engulfing us was enormous. And then we heard him speak: 'Both of us [Hitler and Mussolini], in view of the fact that we have now become neighbours, wish to maintain the natural border which providence and history have clearly drawn up for us … My unshakeable will and my legacy to the German people stands, and this Alpine frontier between Italy and Germany, erected by nature, will forever remain untouchable.'

I believe that at this moment our hearts stopped. It was like a hammer blow; it felt like treason. The saviour, to whom we, the drowning people, had beseechingly stretched out our hands, was not coming to our rescue and had left us stranded, leaving us to our fate. The great Führer on whom we had pinned all our hopes, the only one who could have helped us, had now rejected us. He had spurned our love, he had refused and dismissed us, we who had been the most faithful of his followers.

As if that wasn't enough, he forbade the German people from ever lifting a finger for us, even after his death. We, the weakest and smallest, had sacrificed ourselves for his strategic plans and his loyalty to his alliance. We now heard from his own mouth that he didn't want us, not ever. Nobody could possibly ignore these words or misunderstand them – they were clear, and they struck us to the core.

For us South Tyroleans the world collapsed at that moment. Uncomprehending, paralysed, open-mouthed, we just set there staring at each other, stunned and speechless.

The first to recover from the shock was my mother. She jumped up from her chair and threw into a corner the swastika flag she had been in the midst of sewing – the flag she had wanted to be the first to hang out of the window. She screamed at me, turning furiously red: 'You will never put on a brown shirt, never. You will wear a red one, a red one, a red one.' It was the cry of the humiliated, the reaction of the rejected, the rebellion of the scorned. The shock of the disappointment had in one fell swoop turned love into hatred. Hers was not an acute or political insight, but a purely emotional, spontaneous and instinctive declaration made within seconds and while the possible significance still had to sink in. How might South Tyrolean history have evolved if the entire population had reacted in this way? Fundamentally, of course, it was not important to us which colour shirt it would be. We South Tyroleans just didn't care one bit about National Socialism, Fascism or Communism. We weren't bothered by any socio-political problems, we had nothing to do with dictatorships, democracies, republics or monarchies. Everything would fine if only we could be Germans. Which colour Germany wore never really concerned us as long as it did something for our freedom.

To hear those harsh words from the mouth of a man who had declared his goal to be the unification of *all* Germans into one single Reich was deeply wounding and incomprehensible to us. Yet, it was the unambiguous confirmation of what Hitler had always said and had put in writing in *Mein Kampf*. It was just that we South Tyroleans had not understood it, had never wanted to acknowledge it. We had believed in the patriotic slogans of a Greater German Reich, a Greater German people to whom we also thought we belonged, even though Hitler kept saying at every turn that the affairs of the South Tyroleans and their national aspirations meant nothing to him. We had simply believed in our dreams and had made no room for reality.

The shock that resulted from this 'political legacy' virtually paralysed us. We were seized by a sense of perplexity and helplessness, with no support or advice. We were alone and abandoned. We were totally disoriented and had lost all footing. The Führer had made his decision and South Tyrol had ceased to exist. What remained was bitterness and despondency.

And yet, like a faithful dog who never turns on his master and always comes back to him, licking the hand that beat him, so too did we crawl back to our master's feet, in spite of all the whippings we had endured. Never once did we think of reciprocating those beatings with maulings of our own. Even if there was an odd flickering thought of rebellion, it was instantly repressed with a shudder of horror. The very idea seemed too awful. We, who had just been betrayed, found the mere word 'betrayal' so alien and disgusting that we never even considered doing the same in return. We, who believed fidelity to be the highest virtue, would rather accept humiliation than be unfaithful ourselves. We preferred to endure treachery than commit it ourselves.

We soon did everything we could to come up with an explanation which would make Hitler's decision appear to be in our favour. We tried to understand why he had closed the door in our face. We wanted to deceive ourselves. We sought and clung to the most desperate and absurd interpretations, just so as not to have to accept the tragic facts. We swam in the sea of desperation into which our so-called saviour had callously pushed us. Here we were just drifting, dragged along with the last traces of the hope that had been taken away from us.

None of us knew how things would turn out. Suddenly and unexpectedly the Italians here at home had once again got the upper hand. They strutted through the streets, self-satisfied, their chests swelling with pride and a vindictive look in their gloating eyes. 'What is it that you actually want?' they seemed to say. 'Your Führer doesn't want you! So just be happy that you are allowed to stay with us.'

Indeed, what *was* it that we actually wanted? One group didn't want us, and now the other one didn't either. That was the tragedy of our people. In the game which these powerhouses were playing we simply weren't considered as valuable pawns. So, who should lift a finger for us, spill even a drop of their blood, if we ourselves weren't prepared to do it? If our homeland was indeed worth so much to us, as we had always claimed, then we should be prepared to fight for it, not just with words but with actions. But that would have required more courage, more decisiveness than was being displayed at the pubs, where we looked at the world through a haze of smoke and the whiffs of bacon and roasted chestnuts. To earn one's freedom would require more than just folk dancing in faraway meadows, or organising cloak-and-dagger gatherings and speeches proclaiming heroic deeds, yet at the same time scattering in all directions at the first sound of an alarm. What was needed above all was the overpowering strength and initiative of a leader. What was required was someone who could operate with energy and foresight, and whose vision extended beyond the line that went from Padua to Innsbruck. A man of stature, mentally nimble and decisive. But we didn't have the right leader, someone who would have shown us the way or, if necessary, would even die for his country. Thus we chose the path which, through the years, would prove to be strewn with thorns.

Whenever it was discussed, the vast majority of us made our choice for Germany. We were prepared to give up on our home country, to leave it in order to be settled anywhere in Germany, or wherever suited Adolf Hitler. We were given the choice between freedom and leaving our homeland or remaining, under permanent subjugation. We chose freedom. It was easy for the German propaganda machine to present this option as a palpable choice for us. Hadn't we always declared that we wanted to be German and remain German? Well, we would then also have to be able to obey. And if the Führer gave us an order, we would obey.

Admittedly, at the time we were proud to receive German passports and instantly to become German. German, yes, but without our homeland. We had voluntarily given up our home; we were prepared to leave the country of our ancestors, our country with its cultural history spanning millennia, and we were willing to sell out and capitulate, just so we could be free. Did we not just surrender our homeland without a fight? We didn't know what we were doing! And we knew even less what we should have been doing. Indeed what should we have done in those confusing and hectic times? Should we have opted for Italy? No, never, not at any cost!

Instead of signing up for the German Wehrmacht, should we have withdrawn to the mountains and made a stand against both Italians and Germans? Should we have become the first partisan fighters of the war? There is no doubt that it would have ended with tears, sweat and us meeting our deaths. But wouldn't death at the homefront have been preferable to death in the steppes of Russia?

It remains debatable whether the great number of lives that the South Tyroleans would have had to pay for such a rebellion would have been any smaller than the one we would pay some years later in the war on all fronts.

We didn't go underground, and we didn't become partisan fighters. Unlike all other ethnic groups, we South Tyroleans voluntarily sacrificed everything we had for our Germanhood and for Germany: home and hearth, blood and soil.[5] We fought right to the last day, hoping that Germany would win the war, while we would forever lose our homeland.

What irony! But, as it so often happens, here the old proverb came true: Man proposes, God disposes. Thus, today we can only thank providence that there is still a place called South Tyrol, because as it turned out, we, the South Tyroleans, truly did everything to stand in the way of this. If Hitler had actually won the war, along with Mussolini, then there would no longer be a South Tyrol to speak of. What we would have been left with would have only been the 'Alto Adige'.[6] Nor would there be an ethnic South Tyrolean population to speak of; instead, we would have been scattered in all directions, left to languish somewhere in obscurity, perhaps in the Crimean peninsula, or in a rose garden, dreaming of the Ortler king and Andreas Hofer.[7] To awaken from this fanatic-nationalist intoxication and face reality would have been sheer agony.

Only God knows to which fortunate turn of events and acts of providence we owe our continued existence in our homeland.

— THREE —

Deutschland, Deutschland über Alles

Berlin

I left my homeland to travel to the German Reich on 2 January 1940. It was snowing in Sterzing that day. The ice-cold wind blowing from the Brenner brought light snowfall to our area, the tiny snowflakes twirling in a happy dance through the air. Arched over the street, the lamps swayed dangerously from side to side in the strong winds, their light casting shadows onto the white blanket that covered the roads.

It was early and still dark outside when I left my parents' house. The town had not yet woken, and no one would have ventured outside in this weather anyway. I had my coat collar pulled up, my hands dug deep in my pockets, clutching my lute tightly under my arm. To protect the instrument, my mother had sewn a soft green case specially for it.

I crossed the road and slipped into the narrow Schwalbeneck alley, which was the shortest route to the train station. Before being swallowed in the dark passageway, I stopped, turned around and threw one last glance towards the home of my parents. My mother stood at the bay window and waved to me. I lifted my hand, waved back and ran along the alleyway. The day before, I had tied my heavy suitcase to the sledge, taken it to the train station and put it into the left luggage. My only baggage this morning was my lute. I hurried to the station, retrieved my suitcase and waited for the train.

I was the only one standing on the platform. Even though it was very cold, I didn't feel it. I was far too excited to pay any attention to such trifles. Today would be my first trip to the German Reich; not only that, I was headed for Berlin, the capital. The very thought of that evoked an unbelievable feeling inside me. Curiosity and expectations set my pulse racing and quickened the pace of my blood through my veins, making me completely immune to the temperature of -30 degrees. I was allowed to travel to Berlin – it was wonderful.

Once there, I was to undergo (along with thirty other South Tyrolean youngsters) a four-month training course which was to end with the Matura. We were all pretty much on the same level and of the same age. We had managed, more or less by the skin of our teeth, to reach the final grade at our

Italian high school, where we had qualified to be the first South Tyroleans ever to sit for these German exams. We came from all corners of the country: from Meran and Bozen, from the Unterland, from Bruneck and Brixen, from Klausen and Sterzing. None of us had ever travelled this far, nor even been to Germany. We were the first emigrant South Tyrolean contingency, and we were going to do our utmost to prove ourselves worthy as an ethnic minority.

At long last I heard the train approaching and soon saw the engine lights coming closer. There was a short wait before the train finally came to a halt in the station. Some passengers alighted and hurried towards the town. I found an empty compartment and happily settled down on a wooden bench. The great adventure was about to begin.

In Gossensass, my friend Maxl Gröbner got on and joined me. He too had been selected for the training course. Soon we were approaching the frontier at the Brenner. When the customs officer entered our compartment, we proudly showed him our brand-new German passports. We greeted these officials, who appeared to take control of every carriage, with sheer joy written on our faces, staring in fascination at the emblem fastened onto their caps. In our eyes even the ticket inspector seemed to come from a different world. We arrived at Innsbruck, changed to a train bound for Munich, where we then had to change again. The very fact that we were immediately able to find our train for Berlin and that all connections ran so smoothly was sufficient proof of German thoroughness in planning an operation. How could it be otherwise, when the Germans were at work?

We decided to use our transfer time in Munich to explore the train station. What wonderful things to see! To us, everything was new and interesting. What impressed us most were the many uniforms we saw, though we couldn't tell any of them apart. We just stood there and guessed.

'Look at that one, is he from the railways?'

'No, from the postal services.'

'No, he's just a doorman.'

'And this man, is he from the SA or the SS?'

'Look at that one: he must be a soldier – or even an officer!'

'No, he's a soldier, I recognise those combat boots.'

'Look that way – this guy is wearing *Keilhosen* and mountain boots – that's definitely a Gebirgsjäger!'

'Do you see the edelweiss on his cap? Fabulous, right?'

'Look over there – that guy has a dagger hanging from his belt. Wow, what could he be? Surely he must be a high-ranking officer!'

This went back and forth between us; we just couldn't get over it. Finally, we got onto our train and departed. Night had fallen and we were totally overwhelmed by tiredness. The dim blue night lamp over the door barely lit up our compartment and made us even dozier, our eyelids grew heavier and heavier and at long last we fell into a deep sleep.

It was daylight when we woke up. We had stopped at some station and we were freezing. The heating had been switched off; obviously they were changing the engine. We opened the curtains and looked out. We were in a big train station and the platforms were busy. It must have been very cold. Many men wore black earmuffs underneath their caps. We thought this was hilarious. We got out to walk around a bit and bought ourselves some hot coffee.

When the train departed again, we saw a big sign: 'Halle an der Saale'.

'Look,' I said to Maxl, 'we're in Halle an der Saale!'

'Where's that?' he asked.

'No idea,' I replied.

That same day, early in the afternoon, we arrived in Berlin, got off the train, and lugged our suitcases all through Anhalter train station. People thronged passed us, here and there forming small clusters. The voice droning through the loudspeaker was loud and croaky – we could barely understand a word. A porter offered us his services. We thanked him but refused. He didn't seem to understand a word we were saying. Even though we all spoke German, it sounded very different. We only spoke our Tyrolean dialect and the porter could only speak Berlin German – Berlinerisch – but in spite of that he seemed, in our view, to be an extremely educated man, as his German was so close to the written language. We thought we would need to speak like that too one day, just so as not to be considered ignoramuses.[1] That was probably the first knock to our self-confidence.

Driving in a *droshke*, we reached the Hegelhaus, situated at 4, Kupfergraben.[2] An old building with a large wooden gate, it was situated between the narrow Spree and the Zeughaus. Some barges covered in grey-black tarpaulin were anchored along the riverbanks.

The secretary of this institution, Fräulein Dunke, completed some formalities for us and then showed us to our room. Fräulein Dunke turned out to be the life and soul of the place. Throughout our stay in Berlin it was she who looked after us and cared for us, just like a good fairy godmother.

Some comrades had already settled in, and the rest were due to arrive over the next few days. Some foreign guests were also staying at the house. They had come from some Far Eastern country and we had absolutely no contact with them. The room assigned to me was tiny. It was more like a monk's cell than a real room. Along one wall was my bed and a small wash stand with a porcelain basin and a water jug. At the other end of the room stood a wardrobe. I put my suitcase on top of it. Right next to it stood a small desk with several drawers. The room, if you can call it that, was so narrow that the space between bed and desk just about allowed for a chair. If I wanted to stretch my legs, I had to sit on my bed, or open the door to the cupboard and just let my feet rest inside it. To reach the door, all I had to do was take two steps, but you could only open it when the door of the cupboard was shut. A single window overlooked the courtyard, letting some daylight sift into the room, but no actual sunshine. If a friend dropped by, he had to sit on the bed with his legs pulled up; there was certainly no room for more than one visitor. But at least my little room was well heated, and there was yet another advantage: I was able to reach literally every single thing I possessed without ever needing to get up from my desk. It was definitely the smallest room in the whole building.

My room was therefore not suitable for me and my friends to get together to study. If I wanted to do that, I had to go to another friend's room or – as often happened – we gathered in small groups and spent time in the building's wood-panelled library. The school itself was also housed in the Hegelhaus; only Physics and Chemistry were taught in a nearby institute. In fact, that was practically the only time we were able to leave the house. Everything else took place at the Hegelhaus, even our gym classes. A specialist teacher had been hired, whose goal, as she explained to us, was to teach us rhythmic gymnastics. With a drum, she would indicate the beat to which we had to jump around the room while elegantly swinging our arms. We went along with it for some time, but after a while we got rather fed up and started fooling around and making fun of the teacher until she was finally too annoyed to return.

We were working hard, and there was much to learn. Herr Kühne, our German teacher, went to great pains to introduce us to the secrets of the German language. We were doing all right with our written German, but he wasn't too pleased with our pronunciation. 'German', he explained, 'has to be spoken by moving your lips'; he demonstrated this as he spoke with great exaggeration. 'One says "Schöne Mädchen", not "Scheyne Medchen".' We then had to pronounce the sentence in unison and move our lips as instructed.

That left only Sunday for us to go out, to the cinema or somewhere else. In fact, there really wasn't all that much to do in terms of leisure activities in Berlin. All we received as pocket money was a monthly allowance of twenty Reichsmark.[3] If you took the underground just the once to the Kurfürstendamm, that alone ate away one Reichsmark for the return trip, leaving you with nineteen. Two Reichsmark for the cinema, then we were left with seventeen. We could only rarely afford to invite a girl out for a dance, where we would then be sitting the whole night with just one glass of wine, and naturally only of the cheapest type. We even wanted to save on the cloakroom charges, so simply took our coats inside, rolled them up and sat on them. With all the noise and to-do in these restaurants, that lack of etiquette went totally unnoticed. In those days people still went dancing in Germany; it was the first winter of the war.

We formed a choir which we called 'Die Lustigen Hegelhäuser', a good opportunity for me to make use of my lute. I accompanied them – for better or worse – but our aim was to give a concert at the end of term. It never came to that, and I cannot claim that the Berlin inhabitants missed anything.

My favourite pastime was the cinema. I even found the auditoria to be fascinating and inspiring spaces. All the seats, even the cheapest ones, were upholstered. The walls were entirely panelled in velvet, the floors carpeted so as to muffle the footsteps – all that was just wonderful. We had nothing quite like this back at home. My favourite cinema was on Unter den Linden. It was amazing how the lights just gradually dimmed until they went out completely. Only one box remained lit, which was where a man played on the Wurlitzer. The gradual fading of the lights underscored by the wonderful sounds of the organ were magical to me.

We didn't just devote ourselves to such banal pleasures; no, we also pursued some higher culture. By virtue of lodging at the Hegelhaus, we came to be given very reasonably priced tickets to the Berlin Opera. It cost five Reichsmark to attend a performance, in seats that were probably the furthest from the stage, way up in the gallery, with only a partial view of the stage, in spite of us twisting our necks to a ridiculous degree. Nevertheless we got to see for the first time the whole of Richard Wagner's Ring Cycle. We saw *Götz von Berlichingen* in the Schiller Theatre with Heinrich George playing the main part. Of course, we only waited to hear the famous quote.[4]

Apart from the occasional blackout, we didn't feel any effects of the war. While the food we were served at the Hegelhaus was not familiar to us, it wasn't bad. We were sent parcels from home containing bacon, sausages and

27

butter, which certainly helped us get through the days. We had also come across a small bakery where bread was sold, but not in exchange for food stamps. The old lady who managed the store had taken a shine to us, she loved our dialect and it may have reminded her of some past holiday adventures in South Tyrol many years ago. But of course, we couldn't just turn up every single day – that would surely have sent the poor old lady over the edge, and her supplies would have soon run dry. So we set up a rota among ourselves and took turns to buy from her, and hardly a day went by without one of us coming out of the shop with a loaf of bread under his arm.

We often went to Aschinger, which was a restaurant next to the train station on Friedrichstrasse, and we pretty much became their regulars. You're always hungry when you're twenty years old, and always on the lookout for something to eat. Aschinger was probably the only restaurant at the time where one could pay without food stamps for an *Eintopf* – stew – that actually contained bits of meat. The only trouble was that sometimes we arrived so late that the *Eintopf* was already crossed off the menu. It was a sad occurrence, but we would console ourselves over a plate of vegetables.

One day we received the order to report to the recruiting district head-quarters to be examined to see if we were fit for military service. The time had come; it was starting to get serious. We had accepted the bait – a very cheap bait which smelled and looked awful – and we were hooked to the rod, no wriggling or writhing could save us. Of course, we were all considered 'fit for armed service' and, as a sign of special benevolence, they left us to decide which branch of military service we wanted to sign up for. All of us expressed the wish to be permitted to join the Gebirgsjäger in Innsbruck. We wanted to stay together as a group: it would have been absolutely terrible if a South Tyrolean youngster had been alone among all those Prussians. If we all could just stay together and speak our own dialect and be understood by everyone, it would turn out only half bad. Besides, we certainly preferred the uniform of the Gebirgsjäger. We felt much more comfortable in stretchy trousers and mountain boots than in combat boots, and then of course there was the mountain cap with the edelweiss emblem. We really loved it and it simply could not be compared to those berets that didn't even have visors. At that time, you would come across many Gebirgsjäger in Berlin; every now and again you could spot one of their mountain caps with the edelweiss and we would make wild guesses as to what these guys were doing up north in the Reich.

We were longing to become real soldiers and be permitted to wear a uniform: 'I am embarrassed to walk around as a civilian,' I once wrote to my parents.

The fact that I, along with most of my comrades, looked forward to military service was in no small measure because we wanted to wear uniform. What lay ahead of us – the induction drills for recruits, the weapons, the horrors of the war – we could never have imagined any of it. Even if once in a while some warning comments were made to us, or if deep down we felt fears or doubts emerging, we would quickly bury them. We were simply gripped by the mass madness unleashed by the uniform. Something was the matter with 'the dirty civilian', something was wrong with him. We of course didn't have any inkling of the reality of having to wear the uniform for five full years. We had even less of an inkling that one day we, by then adult men who had been severely tested, would have to make our way home, clad in little more than torn civilian rags. At that time all that counted was the uniform. Those who wore one were real men; civilians were sad losers.

This cult of wearing a uniform was most obvious on the day of the Führer's birthday. The entire city of Berlin was covered in swastika flags, and Unter den Linden, the parade avenue of the Third Reich, was a swarm of bustling crowds, with people fighting for a good spot from where they could enjoy the parade of the Wehrmacht and, if they were lucky, even catch a glimpse of the Führer. Of course, we were among them.

A platform had been erected in front of the Zeughaus from which Hitler would watch over the parades. The whole avenue was one long impenetrable cordon made up of the police, the SA, the SS and the Hitler Youth, and God knows who else. Men stood shoulder to shoulder dressed in different uniforms. Behind them, the crowds were pushing, civilians jostling, everyone wanted to see as much as possible.

When finally, after waiting for hours squeezed in between these extremely patient folk, the motorcade with the Führer drove past, an incredible outcry of jubilant voices erupted. Hundreds of thousands of arms were flung into the air and the cry '*Sieg Heil, Sieg Heil, Sieg Heil!*' rang out of every mouth.

We pulled ourselves up as tall as we could, we strained our necks, we pushed and shoved and jumped, just to be able to catch even the briefest of glimpses of the Führer. We had actually found ourselves a good position, just opposite the Führer's platform, but we were so far away that any individual appeared as a small and fuzzy silhouette. But we were happy nonetheless: we had seen the Führer, even if it was only for a split second and from very far away – but we had seen him.

How our friends back in South Tyrol would envy us this moment of bliss! Now we too were among those fortunate ones who were able to say that they had seen the Führer. Nobody in our group even for an instant thought, 'There's the man who sold us down the river.' When the individual organisations filed passed, our mouths dropped in sheer amazement: a virtual sea of flags, banners, marching bands, tanks, artillery, an ocean of steel helmets and guns, waves of fighter squadrons and dive-bombers sweeping and thundering through the sky. The bright officer commandos and the precisely timed and minutely choreographed steps of the infantry pounding on the avenue had us in goosebumps and our hearts beating faster, shuddering in awe. Our mouths agape, our eyes wide open, we experienced this imposing demonstration of German military strength.

The events and scenes of that day stayed with us. We discussed every detail and our hearts were filled with pride: soon we would be part of this wonderful military strength. These were the days when the German Wehrmacht was able to once more prove its military might.

We were in the middle of our written Latin exams. Those who had finished and handed in their paper were allowed to leave the room. A few minutes later they returned with the news that the German Wehrmacht had marched into Denmark and Norway and that the Gebirgsjäger were on their way to the Arctic Circle, or had perhaps already landed there by parachute.[5] We rushed to finish our test and gathered round the radio, waiting to hear the special messages from the Führerhauptquartier. Marching music interspersed between the news broadcasts underscored the drama of that moment.

We commented excitedly on every single detail of the military invasion. So, here was our Wehrmacht who had hit hard once again, and precisely where nobody expected it. What exactly was Norway's or Denmark's involvement in this war? As we were to find out later, it was a race against time. The British Expeditionary Force was already on its way to Norway and had to be called back, as the German soldiers had pre-empted them and got there first.

We were impatient. Would we arrive too late? Would the war have finished by the time we were ready to participate? As it turned out, of course, we were indeed going to experience war, and much of it at that.

But at the time, in the midst of this frenzy when the virtues of soldiers were being praised above all else, none of us had the faintest idea of the atrocities war brings in its wake. If someone did think of it, they didn't mention it. We, being in our early twenties and full of idealism, certainly had no idea about any danger, any suffering or blood spilling; we really were clueless about any of the horrors war would bring. All we were attracted to was the adventure that lay before us.

Eventually, our stay in Berlin came to an end. Exams had been passed successfully and we set about packing our suitcases. We had accumulated a fair amount of knowledge during those four months. We now knew who the 'Grosse Kurfürst' was, who the 'Alter Fritz' and Götz von Berlichingen were.[6] We knew the route of the Spree, the Memel and the Saale. We knew where such pastures as the Lüneburger Heide lay, the Black Forest and the Müggel Mountains. Also, even though it was still somewhat difficult for us, we were now able to speak a fluent German, we knew that the girls were '*schön*' and not 'scheyn' – but had we really *learned* anything? Not really. From our stay in Berlin we emerged just as entranced by our fantasies as we had been before, if not even more so, as by then we had turned into extremely enthusiastic idealists. The real learning process would take place only later, in the Russian steppes. But at that very moment, all we did was look forward to returning home to show off all that we had seen and experienced! We left Berlin as a group, and our goal was to enlist as a group to the German Wehrmacht some four weeks later.

Along with my friends, I got off the train in Sterzing and hurried towards the town. I was blissfully happy. It was night and I didn't meet anybody. The ancient gnarled trees lining the street stood in bloom and I greeted each one like an old acquaintance. I took deep breaths, drinking in the scented air. The wonderful smell drifting up from the sawmill was intoxicating. When I reached the bridge over the Eisack, which now seemed to be so small and insignificant to my eyes, the bells of the Zwölferturm struck midnight. Abruptly, I stopped in my tracks and listened to the four hammer sounds coming from the small bell before counting the next twelve of the big bell. I had never before realised how pure and clear the sound was, and I would never forget that moment. I will always recognise that sound among a thousand bells and in a thousand years. I was home again. Tears ran down my cheeks.

FOUR

The Beginning Was so Innocuous

The Pfeifermühle, Allgäu

The three weeks I spent at home after returning from Berlin went by in a flash. On 30 May I left my home – this time for good. It was a gorgeous spring day. The sky was blue and the sun was shining bright. This time I wasn't standing all alone on the platform: many people bustled around and I wasn't even the only one leaving my homeland. There were another dozen boys, who had also been drafted, who were being accompanied to the train station by their family and friends. We all carried the same type of small suitcase holding our few modest belongings.

The atmosphere was happy and cheerful, with laughter and jokes abounding, yet it all seemed slightly artificial. We, who were about to leave our home, simply wanted to mask our true feelings by putting on a brave face; deep down we were a bit frightened of what lay ahead of us. Germany was, after all, at war, and being drafted into the Wehrmacht at this particular time was quite honestly something that made us feel quite uncomfortable, though we would never admit it. It is easier being the hero when you're sitting in your living room or sipping on a glass of wine than when you actually have to face reality head on. The die had been cast, and what good would it have done us had we been sad or frightened? We simply had to make the best of the situation, and with a bit of humour and some measure of luck, all would end well. Above all, we didn't want the loved ones we were leaving behind to be in any way affected by our fear – our priority was that under no circumstances should anyone catch a glimpse of our true feelings.

Those left behind may well have felt the same. They didn't want to make our departure any harder than it was by displaying sadness; they were keen that we youngsters shouldn't notice their anxiety, hence all this laughter, all these jokes. But it was all forced humour, all a bit fake. That's how both sides put on a show for each other, both of us suppressing our true concerns and worries.

My father, a veteran of the First World War, stood by in silence, absent-minded. He neither heard what was happening around him nor did he want to take any part in it. He wore a serious expression on his face, and his eyes were sad. Who knows what he was thinking? He was surely the person best placed to know what lay ahead of us, having experienced it first-hand. When someone spoke to him, his responses were monosyllabic and accompanied by a thin smile. He was somewhere completely different with his thoughts. My mother, on the other hand, had tears in her eyes. She wasn't aware of all the people surrounding us, her gaze focused only on me, her son. A thousand pieces of advice rained upon me while she gripped my hand tightly. My sister was with a group of her friends, and it wasn't difficult to see how proud she was of her brother, who was one of the first to be enlisted into the great German Wehrmacht. I had to promise to send her a picture of myself in uniform. The other girls, all in their pretty dirndls, were all of a sudden so friendly to me, even those who had been rather aloof in the past when I had tried to court them. They were all smiles now, and even gave me a peck on the cheek. Each of them asked that I write to them soon, they were looking forward to hearing from me. I think everyone gathered there was quite relieved when the train finally pulled in and put an end to these painful goodbyes.

The train was filled with our comrades, or rather our fellow sufferers. Out of every window peered a youngster, laughing or waving their hands. I looked around for my friends from the Hegelhaus and when I spotted them in their carriage I joined them. A hasty farewell kiss to my mother, a firm handshake with my father, a last wave to the quacking girls, and then the train doors were banged shut. I was still standing at the window waving until the train wound around the first curve and I lost sight of the Zwölferturm. I finally sank back into my bench.

The so-called reception camp for the incoming South Tyroleans enlisted for military service was in Innsbruck-Rossau. There they were assigned to the various troops to then be sent onwards. We had to report as well. There were five of us from the Hegelhaus: Göther, Walter, Sepp, Willy and myself. We definitely wanted to stay together. We informed the officer on duty that we had enlisted in Berlin as Gebirgsjäger, and that we wished to be dispatched to the unit stationed in Fulpmes. Friends who had been drafted in before us had reported home that it was good there and that a really great group of boys were training there. That's where we wanted to go too.

The following day an Oberjäger came up to us. A tall, slim man with a long face and a strong nose, he wore his cap with the edelweiss insignia askew, pulled over his left ear, his stretch trousers with the elasticated stirrups were tucked into his boots, but he didn't wear any puttees. He had sort of lanky movements, his language was simple. We liked this man, Oberjäger Stuhlberger. Holding a list in his hand, he called out names, and we were truly glad to be on that list.

Stuhlberger got all his sheep assembled and off we marched. We must have been some thirty men. Almost all of us were South Tyrolean and farmer boys. As it later emerged, we five boys from the Hegelhaus were the only ones who had completed secondary schools with our Matura. This would become apparent very soon …

We packed our small valises and marched to the train station. But it wasn't Fulpmes we were heading to, instead we travelled to Wertach in the Allgäu. 'Why not Fulpmes?' we asked Stuhlberger. He told us that they didn't have any space there, but that we still belonged to the same unit and we were definitely going to like it at the Pfeiffermühle, which was to be our final destination. One day we would be meeting up with those from Fulpmes, and we contented ourselves with this information. What else could we do?

From Wertach, we still needed to march for another hour or so, suitcases in hand, until we finally reached the Pfeiffermühle. On the banks of the narrow torrent stood an old mill, and next to it a small, simple guest house. Close by lay a camp made up of some twelve barracks. It had been constructed originally as a camp for labourers, but now we were going to live in it. The camp was accessible only by crossing the bridge over the river, at the end of which stood a small hut next to the barracks reserved for the guards. Six large double-sized barracks were allocated to the squads, all facing the valley and situated one behind the other along the gently rising slope. A little bit further below the barracks and beyond a small meadow was the hut housing the hospital, the orderly office, and the flats for the corporals. Next to the first squad barracks, at a right angle, stood a hut in which clothing, tools and weapons were stored, and annexed to it was a cabin where the kitchen and a large dining room or lecture room were located. To the very back of the camp was a hut with the latrines. Two wooden planks, each with six cut-out holes, were arranged in rows, and behind them, along the wall, tin gulleys; that was it. In that same place were also some toilet cubicles, one for the officers, the other one for the corporals or sergeants, but they were off-limits for the squaddies. Woe betide anyone caught using them. I did once. To the far end, at the furthest corner, stood the barracks with flats belonging to the officers.

The entire camp was surrounded by a wire fence. We were going to be spending five months there. As a start of a soldier's life it actually wasn't bad; we rather liked the camp. We were the first soldiers to lodge there, even though we weren't real soldiers yet, but it felt real. We took possession of the rooms and arranged them as we thought best.

Apart from Stuhlberger there was one other corporal. A small man, hailing from Swabia, his name was Corporal Messerle. We thought that everything about him was funny: his name, his language, his bearing. The little discipline demanded from us by Stuhlberger and Messerle seemed to us to be reasonable and we had no problem abiding by their rules. If only that had been all there was to it.

The kitchen did not work properly yet. We were more than happy to go to the Pfeffermühle inn and take our meals there. We were served by the innkeeper's wife and a waitress. In the evenings we would sit together and chat. Some played cards at the inn, some strolled through the camp, others wrote letters and others still drank themselves silly, as if they had an honourable soldier's life behind them already.

At the very top of the camp I discovered an idyllic place where a rough wooden table stood, surrounded by some simple benches. It seemed like the kind of peaceful spot that might be found along a promenade with a wonderful panorama. Indeed, the view from here was spectacular. Below us the whole camp was spread out, and one could see the river encircling the valley, the mill and the inn, the dusty road leading to Wertach and the meadows opposite, with their dense forests and odd-shaped trees – it all seemed so close you could touch them. Behind rose the steep Sorgschrofe, and far away you could just about make out the church steeple of an Allgäu village.

We liked getting together up here and would sit on the benches or the grass, looking across the wide countryside and waiting for dusk to fall, when the deer and rams came out to graze in the clearing of the forest. Somebody would start singing a song from our hometown, and soon everyone chimed in enthusiastically. There were a few outstanding yodlers among us. When the yodlers' voices pierced the darkness of the falling night and echoed back, we were able to relax and were satisfied with our lot.

Corporal Stuhlberger had to travel to Innsbruck again to fetch new 'supplies'. Indeed, just a few days later he returned with another group of South Tyroleans. We steadily grew into quite a respectable bunch of men. There was, however, no sign of any official action on the horizon. We hadn't even been given our uniforms.

The moment Second Lieutenant Siegfried Grabert and his cohort stepped foot in our camp to take over the leadership of our group, our life of leisure came to an abrupt end, and the peaceful setting suddenly lost all its romance.

The campaign in France was approaching its final stages. Grabert and his men had participated in it and had proven themselves as worthy soldiers. In our eyes, Grabert personified the hero of the *Nibelungen* and was, as it happens, also named after him. Each of these men held the Iron Cross, Second Class, Grabert had even received the Iron Cross, First Class. We were totally in awe of them. These were Sudeten Germans, but there were some Baltic Germans among his group. In contrast to the Sudeten Germans, the latter were calm, thoughtful and friendly. They were all intellectuals: law students, assessors or something on that level. Grabert himself was twenty-five years old and a medical student in his sixth semester.[1]

We were put into platoons and squads. Somehow our group from Hegelhaus managed to be in the same platoon, with Sergeant Hiller as our leader.[2] Hiller wasn't a very tall man, but he was extremely agile and fast. With his metal-framed glasses sliding down his nose, he reminded us of a librarian or a Latin teacher. But the look in his eyes was that of a savvy civil servant who knew his numbers: sharp and suspicious. He was extremely officious and had only one goal: that his platoon always be the first, and his people always the best.

Grabert himself didn't care so much about our group, and we didn't get to see much of him. He essentially left it all to Hiller, whom he trusted fully, and so Hiller did everything. He was ably supported by his other NCOs and lance corporals, who were more or less cut of the same cloth as him. NCOs Rosenkranz and Slama, Lance Corporal Pils and others whose names I have forgotten were in no way any less driven than Hiller. Hiller viewed us as material which he could hammer, file, polish and drill so that we became malleable tools, with the help of which he could obtain personal glory and distinction.

The contrast between us youngsters – idealists and pure as the driven snow – and our instructors – whose mentality was the polar opposite and fuelled by self-interest only – was significant and would remain that way throughout the war. We South Tyroleans only understood very late in the game that we were but a means to an end.

In the eyes of our superiors we would always be uncouth, slow and slightly dumb country hicks who, precisely because of these characteristics, could be fully relied upon to obey all orders faithfully and blindly, to hold out and stand their ground to the bitter end. The trickier the situation, the more they would persevere and get out of it. They were forged of some special metal, these South Tyrolean peasants. The more you hammered them, the stronger they became. When a task was completed they were patted on the back, just like some stupid animal. They were fed a handful of oats, so to speak, which would surely make them happy enough not to make a stink. But they certainly weren't to be trusted with anything more than just carrying out simple tasks. Oh no, thought our superiors, these idiots certainly couldn't hold a candle to us real soldiers and higher-placed men who could take on demanding leadership roles – that's not something these boys could ever learn. Things like commanding and managing would have to remain *our* remit and ours alone.

No wonder that, beyond serving in the army, there was no social contact or relationship between these two groups. In part, this was due to the groups being so different in character, but it was also due to the hierarchy – the divide between instructor and recruit was simply far too wide.

It couldn't have been easy for Hiller and his men to turn us simple, slow and plodding South Tyroleans into useful soldiers to fit the German pattern. After all, they themselves lacked the professional drill for which the Prussian recruit was known. Neither were we shoved into freezing cold military barracks, which would have been the environment in which this inflexible, relentless and back-breaking instruction could have succeeded. Thank God! We were never acquainted with such situations. We were always accommodated either in romantically remote camps or in hotels, where none of these drills would have been feasible. But perhaps, considering our later deployment, this wasn't even their aim. Their actual goal wasn't to turn us into soldiers who could march in a parade, but into men who would be equipped to join a combat unit. Even though Hiller and his company tried everything to make our life miserable and to grind us down to nothing, into an amorphous heap of spineless creatures, they didn't succeed. We remained the stubborn individualists we had always been.

We received our uniforms, and this marked the end of our quiet and peaceful evenings spent at the picturesque table and bench above the camp. Dressed in our jackets and mountain caps, we no longer recognised each other. We had a good laugh when we eyed each other up and down and realised how weird we looked – but we soon stopped laughing. Dangling from our belts, the rifles bothered us during our marches. The steel helmets pressed too hard, regardless of whether we wore them or carried them on our belt hook. I just couldn't stand the helmet and only wore it when specifically ordered to do so. I never wore it when fighting at the front. The collarless mountain shirt, and especially the long gaiters with the bands top and bottom that needed to be tied up, gave a whole new meaning to the term underwear. I found it difficult to get used to. The mountain boots, heavily studded and cleated, were as hard as stone and caused many bruises. But at long last we had what we had yearned for: we were in uniform and no longer had to feel ashamed. The military drilling was about to begin.

We were dragged out of bed at 0500. Then everything seemed to happen at once: in a flash we washed, shaved, brushed our teeth, dressed, got our coffee, ate our breakfast – everyone was pushing and shoving at the latrines, followed by barrack room duty. I would never understand why everything had to be done so early and at the double in the army, and then you were simply left for hours, waiting for something to happen.

Making our beds was a real problem. Countless times, upon arriving back at the barracks, dead-tired from the exercises, and dragging ourselves to the beds, we would find them completely rumpled. The *Spiess* had found them wanting.[3] Either the blue-and-white checked bed cover had a tiny crease and didn't sit in a straight line, or the corner of the pillow wasn't sufficiently sharp. There were thousands of misdemeanours this informant found while inspecting our rooms after we had marched off. It wasn't only the beds which gave cause for trouble: our lockers too were a whole other sorry story. Once we had arranged our lockers and everyone seemed happy, we hardly dared touch anything ever again. The handkerchiefs remained forever pristinely folded and untouched. When we had to blow our nose, we preferred to use our bare hands for that rather than destroy what we had meticulously put in order. I had acquired the knowledge of how to navigate these locker rules thanks to several weekends spent on guard duty.

Even though everything had to get done at the double, it still took quite a bit of time for us to get ready and organised before reporting to the sergeant. At long last we were permitted to depart. As soon as we had crossed the bridge we got the order: 'A song! Two … three!'

We never got the tune quite right and we were instantly thrown into the mud by the sergeant's thunderous voice: 'Lie down!', 'Jump up, march, march!', 'Lie down!' That's how we painfully moved forwards; we never got to sing a song to the end. Finally, we reached the soggy field where our drills took place. And the fun didn't stop there. But while it was physically very demanding, it did all train us up to peak condition.

We ran, crouched, crawled, hopped back and forth, or stood still for ages, our hands pressed to our trouser seams, our middle finger placed precisely on the seam, the thumb snug along the hand in line with the fingers, without moving an eyelash or eyeball, while the sergeant circled us, inspecting us from top to bottom: 'You will catch pneumonia if you keep running around like this, half-naked!'

Why did he say that? I wondered. And then, much to your surprise, you'd notice that the button of your breast pocket had not been fastened properly.

We took aim and cocked our rifles in readiness until we lost the feeling in our arms and had bruises on our shoulder and left collarbone. We marched for hours, one behind the other, past a private, saluting him with our heads flung sideways, our noses pointing towards him. We learned how to stand in parallel rows, count off in line formation, and do military about-turns. We were taught how to march in step and how to sing the songs. This was the crucial time for our combat skills to be honed and perfected.

At lunch we returned to the camp, but that didn't spell the end of the hounding. Once back, our instructors handed us over to the *Spiess*, who had been expecting our arrival, just as we'd been expecting his presence upon our return. We had to change instantly, which meant swapping the uniform jacket with a black *Drillichjacke*, a pretty horrible piece of clothing; I truly despised it. I felt like an inmate, the only thing missing was the prisoner's number on the breast and the iron shackles on my leg. We learned to queue when waiting for our meals to be handed out, nice and orderly, one behind the other. Those who were faster changing out of their uniforms got to get to the front of the queue. We also learned how to wash dishes and peel potatoes.

Our midday break was little more than a fleeting moment. We didn't dare lie down on our beds and stretch out our legs. If the *Spiess* had caught anybody doing that ... well, good luck to them. So we just sat on those long benches with no backs to them, smoked our cigarettes and vented our anger at everything and everybody.

The blow of the duty sergeant whistle, timed like clockwork, tore us out of our reveries and back to work. The sound was brutal, impossible to ignore, and always came on time – and always at the most inconvenient time. Nobody dared miss it.

In bad weather – only considered as such if it literally poured down in buckets – teaching took place inside. We had German lectures, lectures on foreign weapons and vehicles, learned the different ranks, the manufacture and use of explosives, hand-to-hand combat, silent killing techniques and the customs, traditions and lifestyle of our target regions. We learned how to take weapons apart, clean and then assemble them again.

And then, of course, we had the roll calls. Roll calls to inspect uniforms and weapons, roll calls to inspect shoes and leather-ware, room and locker roll calls ... the list went on.

Every single one was brutal in its own way, and usually ended with further punitive drills or guard duty on Sunday. That's when we learned how to polish our shoes and our buckles so well that you could see yourself reflected in them. Even the inside of our seams was polished to perfection! I was often assigned to weekend guard duty until I finally got the hang of it. We learned how to clean our rooms and specially to dust those remotest of corners. The camp was rarely quiet, not even after curfew, as more often than not the NCO or the sergeant would find a speck of dust, which he'd use as a pretext to haul us over the coals yet again. He chased us in our underpants through the camp, up and down the roofs of the barracks. The minute we were all up there, we'd have to sing. Then, down again and into our beds; we'd fall asleep instantly in the hope that he too was tired out.

After a month had passed, we moved on to field-training exercises. While we had hoped that our drill would ease off, the opposite was true, and training was so harsh we actually prayed for the clock to turn back. We marched through one valley after another, climbed all the mountains in the surrounding area, stormed up every hill, often several times, one after another. We trawled and hopped through marshy fields. When we had to change positions and where the mud was too deep for us, we just dived in.

Fortunately, Second Lieutenant Grabert and his NCOs spent the evenings in the restaurant in Jungholz, sitting around with a bottle of red wine and indulging in refined small talk. At least this gave us some peace and quiet during the nights, other than the occasional tantrums by the officer on duty.

Throughout that summer it rained practically every single day, and our knees and elbows were permanently covered in wet bandages. That year, the sunny Allgäu resembled a flooded laundry room. Every second Thursday we marched to Wertach's shooting range. That was the only part of the whole instruction course which we loved. We just lounged around there the entire day, emptied our magazines in futile shooting exercises and lazed around some more.

We soon caught on that it was not helpful to draw attention to ourselves in any shape or form, not in a positive and certainly not in a negative way. Always keep your head low, don't ever raise it.

But for us boys from the Hegelhaus who had actually earned our Matura, it wasn't always so easy to keep a low profile. We were noticed all the time: during our classroom training, when we were the first to be tested to see whether we had understood the stuff and then made fun of when we got the answer wrong, or during the field-training exercises, where we just never ran fast enough, always seeking out the dry spots when ordered to change positions and cleverly avoiding the puddles before hitting the ground.

At the time, it was still the five of us in the same team, and when we fanned out, storming across the fields and were on the far end of the platoon, we were referred to as the 'miracle wing'.

'Why, have a look at these slowcoaches here, these lazy student folks,' the sergeant screamed, pointing at us. 'You probably think you're above it all and don't have to get your hands dirty, or throw yourself into the mud!' … 'Just you have a look at how they're holding their guns! Do you really think that the rifle is a writing pen? Oh, do be careful not to hurt yourself with it,' he continued sarcastically. 'Imagine, trying to win the war with lame ducks such as these!' … 'Well, Tommy will laugh himself silly once he sees you rabbits hopping along.' … 'But just you wait and see, you know-alls. I will make damn sure that your arses fly off the desk chair. Yes, mark my words, I sure will whip you into shape – I will mould you and grind you down until the water starts boiling in your arses.'

And while the others were resting, we, the so-called student wing, were subjected to their 'special treatment'. The drilling exercises themselves didn't actually bother us too much, even though we were decidedly sick and tired of the whole thing after a month had gone by. We were young, healthy and full of idealism. We looked upon the drill as a kind of obligatory sports activity and realised that it wouldn't last forever.

On Sundays, when it wasn't our turn to stand guard and when we had more or less survived the week unscathed, we were given permission to leave the camp. We would usually then go up to the Jungholz. This small village, some twenty kilometres away on foot, became our regular Sunday destination. What was there to do other than go to a few inns? Nothing. Soon, all the young and available girls had been claimed by those who were there first and who took firm possession of them. The less fortunate ones just got together in some pub over some spirits and beer. The innkeeper's wife at the Hotel Adler prepared some wonderful pancakes with apricot jam and pear compote for us. We guarded this secret religiously.

Summer went by and autumn drew near, and we had had our fill, as far as the army was concerned.

'How long do you think this will last?' I asked my friend Willy one day when, sitting lost in thoughts, we were walking from Jungholz towards the camp.

'Well, not too long, I would think,' he answered. 'The war will soon be over, and anyway, we will obviously be too late for any action.'

'Do you think we could still sign up for the winter term at university?' I continued.

'Well, I don't think we'd be in time for that,' responded my friend, 'but certainly for the summer term we could.'

'Yes indeed. By that point we would have one year of army service behind us – that's enough, don't you agree?'

'Yes, that would suffice,' answered Willy.

With that we walked on, feeling quite content. We now knew exactly how this would continue. Whistling a merry tune, we returned to camp.

— FIVE —

Zur Besonderen Verwendung

Bad Vöslau[1]

The sun was sinking below the horizon like a burning red sheet of metal. The sky turned yellow, then burnished orange, and gradually changed to purple with the sliver of sun turning darker and smaller until it disappeared completely behind the hills of the Vienna woods. Gone was the kaleidoscope of glorious colours with which the autumn had painted the countryside around Vienna. It got dark quite quickly. The sky which had glistened only a few minutes beforehand with different shades of red suddenly turned grey. The air was crisp. Thin wisps of mist formed in the lowland. One or two magpies – or were they crows? – flew out from the cornfields, flapped their wings, screeched briefly, made a turn and then settled in the next field. This is their season; there is no shortage of food, the corn is ripe, and there is plenty of it.

Lost in thought, I sat on the tram that went from Vienna Bösendorfer Strasse to Baden bei Wien, just outside Vienna. I was fascinated by the wonderful sunset, which was so very different here in the city from the mountains where we came from.

People got on and off at the numerous stops as the tram came to a shrieking halt. I paid little attention to them; I was too preoccupied to take any interest in strangers.

After a short leave from the army, I was returning to my unit, which had been moved from the Pfeiffermühle to Bad Vöslau. Our training was over. No longer were we new recruits; we had become real soldiers. We were prepared to be deployed at the front, and the order to report could come any day.

But where were we going to fight? France had surrendered. There was England left. The Tommies were isolated on their island, and even though they were putting up quite a fight against our air force, they would surely have to back down soon. Winter was knocking at our door. England would surely not survive. Our Marine Corps was blocking its ports – fabulous boys, those U-boats. There they were, criss-crossing the Atlantic, sinking everything in sight. And there it was, the mighty British Royal Navy, anchored in the ports and not daring to sail out because there, just beyond, were our 'Blue Boys' eyeing their prey like greedy sharks.

With our training having finished, so too had our stay at the Pfeiffermühle. We missed it. We had been kept so nicely hidden and tucked away in that remote and forgotten region of the Allgäu. Nobody had bothered us, nobody had controlled us. The highest authority had been Second Lieutenant Grabert and his sergeants. For us, at the time, there was no higher authority. But now, in Baden bei Wien, we would be pushed into the limelight. We were told that the major of the battalion was there, a man called Jacobi; we weren't at all curious about him.

Our motley group had turned into a real company. A very strong company at that: we were some 300 men. Suddenly, we also received a name – we were a unit in the 800th Special Purpose Construction Training Regiment. We were never able to find out what exactly we were supposed to be training in, or whom we were meant to train. We were somehow suspicious of the acronym zbV, 'for special purposes'. It didn't seem to say anything about the Gebirgsjäger division, it sounded more like a special unit. 'For special purposes!' What were these special purposes that others couldn't be ordered to undertake, and to which we were now assigned?

In war, special operations are always very risky. Wouldn't it be preferable for special operations to deploy special men? Men who were, above all, prepared to run any and every risk. Wasn't it be true that volunteers would be much more suitable for such tasks, reckless men who had only contempt for danger? Were we these men?

This wasn't what I had envisioned when I had enlisted for the German Wehrmacht. I would never have thought of signing up for a special unit. I had simply wanted to join the Gebirgsjäger and do my duty. Just as my father had been Kaiserjäger before me, and my grandfather before him.

I wanted to defend my homeland as an honest and sincere soldier, as befits every upright German. Which homeland did I want to defend? The fact that at the time I didn't even have a homeland to speak of, as my parents had already moved to the Reich, didn't even occur to me. And now I had landed in a special unit: the one 'for special purposes', zbV!

I arrived at the final stop: Baden. I stepped from the tram and asked how to get to my connecting train which would take me to Bad Vöslau. I was pointed towards another tram. This puny narrow-gauge railway rattled and rumbled through cornfields and vineyards. After half an hour I arrived at my destination. It was already dark when I got to my lodgings, and I immediately reported to my sergeant. The Park Hotel, where my company was being put up, was quite close to the city centre. Two roads led up the incline to the hotel. One street was meant for vehicles and the second was just a narrow pathway which wound through a beautiful park full of old trees and past a romantic terraced open-air pool. The hotel was an old building, which had certainly seen better days.

Each platoon occupied half a floor, each squad one room, all with a balcony. The rooms once used for breakfast and as a dining area had been converted into classrooms. At the back of the hotel a broad terrace ran the entire width of the building. It had once been the veranda where spa guests would take their tea. In one corner was an alcove that had once been reserved for the orchestra. For us, this terrace was where roll call took place. Behind the hotel, concealed by bushes and trees, stood a small villa. This was where Second Lieutenant Grabert resided.

The company, after having once again been turned upside down, was now unified and ready for combat, yet too large for a single lieutenant to manage. We were therefore given a new boss, Captain Buchler. We had become so used to the gentle manner of Second Lieutenant Graber that our new chief seemed particularly arrogant.

During this rearrangement, the five of us from the Hegelhaus were separated. On 1 November we had been promoted to lance corporals but were each assigned to a different platoon. I remained with the Grabert platoon. Full of pride, we set about sewing our armband onto the left sleeve of our blouse and coat, and from then on in we weren't just regular soldiers – we had officially become lance corporals. I had become section officer of the engineer branch, and three men were under my command.[2] We trained in demolition, learned about explosives, ignition cables and wire cutters, and were taught all kinds of rules and regulations related to combat and reconnaissance. In a remote quarry we hand-crafted our own explosives, round and long-shaped ones; we practised blowing up tree trunks and throwing hand grenades. When we marched home after our reconnaissance practice, we sang our Bozen mountaineer song.[3] I believe that this was when the lyrics '*Wohl ist die Welt so gross und weit*' were first heard on the streets of Vöslau.

Permission to leave after our duties ended took on quite a different meaning here in Vöslau. We swarmed through the city, went to the cinema or dancing – and on Sundays we did both. During such outings, we frequently got into trouble with members of the air force. The reason for these fights was always the same: the Vöslauer girls, whose favours every single one of us was vying for.

When our superior spoke about what was special about our potential future deployment, he was hesitant and restrained. We were never properly informed about anything. References were made and half-sentences spoken, and those began to circulate, but they just led to speculations and heightened the sense of secrecy and mystery that enveloped our unit. We heard about military actions carried out in civilian garments or foreign uniforms. But these were just some vague hints, nothing concrete. We never paid much attention to what was said. While it was interesting to hear about such operations, and while we certainly admired the courage of those who had been involved in them, we felt that this didn't really apply to us.

Until one day, that is, when Second Lieutenant Grabert addressed our assembled company. He started with a threat. He threatened court martial if so much as one word of what he was about to say got out. We paid attention. He described actions that he and his men had already carried out in Poland, Belgium and Holland and where, as we had heard rumoured, the men were indeed wearing civilian clothing or foreign uniforms during those actions. If it hadn't been Grabert himself telling us these things, we wouldn't have believed them. We were also told that the highest authority wasn't General Dietl, but Admiral Canaris, that we didn't belong to the regular Gebirgsjäger division, but to the Abwehr II.[4] He told us of the advantages our unit would enjoy in contrast to all the other units, and that it was precisely the fact that we were so special that justified our special operations. He explained why it was that we, the South Tyroleans, had been recruited to the Lehrbataillon Brandenburg zbV 800. Since we were ethnic Germans, we were particularly well suited – we had lived abroad, experienced foreign countries and spoke foreign languages – and would be especially valuable in such operations.

He then announced that the waiting had come to an end and that, finally, we were ready to be deployed. We were going to be transferred to Romania in order to protect the security of the oil refineries in Plösti, which could be significant for the war effort. Yes, Romania was our ally, but it was not equipped to protect its oil plants.

In concluding his presentation, Grabert just sort of mentioned in passing that each of us was free to be transferred to another unit if we were not in agreement with how the battalion was conducting the war. 'I only want to have those men in my unit who have volunteered to be with me out of their own free will. I must be able to rely on each one of you, rely on your full commitment, your courage, your responsibility and your absolute obedience. I will not ask anyone to do something that I myself wouldn't be prepared to do, or have done already. If someone wants to quit, he can do that now; once we are out there at the front, we will deal with anyone who defects with the utmost rigour.'

Grabert had spoken. We knew the score.

Goodness, what had we got into? All those rumours that had been circulating for some time now had been confirmed. Now we knew what a 'special unit' was, and what special purpose it served. After Grabert's explanations, and once back in our rooms, my comrades could talk only about the forthcoming action, repeating how adventurous and special the operation would be and how excited they were that at long last it would start. They thought wearing foreign uniforms was going to be fun and a good laugh; I was tormented by doubts and misgivings. I was barely able to take part in the lively discussions my comrades were so keen to have, and the moment I was off duty, I left the barracks to take a walk in the woods. I had to be on my own. I had to sort out my thoughts and doubts. Nobody could help me with that. Everyone had to decide for himself.

I tried to go through and carefully analyse Grabert's speech to us. So, it had turned out that we weren't Gebirgsjäger. We were only wearing their uniforms. Wasn't this fact in itself proof of a deception? Weren't we actually lying to ourselves? What was Abwehr II, whose chief was an admiral? Were we now part of the Marines? What were we meant to defend against? If indeed our task was to defend, then why on earth had we been trained to attack?

Lehrbataillon Brandenburg! What did Brandenburg mean to us? Never heard of it! Where is it even situated? Ah yes, up north somewhere, close to Berlin.

Back there in Berlin, when we were first examined, hadn't we deliberately reported to the Tyrolean Gebirgsjäger? Yet now we seemed to have landed with some Prussian forces!

Who on earth would dare jump off the bandwagon now? Why was it that we South Tyroleans were so suitable for these special operations? Our language skills? That made me laugh! Granted, we certainly understood Italian, but what with our pronunciation we never could have fooled an Italian. All we had to do was open our mouths and every Italian would know instantly that we were Germans. And anyway, Italy was our ally. Surely we wouldn't be deployed wearing an Italian uniform? But, after what we had just heard, anything was possible!

What indeed were we to do with our knowledge of Italian in a war against Britain? We only knew a few words of English.

Experience in foreign countries? What did that mean? Did we really have any? One surely couldn't refer to growing up in South Tyrol as having lived abroad. In fact, if we were talking foreign experience, what we were experiencing now – in the Allgäu, in Vöslau – that would be closer to the mark. This could actually be called 'experience abroad'.

'All that is nonsense. They just want to make us look foolish.' Those were the thoughts that plagued me. I was bitter, angry with everything and everybody. But above all, I was furious at myself for having taken the bait.

It wasn't that I didn't like being in that team. The opposite was the case; in fact, I couldn't have hoped for a better unit. We were all cut of the same cloth, we got on extremely well with each other and there was an incredible sense of camaraderie. No, assuredly, we really were a top-notch team. What made me bitter was the way they had caught us out, how they had manipulated us into a special unit and were now, a few days before engagement in the theatre of war, presenting us with a new decision they seemed to feel was a fait accompli.

What bothered me above all was that thing with the foreign uniforms. I personally felt that engaging dressed in the uniform of the enemy was wrong, unfair and unjust.[5]

Did the German Wehrmacht truly have to resort to this? Did it have to deceive the enemy in such a treacherous manner in order to dominate? I couldn't get my head around it. It contradicted every single one of my moral principles. I was still filled with youthful idealism, the crystal-clear purity of which did not sit comfortably with such shady dealings.

'I don't want to buy my life with a lie.' Wasn't that what the innkeeper at the Mahr had said, and he faced the consequences? Wasn't he honoured by us as the hero of truth? Wasn't he our model – a real man?[6] Could I really remain with a unit whose code was deception, deceit and disguise?

Or was it simply fear? Fear, because we were now all ready, and the moment of truth lay before us. Was I unconsciously trying to avoid going to the front, and was I just using the unusual Brandenburg manner of fighting as a pretext for skiving off?

No, it wasn't fear. I wasn't any more or less frightened than my comrades. In truth, we couldn't even imagine what it would be like. And who thinks about death in their twenties? One speaks about such things, perhaps, but nobody consciously acknowledges it. No, it wasn't fear of death per se that made me have doubts; rather it was the 'how' of my death – should I be captured – which worried me. Absurd though it may sound, it was how I would die that was more important to me than whether or not it was going to happen. If I was going to die, I wanted to die 'on the field of honour', fighting for the glory of my nation, in a fair fight, hit by an honest bullet and not dressed in a foreign uniform or sentenced to death for sabotage or even espionage, hung from a tree in enemy territory.

Grabert had said that he only wanted volunteers in his organisation. Wasn't this now the last opportunity to pull my head out of the noose?

But was it even possible for me to walk away? Leave all my friends, move to a different unit where I didn't know a soul and be a simple private who had to rise through the ranks again? What would people think of me? Everybody would see me as a total coward, an army dodger. Wasn't it my moral duty to walk side-by-side with my comrades, through thick and thin, whatever the result? 'Cling together, swing together', or the other way around, as the case may be.

Tormented by such worries, and pained by such doubts, I got lost wandering in the woods. I returned late to our lodgings. None of my comrades was suffering as I was. Nobody spoke about the impending action. It seemed to be the most natural event for them. Some were already asleep, lost in pleasant dreams.

I couldn't sleep. I tossed and turned in my bed, and all of a sudden, I came to a decision: I would speak to Second Lieutenant Grabert.

The following day I reported to Grabert and asked for a meeting.

'What's it about?' he asked. 'Official or private?'

'Private, sir,' I responded.

'Is it connected to the operation?' he probed.

'Yes, sir,' I responded, 'but it cannot be dealt with so quickly. I would respectfully request to speak with you in private.'

'Fine, well, come to my quarters today, later in the evening – let's say 8 p.m.'

'Yes, sir, at 8 p.m. at your place, tonight.'

I clicked my heels while flinging my hand upwards to my cap in a salute, then made an about-turn and left the room.

There was no turning back now. I had to speak with Second Lieutenant Grabert. And in that very moment all uncertainty had disappeared. Now that things were underway and there was no way out but going forward, I had regained all my self-confidence and I was calm once more. I would be open and frank with Grabert and leave him in no doubt as to what my thoughts and feelings were about camouflaged operations. He should know that I wasn't just a robot that you could simply switch on to perform according to his programme. I would explain to him that I wasn't just a stupid and stubborn yes-man who just let everything pass him by, who couldn't think for himself and accepted everything, no questions asked, a man who had no honour and conscience, but that I was a human being who had a good brain, who knew about moral principles which – though they may not be needed at that moment – were inherently meaningful and valuable. I would feel free to speak my doubts.

This was in the middle of totalitarianism, in the middle of a war, and I was facing an army where orders were never ever questioned, where the officer had unlimited authority over his unit, and where the gap between commanding officer and the obeying ordinary soldier was enormous, perhaps even insurmountable. It was certainly most unusual for a private to request a meeting with his chief, in confidence and behind closed doors, to discuss operational methods, his sense of honour and his pangs of conscience. No question, this required a good dose of courage and a whole lot of brazenness.

The closer the hand moved towards 8 o'clock, the more nervous I became. My knees started shaking, and I felt queasy. All of a sudden, I was scared of my own courage.

Nonetheless, at precisely 8 p.m., I reported to Second Lieutenant Grabert. He opened the door himself, having dismissed his boy for the evening. He invited me into his room. He was in his riding breeches and boots and had taken off his tunic, wearing only his collarless shirt, which was unbuttoned.

'Come in, Private Tschampetro,' he said, and then got straight to the point: 'What seems to be burdening you?'[7]

So, it was my turn to speak. Gone was the beautiful speech I had prepared. At that moment, I just couldn't think of where to start.

'Second Lieutenant, sir,' I began hesitatingly, 'here is the thing: how should I put it? Well, I respectfully request for transfer into a different part of the troop, as I don't consider myself suitable to carry out the camouflage operations, disguised in foreign uniforms, such as you have described.'

That was it. I had said it out loud. Grabert turned sharply to face me and stared at me long and hard. I held his gaze, even though it pierced me to the core.

'Let's sit down,' he said finally. 'Help yourself to a cigarette and say that once again.'

We took our seats in velvet-cushioned armchairs and lit our cigarettes.

'Well, Second Lieutenant, sir,' I began, 'I feel that fighting in foreign uniforms is unfair and cruel. In any event, it is blatantly against the principles of honour, honesty and loyalty, which, in my opinion, all have to be part of our combat methods, even against the enemy.'

I paused. We eyed each other in silence. I put my cigarette in an ashtray. 'I don't fear death, Second Lieutenant,' I continued, 'but if I should fall, it should be an honourable death. We South Tyroleans consider ourselves part of the German people, we have left our home country, and we did so without being forced into it, but simply because we are convinced that this is right. I reported to the German Wehrmacht as I do not want to stand on the side lines and look on while the German people are fighting the war, and because it is my duty to help bring victory. But I fail to understand why I should do this while wearing a foreign uniform.'

I had said my piece. Grabert had listened to me carefully. He had not taken a single puff on his cigarette, which was left smouldering in his hand. Finally, he broke his silence.

'Have you spoken to anybody about this?' he asked.

'With nobody, Second Lieutenant, sir,' I answered. 'Coming to speak to you was entirely my own choice. I have made this decision all by myself.'

'Well, then,' said Grabert, 'now you listen to me carefully. I respect your feelings and commend you. If all men, our enemies included, thought the same way, so much in our world would be easier and simpler. But sadly, this is not the case. As long as there have been humans on this earth, there has always been war, and there always will be. Nothing will change that; it is simply part of being human, it's within our nature. And every war is cruel and brutal because everyone does his utmost to win and, in the final analysis, destroy the enemy. Everyone! To achieve this, everyone does whatever is in his power, and uses every tool he has, as it is a struggle between life and death. Not just his own life – no, it's the lives of his entire people. We are seeing ever more resources being utilised, ever more powerful weapons deployed, and these serve only one purpose: to destroy the enemy.

'With each new war, the battles fought become more atrocious and more inhumane than in the one before. War will be waged more relentlessly and more ruthlessly than ever. We soldiers, who carry this war's entire burden and witness its harshness, cannot alter these facts. All we have to do is ensure that we are prepared to deal with it as best we can. We have no choice but to resign ourselves to this reality. We also have to make sure that we are faster, stronger, more able and, yes, indeed, more cunning than our enemies.'

Grabert had got up and was pacing the room. I was sitting on the edge of my armchair with my elbows on my thighs, hands clasped.

'What does it mean to be cunning?' he continued. 'Let's have a look at history. You know history, so I am not telling you anything new. Isn't it true that every war throughout the ages reveals ruses which all had that one goal – to deceive the enemy. Why do you think that was? The goal was to defeat him. There is nothing dishonourable about that. There are countless examples. Just remember what happened in Troy. Didn't Ulysses sneak his warriors into the city, concealed in the belly of the wooden horse, and so position himself to conquer Troy? That is a classic example of a camouflage operation. Yes, he needed some special men to go through with it, and these were especially brave and determined men, who were prepared to be locked up inside the wooden horse. What do you think would have happened to them had they been detected too early? Not one of them would have survived! They would all have been killed, dying a painful death; and on top of that, they would have been ridiculed and derided. Nobody, however, would ever think of condemning these men, of ostracising them for being false and cruel, of being men without honour. On the contrary. They are praised in history as heroes, and Ulysses, who had come up with the plan, is considered the biggest hero of them all. And why? For the single reason that they were *victorious*. If they had been discovered, nobody would care two hoots about them, and no Homer would sing about their past glories. They would have been branded forever as traitors, or even as criminals. As for Ulysses's idea, it would be decried as the product of a sick and perverse mind.

'No, my dear Tschampetro, it is not a matter of "how" one wins the war, that should never be our concern, but only "if" one wins the war is what interests us soldiers! The winner, and he alone, can decide whether the ways and means deployed to achieve victory are honourable or despicable. The ends justifies the means, and not the other way around!'

Grabert fell silent. He lit another cigarette, walked over to the sideboard and poured two glasses of cognac.

'Come, let's have a drink,' he said, handing me a glass.

'But it doesn't change the fact that camouflage and resorting to a foreign uniform remain dishonourable and unworthy of a strong Wehrmacht,' I objected. 'In the end, why does one wear a uniform, why is there such a thing as uniform?'

'Goodness gracious, what do you mean by "honourable" and "strong"?' Grabert got quite worked up. 'What do those words even mean if it's a case of survival or not surviving? Doesn't the lion have yellow fur precisely because he needs to hide in the savannah? And the tiger a stripy one, the leopard a mottled one and the panther a black one so he doesn't get spotted? Isn't that all for the same reason? And isn't the prey animal that is tricked and then carried between the predator's jaws always, without exception, the much weaker one? Would you say that because of that the lion, the tiger and the leopard are despicable? Doesn't the Native American hide under the buffalo skin when approaching an unsuspecting herd before going on the kill? And why is he doing that? Because if he didn't, he wouldn't be able to get close, and he wouldn't have anything to eat. Or, I could give you another example: think of Siegfried, the hero of the Nibelungen. He went even further. He disguised himself beneath a magic hood, rendering himself completely invisible, so he could defeat Brunhild. Were his actions dishonourable? If so, then it is King Gunther who should be shamed, not Siegfried.'

Grabert sat down and downed his cognac. 'But let's not talk about this any more,' he said. 'I could give you many more examples of subterfuge and disguise, from history, mythology, and even nature, which is full of such stuff. We soldiers need to adapt to the circumstances. We have to fight so that our people can live. We cannot think of anything else, have any other goal in mind than to defeat our enemies. It is a moot point as to *how* we do that, it's a matter of life and death. Long gone are the romantic times of the noble knights. You can offer your nobleness to the enemy once you have defeated him; yes, then it's appropriate, but not before – that would be tantamount to stupidity. Indeed, don't you think that our enemies also do all they can to deceive and outwit us? They certainly employ the same methods as we do, and they certainly have neither regard nor sentimental feelings towards us or anybody.'

Grabert had got up and was pacing the room once again as he spoke. Then he stood still, looking for another cigarette. The ashtray was becoming full, and thick smoke wafted through the air.

'Look here, Tschampetro,' he said after a while. 'Disguising yourself in a foreign uniform, in the uniform of the enemy, isn't a German invention. Not at all, it's not us who came up with this. A very long time ago, there were many other nations who engaged in this practice. In fact, it was above all the Brits who were masters of disguise. You cannot imagine how often and how many ships sailed under a false name or a false flag, and it's only in this way, by using such trickery, that they conquered the oceans, and indeed entire continents. Just remember Captain Drake. Didn't he change the appearance of his ship countless times so that he could carry out raids privateering? Was he hanged for that? The Spaniards certainly would have done so had they been able to lay their hands on him, which would have put him in the history books as a buccaneer and criminal. But because he emerged victorious, and with rich booty, his queen made him a nobleman. Sir Francis Drake, the pirate!' Grabert downed another cognac. 'No, there is nothing dishonourable in what we are doing, if, well, if we are successful! Come then, Tschampetro, drink up, have another one!' he said. 'You know something? As for me, I couldn't give a shit about how I fall, quite frankly. But what I do care about is whether or not I fall. I too love life, I'm not one to commit suicide. I love my profession, and I want to continue my studies and become a good doctor.[8] But now, in these times, in this war, we first have to win. How we achieve that doesn't matter. Everyone is put where he is of most use, where he can achieve the most.' He paused again.

At this point, I no longer knew what to say. I no longer felt I was on solid ground. I actually had to agree with him. I had been such a naive idealist!

'We thought', he continued finally, 'that you South Tyroleans above all would be the real Brandenburgers. You have all the character traits that are required. You are reliable, loyal and tough lads, particularly when you've made up your minds about something. You aren't rigid, but full of ideas, you are capable of improvising, and you are intelligent. You know how to deal with foreign nations and have lived under one long enough. All in all, we simply believe that you guys are much too valuable to just disappear, to submerge nameless, as you would in some of the other units. Alone, you won't achieve anything, but together – big stuff! There's no life insurance in a war, not with us, nor with another troop.' And then, after another pause, he concluded: 'But, if you really want it, then I will have you transferred tomorrow to the bicycle battalion in Stockerau!'

'No – no – just please not that!' I exclaimed, horrified.

That was what decided it for me. Just the thought of being part of a bicycle battalion was enough to make me shudder with dismay.

'I don't want to go away,' I added slowly. 'I promise to be a good soldier – to become a good Brandenburger.'

We shook hands.

This one discussion with Grabert was of enduring importance to me in my role as a Brandenburger. It had two effects: one was immediate, the other would only become obvious later on. The immediate result of this conversation with my company commander was psychological. Instantly I felt relieved, a heavy load seemed to have been lifted from my heart. Just as a new day dawns after a night filled with dark nightmares and the first rays of sunshine break through the blustery winds and stormy clouds, all my reservations and troubles, my fears about the impending operation, were blown away. Once again I felt myself part of my circle of friends, as if I had returned to the fold, back to my big family. The sense of responsibility for my group of men filled me with extra strength and took away my fears. I had become a member of the Brandenburger club.

The second result of my discussion with Grabert would emerge later in life, and not in any positive way. Of course, Grabert had informed my platoon leader, Sergeant Hiller of the conversation, as well as informing my individual junior squad leader, Rosenkranz. Both men kept a close eye on me. Even though they never made any reference to the discussion I had had, I would nevertheless feel that they treated me with suspicion, especially when it came to the Balkan campaign. They certainly scrutinised minutely how I behaved vis-à-vis the enemy. Hiller simply couldn't grasp the fact that a soldier, and one of his men at that, would have a debate with the company commander on how war was to be waged, and even go so far as to question its justification. Such a soldier would either have to be kept under close observation and control, or be sent away, far away. Over the course of time, a sort of love–hate relationship was to develop between Hiller and myself, which only ended with Hiller's death in Bataisk.

Suddenly the day of our departure to Romania had arrived. My final act was to send home my suitcase with my remaining civilian clothes, send my last Reichsmark to my sister and prepare for war.

— SIX —

The Balkan Campaign

Via Romania to Greece

Saturday, 5 April 1941. The tent camp at Petric, Bulgaria, had been calm and peaceful but was now a hive of activity. The company was preparing for action. The moment had come: the actual war, with all it entailed – shooting, throwing hand grenades, all accompanied by the sound of artillery and tanks rattling – was to begin.

Until now, everything we had experienced in the Balkans had been little more than child's play, a sort of KdF trip, albeit not short of interesting and sometimes even thrilling events, in Romania and Bulgaria.[1] But now, the very next day in fact, it was to get serious. We had occupied the oil rigs in Campina, north of Plösti, standing guard was endless, but other than that there was nothing, absolutely nothing. We hadn't seen one Englishman, nor heard any. There was nothing but mud, snow and freezing temperatures.

One snowy and ice-cold day, we all – that is, the entire company – had driven in our army lorry through Bucharest to Giurgiu on the Danube. We had been ordered to arrive there in the middle of the night when it was pitch black. We stopped the truck once in the middle of a field to take a leak. Darkness surrounded us. We had to fasten the tarpaulins that covered our trucks tightly and were ordered not to stick our heads out, under no circumstances, no matter what happened. There should be total silence, no word must be spoken.

The drive continued. The night was coal black; it was still snowing. At midnight, we reached the port of Giurgiu. We stopped and waited. Here and there we heard somebody speaking but didn't understand what it was about. At last, somebody from the outside lifted our tarpaulin by just a crack and our squadron leader, Oberjäger Rosenkranz, stuck his head in. 'Get out,' he whispered, 'bring only your weapons and ammunition. Clothes remain in the truck. Quick and not a word. Don't make a sound. Come on, make it quick, down you get.'

We obeyed the order. We had to report. We then marched down to the river. There was no light. Each of us closely following the person in front, we moved in one tight group. It was absolutely still. Our heavy mountain boots crunching in the snow was the only noise in the dark. We crossed a wooden plank and boarded a large ferry anchored on the riverbank. Swiftly, we disappeared through the hatch into the belly of the ship. Once inside, nothing but a flickering oil lamp lit the space. There were several large wooden crates and, on the floor, heaps of brown uniforms.

'Take off your uniforms, pack them up into your rucksack. Put on that brown clobber – nobody gives a shit whether they fit you or not. You can switch them around later among yourselves,' ordered Oberjäger Rosenkranz. 'Quickly and keep silent. I don't want to hear a word.'

While we were busy with these uniforms, we felt a slight rumbling travel through the ship. The ferry had moved off the jetty and was making its way along the river. That's how we crossed the Danube, in the middle of the night and in heavy snowfall.

When we reached the other side of the river, landing in the port of Russe, Bulgaria, we left the ferry disguised in Bulgarian uniforms. Without wasting even a second, we dashed to the waiting train and boarded it. The compartments were dimly lit. Curtains were drawn shut, not allowing any light to filter outside. It was only now that we could actually get to look at each other and admire ourselves. Even though we were ordered to remain silent, we couldn't help bursting out laughing. We just looked too hilarious in those brown Bulgarian uniforms, and we could hardly recognise each other.

The train began to move, gathering speed and then rattling through the night. Only then did we feel it was safe for us to switch uniforms around, trying them on until everyone had found the right size for himself. When morning dawned and we were well inside Bulgaria, we looked like handsome Bulgarian soldiers – at least at a distance.

Throughout the day we criss-crossed the country by train, and never once did we know where we actually were. Even during daytime we had to keep the curtains shut. Every so often we would stop, and some groups would leave the train and march away. And there were groups who changed onto our train. We were being distributed across the entire country. Every strategic point, every bridge, factory, every railway junction, power plant, every dam and mine – our company had its men at every single position. The size and importance of the sites determined the number of the security force put in place, but it was never bigger than one squadron. In some instances, one squadron had to guard two sites.

Our destination lay deep within the countryside. To be precise, it was in the easternmost part of Bulgaria, at the intersection of Greece and Turkey. Our task was to protect both a power plant and a railway junction and prevent any sabotage.

It was night when we arrived in Svilengrad. We were expected by a Bulgarian officer, a genuine one, who accompanied us to the barracks. This was a large square building, which seemed more like a fortress due to its location and its construction. The courtyard was surrounded by a large and very strong wall. We were allocated a huge room up on the third floor that held twelve beds and one locker each. The floor was recently scrubbed clean, and the beds were freshly made up.

In the early hours of the morning we were shown, still by the same officer, what we were meant to be guarding. Together with a colleague, I was to guard the train station. That's where we spent the whole long day, or the whole long night, taking the guard duty in turns. We sat in the station building watching the station master make telephone calls, turn control levers or, with his red cap on, dispatch trains. We prowled between the train tracks, observing Bulgarian farmers unloading their straw baskets of vegetables and filling their carts. We never came too close to them – we tried to avoid any contact with the people so we never had to speak to them. We honestly believed that nobody would notice that we weren't real Bulgarian soldiers. But, of course, even from a distance, everyone saw that we weren't the real deal. They stared at us with curiosity and the word 'Germansky' was always heard being uttered under their breath. When off duty, we were in our room in the barracks. We had a beautiful view from the window. The fortress was situated on a hill, allowing us to see far off into the country. What else was there for us to do? We cleaned our weapons, slept or watched real Bulgarian comrades doing their drills and exercises. We had no contact with any other squads of our company. We didn't know where they were, what they were doing, or whether or not something was going on with them. It was hellishly boring.

Weeks passed. How much longer were we meant to do this guard duty?

Finally, there was some news: the German Wehrmacht was invading Bulgaria. Well, that put an end to our task. Two days later our lorries arrived. We changed out of the enemy uniform and once again we were German soldiers. We departed that same day: first we drove to Plovdiv, meeting up there with the rest of our company, and then onto Dolna Banja. There the entire company, previously distributed all over Bulgaria, finally convened.

The journey to Dolna Banja was anything but pleasant. At points we drove at a snail's pace. Endless military columns caused heavy congestion on the streets. The German Wehrmacht made its way south. Tanks, trucks, heavy artillery, vehicles of all sorts wound their way slowly, one behind the other, through the narrow pass roads of the Rhodope mountains. Meanwhile, the Gebirgsjäger had a terrible time on their mules and horses, with their backpacks and weapons heavy on their shoulders, and unwieldy ammunition boxes under their arms. Their faces, pouring with sweat, showed how strenuous the march was. Panting and swearing, they dragged their rifles up the mountain pass. Boy, weren't we the lucky ones, us fine folks who were at least allowed to drive? While we also swore, it was mainly at the driver when he wasn't paying attention and hit one of the countless potholes, which had us flying off our benches.

It was night-time when we arrived in Dolna Banja. Since the field kitchen hadn't even arrived yet, there was no food for us. It rained. We crawled into a shed and threw ourselves onto some damp and filthy straw that was lying there. It looked like the Bulgarian military had camped out here before us. It certainly smelled like it. Already by the following day, I felt that my back was strangely itchy. I scratched myself, but it didn't go away. 'Damn,' I thought to myself, 'I've caught lice or fleas.' I crept behind the house and examined my whole body. Yes, it was lice. I hadn't yet become the hardened Landser who didn't care the least bit about such things: I was shocked and felt embarrassed in front of my comrades. I thought that I was the only one who had caught these lice, so I didn't mention it to anybody but reported instead to the doctor. I had to wait outside his room until he was free. Finally, the door opened and he came out – it was Second Lieutenant Grabert. In his hand was a bottle of Cuprex, the insecticide.

'You too, Tschampetro?' he asked with a big grin on his face.

'Yes, sir, Second Lieutenant, me too,' I responded.

It turned out that half of the squadron was plagued by lice. We tossed the straw and scrubbed all the floors until the entire squadron stank of Cuprex. Luckily, Dolna Banja had some hot springs where we would spend hours.

Spring had arrived. A warm sun was shining down, the sky was clear, the meadows were green and the trees were in bloom. We had pitched our tents and built a campsite in the Struma valley, which was actually more of a broad crater. Surrounded to the north and the east by the Rhodope mountains, it looked out southwards onto an extremely high and steep mountain range. It rose before our eyes like a wall, inhospitable and forbidding. The mountain peaks were covered in snow. The length of the crest marked the border between Bulgaria and Greece. Into the rough gorge and the rugged rocks, the Greeks had, often with the help of explosives, cut out a huge number of bunkers and gun positions and dug trenches, MG nests and casemates. In between lay barbed wire and minefields. They had erected a fortress belt largely considered impregnable. Even the heaviest bombs would simply evaporate when hitting these rock walls, and not even the most reckless of assault troops would be able to come anywhere close to the bunkers.

The Greeks felt themselves totally secure behind their Metaxas Line. Now, way below, deep in the valley of Petric, the German Wehrmacht had assembled. Here, a powerful force had come together to prepare for a momentous assault, like an animal ambushing its prey. The moment had arrived – zero hour was here.

Some of our company had left early that morning. They were to infiltrate Greece by crossing the Metaxas Line disguised in Greek uniforms, capture a bridge behind the line and prevent it from being blown up. Well, all I could say to them at the time was: good luck, comrades!

We too got ready to decamp. Nothing but absolute essentials was to be packed into our rucksacks: toiletries and one change of clothing. The rest of the kit was stuffed into our laundry bags and thrown onto the baggage vehicle. We checked our ammunition, oiled our MG belts, filled our rifle cartridges with new bullets to prevent anything from getting stuck and cleaned our hand grenades. Finally, we filled our flasks with hot tea.

Those who had finished their preparations quickly wrote a letter home. We were still able to post some letters before 1800 hours. When would we get our next opportunity to do so? For how many of us would it be their last letter? Let's not even think about such things!

The snow-covered mountaintops turned blood red with the setting sun. Dusk fell. Lost in thought, we spread out underneath the blossoming trees. Nobody felt like talking any more.

'Get ready!'

The order tore us from our dreams. We dismantled the tents and lit a campfire just as always. The Greek observers weren't to notice that we were decamping. Tunics were buttoned up, belts slung around the waist and fastened to their hook were the steel helmets. We then grabbed our weapons. We were to report to the allocated spot, in front of the lorry, which was all set to leave. Second Lieutenant Grabert reported to the company commander that the squad was ready for action.

The sergeant addressed us: 'Men of Company 8, finally the operation that we have been expecting for so long is about to start. At dawn, the German Wehrmacht will traverse from the Karawanks to the Rhodope mountains to destroy the enemy of the German people on Balkan territory. We will chase the Tommy away from this corner of Europe, the corner he is so desperately clinging to. You should be proud to be able to take part in this historic event, and I am certain that you will make the Führer proud that he has put his faith in you.'

Sitting in our trucks, we drove in the direction of the Yugoslav border. Together with the 2nd Panzer Division, we were to push forwards deep into Yugoslavia and along the Struma river, turn into the Vardar valley and reach Salonica. This would allow us to circumvent, and indeed avoid, the Metaxas Line.

We reached the staging area. Tanks came rolling in from side valleys, forcing us off the road to make room for them. It seemed to go on forever. The hours passed slowly and none of us could really think of sleep. Some comrades gathered their blankets, spread them under a tree and had a smoke. Others remained on the truck, put their head on the petrol can or used their steel helmets as pillows, and dreamed with open eyes. I just dozed into the night.

The following day was Palm Sunday. In Sterzing, all the boys would march through the city holding up their palm rods, and I remembered how I had often balanced this long and heavy stick during the street procession. As images of my childhood rolled in front of my eyes, I mused how long ago all that seemed! I remembered how we had put paper helmets on our heads, slung wooden sabres over our shoulders, made cannons out of cartons and built trenches in the fields, but then, shocked by the sight of a small slowworm, ran away. Now it was no longer a game and the day had come.

I also remembered evenings spent in dank cellars, lit only by candles, when we listened to patriotic speeches and songs from our homeland. And then there were the sport camps held in remote Alpine meadows where we had organised competitions and games. And now, here we were, at the front, in the staging area. In just a few hours a war would be starting. Was this really what we had wanted? Was this what we had been aiming for? Yes, we did want to be part of it, that was certainly the case. I had to think of my parents, who were going to church tomorrow morning not suspecting anything, and I was imagining their fear, their anxiety for their son when they heard the special broadcasts. I had a strange sensation. Was it fear? What would tomorrow bring us? Would I have the strength to perform what was expected of me, would I find the courage? I rather thought that I would be scared shitless. I had to conjure up the picture of my girl – and all of a sudden, I felt brave. Anxious? Me? Ridiculous! I would stand my ground, I would wage war and I would win. She was going to be proud of me!

A train rattling by tore me out of my reveries. I got up. Some comrades had actually fallen asleep; I really envied them for being so calm, and stepped over them carefully. On the road, one tank was lined up against the next, a horribly beautiful band of lethal iron and steel.

I lit a cigarette as a tank division was being deployed across from us. I had never seen anything quite like it. As if pulled by a string, these black caterpillar vehicles weaved through the concourse while motorcycle messengers whizzed back and forth. The luminous dial of my watch pointed to 4 a.m. There were only a few minutes before crunch time. 'Helmets on, lock and load.'

A strange stillness swept over the mountains and valleys, while along the entire front, at every point, the stormtroops stood ready, waiting with bated breath to hear the commander bark out the order to attack. Somewhere, in the background, you could hear Stukas revving up their engines, and combat squadrons starting up.

Sitting on our trucks in silence, the leather straps of our helmets fastened tightly under our chins, we nervously fingered our weapons. Suddenly the driver of the tank in the vanguard pushed his arm up into the air, yelling, 'Tanks – forward, go!' The command passed from one mouth to the next, through the entire column. The war had started.

Lightning erupted on the mountain ridge, we could already make out the sharp contours as the early morning mist lifted. The sounds of crackling gunshots and thunderous explosions filled the valley. White fireballs ascended in the sky, extinguished and fell. Up there, the Gebirgsjäger stormed the Metaxas Line.

It became lighter. All of a sudden, we heard the drone of turbines ripping the air with nerve-wracking howls. A Stuka squadron thundered above us, getting ready to make a crash-landing. We heard another splintering howl, and then it was over.

We joined the column lining up behind the armoured reconnaissance vehicle and crossed the Yugoslavian frontier. The guardhouse was on fire, burnt-out vehicles lay in the trench. The lead tanks rolled forwards, firing continuously. We saw the areas that had been hit by shells, with smoke still rising. Motorcycle messengers wound their way between tanks and vehicles, clenching paper messages between their lips. The narrow road was totally blocked by all kinds of vehicles. The column slithered forwards like a snake covered by a thick cloud of smoke. From the reeds and the ponds you could hear frogs and toads croaking in protest.

The first captured soldiers were already coming towards us, hands held high and terror in their eyes. Some were wounded and were being supported by their comrades. We removed their overcoats and caps; we were going to need them for our next operations. We examined their pockets, looking for their identity cards – these could also come in useful, we thought – but we found nothing. What must these poor devils have thought of us scoundrels stealing their coats and caps and emptying their pockets before sending them into captivity? Even our comrades from the tank brigade looked at us in disbelief, shouting at us. They couldn't make sense of our behaviour either.

The column had come to a standstill. Ahead, the resistance seemed to have gained in strength. We heard machine guns rattle and the dull sound of tank cannons going off.

Slowly we moved on. The first soldier was killed. One of our boys put his comrade to rest, next to the road, covering up his body with a tarpaulin. All of a sudden, we became profoundly aware of the bitter reality of war.

No time for mourning. A farm in the middle of the field became the object of our attention. We saw some people running around but couldn't make out whether they were soldiers or civilians. I was tasked to find out. One of the members of my pioneer squad volunteers was to accompany me. We sneaked around, protected by the bushes and shrubs. Circling the field, we approached the house, stopping some fifty metres in front of it. I left my comrade behind to stand guard. He was to provide covering fire while I ran towards the building, machine gun in hand. I couldn't detect any movement. Only some chickens, clucking away in the yard, flapped their wings and behind a shed a lonely pig grunted away, oblivious to us humans. I kicked open the door and cautiously peered in. There, in the corner, two men and a woman were crouching on the floor, trembling from head to toe. Beseechingly they stretched out their arms to me. My comrade joined me. We inspected the house and returned to our group.

Slowly the defilade drove on.

'Clear the road, the general is arriving.' The call spread like wildfire, reaching the rear in seconds.

Swinging to the right, we craned our necks to see the general. And he was there, standing erect in his Kübelwagen, holding in his hands a map, his Iron

Cross gleaming in the sunlight.[2] This was the first time we had seen a general, and here was, in the vanguard. He really made a huge impression on us, as we hadn't expected this.

We were able to move forwards only haltingly. The Serbs put up quite a bit of resistance. Noise from the battlefield grew steadily louder as we drove, and along the side of the street we came across four German tanks with broken tracks. They had obviously hit a mine. Some crewmembers were already hard at work, fixing the damage.

Second Lieutenant Grabert had driven ahead to the general. Anxiously we awaited his return. He came back after just a few minutes, ordering us to the front. We were tasked to move into Novo Selo, a small Serbian village, and eradicate the enemy within.

Covered in a thick cloud of dust, we zoomed to the front along the bumpy country lane, passing tank barriers. A barricade of train tracks and cement blocks rammed into the ground spanned the terrain. Obviously, the enemy had intended to stop our tanks getting through. But our grenades had blown the tracks apart and the caterpillar tracks of our tanks had ground down the cement.

Some tanks had already traversed the village. Sitting in our trucks, speeding towards the settlement, we were ready to jump out at a moment's notice. We could, before we even knew it, be under enemy fire. Nothing happened. We reached the town centre and jumped from our trucks. Combing every house, we couldn't find a single person. They had all fled. In a pub, we came across some bottles of wine, which we emptied in one go, and a few eggs, which we ate just as quickly. No soldier on this earth would ignore such a booty. Then we caught up with the front of the tank column, which had already reached Strumica.

On the hills that surrounded the town on the left and right we could make out field positions and bunkers. Tanks opened fire on them. Guns and mortar fire from the town responded. We jumped down from the vehicles and, ducking the whole time, ran along the roadside ditches, right up to the tanks at the very front. They didn't dare proceed further. They feared that somewhere in the town entrance, a PaK anti-tank gun might be lurking.[3] Then General Veiel returned once again and threw himself down next to us in the ditch.[4]

What on earth was he doing here? We could manage on our own, but perhaps we weren't fast enough. His position was supposed to be further back, not here at the front. But wasn't it Guderian who once said that tanks must be led from the front? General Veiel followed this law to the letter. He ordered Second Lieutenant Grabert to invade the town. We worked our way through towards Strumica, ducking and moving cautiously along the sides of the street, just as we had been taught and had practised hundreds and hundreds of times back in the Allgäu. Under the cover of machine-gun fire, the soldiers moved forwards, all while we were coming closer to the target.

The gunfire had mostly died down, only a few shots could still be heard. It seemed that the enemy had fled. We had reached the first houses but encountered no resistance. Carefully, we moved further in and made it to the centre of town without having to fire a single shot. Some civilians came out of their houses, and here and there we saw somebody opening their window shutters, tentatively, just a narrow slit. A nosy woman poked her head out. Soon we were encircled by a bunch of civilians. Everybody was confused and all talking at the same time; we couldn't understand a single word. They stared at us, looking us up and down, before bringing us some wine and salt.[5] Even the town priest came, bringing the mayor, who made a big song and dance of presenting us with the keys to the town. We thoroughly enjoyed having honours bestowed upon us, and we felt like proper heroes.

In the meantime, the tanks had caught up with us, and along with them two rifle squads who combed the entire city in search of anyone suspicious. After two hours, we drove on.

We had come from the east and now turned southwards to the Greek frontier and the Vardar valley, from where we were ordered to push forwards along the coast up to Salonica.

We didn't get very far that day. While the valley is quite broad around Strumica, it narrows down towards the south, finally forming a ravine that is barely traversable and extremely rocky. The plan was to get across, but already one kilometre outside Strumica we had come to a complete halt. In front of us lay a bridge that had been torn to pieces by an explosion. Military engineers were already hard at work building a makeshift crossing. That suited us fine. We threw ourselves onto the grass and enjoyed lounging in the sun for a while.

But there is no rest for a soldier if the sergeant won't have it. And what possessed Sergeant Rosenkranz to be curious and scour the surroundings with a telescope, I will never know. In any event, that was the end of our supposed rest time.

West of the road, the terrain ascended, first only gradually, then becoming steeper and steeper. Meadows and fields were flanked by bushes and clusters of trees, and further up lay a vineyard, accessible through a small walled pathway which was broken up by some paved steps. There was nothing spectacular about this, unless you took a closer look, which was exactly what Rosenkranz did. He had a thing for walled constructions and curious-looking inclines. If he hadn't simply wondered about this in silence and to himself, our break would surely have remained uninterrupted. But no, Rosenkranz felt it behoved him to report his findings to Second Lieutenant Grabert, who was clearly of the opinion that we had lazed around long enough, as he ordered a reconnaissance patrol to ascend the slope and investigate. Purely out of curiosity, and to keep us on our feet. And upon whom did he bestow this honour? Yes, it was the Rosenkranz group.

While our comrades lay on their backs and continued dozing, we jumped to our feet and fell into formation. Oberjäger Rosenkranz headed our squad, walking along in his usual characteristically gangly gait, probably conditioned by the length of his legs. Serves him right, why on earth did he have to be so nosy? Together with my squad, I followed, all of us with two hand grenades on our belts, machine gun in hand. We were followed by the MG squad, the patrol squad taking up the rear. We stumbled, swore and cursed our fate as we climbed the steep path up and along the vineyards, finally reached a track that took us right across the slope.

Suddenly we were wide awake. There, in the middle of the pathway, lay an upturned cart with two dead horses sprawled out next to it. Hurriedly we examined the situation and realised that this must have been the transport for a Serb officer's luggage, as what we found was not only laundry bags and boots, but also a shirt from a Serb uniform. So, something must have been happening up here. We left the road and climbed the mountain, walking along a row of bushes that protected us. The climb was steep and arduous, and then we came to a halt: a stoney step-like construction blocked our way. We helped each other up it, step by step, until we couldn't get any further. The last bit of wall rising vertically above the last step was about one and a half metres high and covered by entangled barbed wire. On this last step, there was just about enough standing room for Sergeant Rosenkranz, me, and one of my men from the reconnaissance squad. The others stayed on the steps below. After cutting a hole in the wire with our wire cutters and half-standing, we were able to at least put our heads over. In front of us lay a meadow sloping slightly upwards for some eighty metres, at the end of which we could make out some freshly dug earth mounds. These seemed very suspicious. As far as we could judge from where we were positioned, these were some sort of field fortifications. Without serious fire to give us cover, there was no way to get across that field, either by crawling or running through it, as it lay wide open and within firing range. We withdrew our heads and consulted about what we should do.

Oberjäger Rosenkranz ordered me to inch along the small wall to the left and investigate if there was a possibility of moving forward under cover, and whether there were any bunkers or field fortifications I could make out on the hill opposite us across a small valley. Trying not to make any noise, pointing my MPi submachine gun in front of me with both hands, supporting myself on elbows and knees, I crawled along the wall, my comrade following close behind. I didn't get very far: just fifty metres along, barbed wire blocked the way. I pressed myself hard against the wall, prised the wire apart, took off my steel helmet and cautiously put my head through the wire. This allowed me a better view of what was happening on the mountainside opposite. Damn and damn again! More bunkers and more trenches. I drew my head back and turned to my comrades, just about to inform them, when … There! I heard a cracking noise and looked up. What was it? There, I heard the noise again, the same soft metallic sound of someone fumbling with his machine gun.

Goodness, this guy must be sitting right above me. I came out in a cold sweat. My friend behind me had also heard the clicking. We looked at each other, both of us fearing the exact same thing. I winked at him and motioned upwards; he nodded. I breathed in deeply a few times, just to calm myself down, and slowly cocked my gun. For God's sake, let's not make any noise. If the guys above us notice us they will simply hit us over the head. It was a miracle that they hadn't spotted us yet. I carefully pulled up my legs, straightened my muscles slowly as I got to my feet, and twisted my neck to peer over the wall. I saw a Serb steel helmet, nothing more, but so close I could have touched it.

Gun in position, I jumped up and yelled: '*Hände hoch!*' – I saw myself, standing right in front of an MG nest with four Serbian soldiers. They were terrified, staring into the muzzle of my gun.

Slowly they lifted their arms, then they came out of the alcove in the wall where they had been hiding. While my comrade held them in check with his gun, I simply reached out and confiscated the two machine guns. We returned to our group with four prisoners and the two machine guns we had captured.

Oberjäger Rosenkranz listened to my report and patted me on the back in recognition. The decision was made to return. It would have been sheer folly to attempt, with only the four of us, to storm the whole mountain. Besides, we had fulfilled our task – in fact, gone beyond the call of duty: we had ascertained that the mountain was occupied by strong forces who had set themselves up in field camps. Our proof was the four captured men.

We aborted the reconnaissance mission and returned to the valley, but not before we gathered fresh laundry from the overthrown cart with the luggage belonging to the Serbian officer. Night was falling and it was too dark for us to eradicate the enemy from the entire mountain area, even with the support of reinforcements. The four captives were transported to Strumica.

The time had finally come for us to look after ourselves and our growling stomachs. The field kitchen had got stuck somewhere in the back of our column, so there was no food. But we had the iron rations to fall back on. While the rules said you were only allowed to access them after three days of hunger, the truth was, by that point, we were so hungry it felt as if we had indeed eaten nothing for three days. We therefore didn't hesitate to open up our reserves and eat the lot.

We quenched our thirst with what was left of the boring tea in our flasks. Then we prepared our truck for the night. That was always a big job, but eventually we had got the hang of it. We realised that the best method was to lay rucksacks on petrol cans on the base of the truck, and by using the benches too, we managed to prepare quite an even surface on which we could lie. Each of us then wrapped himself in his blanket and after a short while, once we had found our most comfortable position, we all quickly fell into a deep sleep, even those who had their legs hanging out over the truck's tailboard, or were lying curled up on the hard planks. Soon all you heard was the loud snoring and the footsteps of the guards who protected us during the night. The first day of war had ended.

As soon as the morning mist lifted, we crawled out of our blankets and then did some bending and stretching exercises to loosen up our bones and muscles. There were black clouds in the sky; it would certainly rain today. We had to skip the morning toilet routine, as there was no water other than a stinking and poisonously green murky puddle, in which frogs had been croaking all through the night. If you pushed down firmly on the algae covering the ponds with your two hands, you might be lucky and get yourself a handful of water. It was probably just enough to smear the grime and filth around your face a bit more evenly.

Time passed, and we had nothing to do but wait. So, wait we did – an activity that isn't so unwelcome for a soldier.

The Serbs started descending the mountain, either one by one or in small groups. We checked them for any weapons and then moved them on to the prisoners' camp. Some really cheeky ones wore civilian clothing and tried to squeeze by us, looking all innocent. Such ludicrous camouflage! Nobody could fool us. We immediately recognised the army boots or the cleanly shaved heads, even if they tried to conceal them by hats. Some just wore a civilian overcoat on top of their uniform. We called this semi-camouflage. But they all ended up in the prison camp. Who would have thought then, that one day the glorious German Wehrmacht would suffer the very same fate?

In the afternoon, an armoured car arrived and we were ordered to move to the front line. We drove through a narrow ravine. There was just enough space for a road and the river, with foamy water breaking against the rocks. Halfway up the ravine, the Serbs had blown up a bridge. That was the reason we hadn't been able to continue yesterday. The military engineers had worked through the night just to get some sort of crossing built. Finally, we managed to get ourselves out of the gorge. Being so closed in and threatened by nature felt very oppressive.

The valley broadened out and the path wound its way up the mountain. Somewhere, surely, there had to be a pass.

At the first turn we met up with the advance detachment, who informed us that we couldn't move forwards due to the shelling in the road. We wanted to reach the front of the column despite the warnings but quickly had to jump off our vehicles and dive into the ditches as we were being targeted by machine guns. Shots missed us by a hair's breadth. Protection squads fought their way up the mountain. A Fieseler Storch circled the pass, but kept disappearing behind the mountains and reappearing again, dropping purple flares that illuminated the sky. It was the signal for 'enemy tanks attacking!' That got us lot moving.

'PaK to the front!'

'Flak to the front!'

These shouts made the rounds, passing from one mouth to the next. Motorcycle messengers hurtled back and forth. Tanks, which had been waiting at the sides of the road, now spread out in all directions. Tank destroyers equipped with Flaks came rattling by, along with half-track vehicles carrying artillery, and commands were bellowed back and forth. Swiftly, the tank squad set up the weapons in firing positions while the other vehicles took cover on the rear slope.

Ordered to move to the top, we were to secure the PaK positions on the left. Panting up the slope, we arrived at the summit. From there, we had a good view far across enemy territory. The enemy fire increased. Shells exploded above our heads, then crashed down on the far side of the valley.

Next to us, an additional PaK position was set up with a wide target range. We were lying in wait on the rear slope with just our heads poking over the top. Where were those enemy tanks that were meant to attack us? They must be somewhere on the pass road, as the terrain was much too steep for them to have spread out. We attempted to penetrate the bushes, which partially obstructed our view of the road, but no enemy tanks were in sight.

But then, a bit further away, all of a sudden, the first Serbian tank appeared just beyond the turning. The PaK gunners had also caught sight of it. Furiously they cranked up their guns, targeted and – there – the first shell was hurled across the terrain. In amazement, we followed its trajectory. Mud flew skywards – the shot had missed its target by a few metres and the tank, unscathed, drove on. But a few seconds later the second projectile flew and now, finally – boom – a direct hit. A jet of flame shot up and the entire tank was ablaze. We jumped up and cheered loudly.

A second tank appeared close behind, and then a third one. Our PaK and Flak got them immediately, showering them with a hail of bullets. Boom – another direct hit. Only a few minutes had passed and already three tanks were in flames. A fourth one would soon suffer the same fate. For a while, calm set in.

Black clouds had gathered in the sky; it was getting dark. A torrential downpour with thunder and lightning added to the noise of the artillery. We were soaked to the skin in seconds but we didn't notice.

Other tanks followed and were immediately met by our PaK. One or two shots ricocheted off the rocks and bounced into the sky. Crashing, banging, and rumbling mixed with the thunder and lightning to fill the air. Again and again, whoosh – direct hit. As night fell those Serbian tanks burnt like torches, a gruesome sight; I almost lost count of them: thirteen or fourteen?

We had successfully stopped the Serbian tank assault without any of their soldiers being able to fire a single shot.

And with that the advance detachment was able to carry on while our squad members returned to our vehicles, running as fast as we could. Two columns of vehicles wound their way, following each other closely, up the pass, coming within inches of treacherous crevices and mountain crags. Just the tiniest mistake by the driver, and we would have tumbled down the mountain. Our fate lay entirely in his hands. Sitting way up on the vehicle, we could only hope and pray that the wheels wouldn't slip in the soggy marshland.

For a while, we drove alongside a field kitchen. What a welcome encounter that was, and one which we of course made sure to take advantage of. We asked for our flasks to be filled with hot coffee as we were bitterly cold and drenched through. A small army field mailbox was attached to the back of the car, and I seized the opportunity to scribble a few lines to my folks back home. All in all, an agreeable break.

When we finally reached the top of the pass, night had fallen. Through a narrow slit in the tarpaulin, we could just about make out the road. The black-painted headlights gave off only a dim light, making it even more difficult to navigate. No moon and no stars could be seen. Clouds, heavy with rain, hung menacingly over the pass. The serpentine road leading down to the village seemed dangerous and endless. To our right and left, the wrecked Serbian tanks were still smouldering, some were even ablaze. Charcoaled bodies were scattered next to them. Some tanks had been spared from damage; vehicles which their crews had obviously abandoned now stood at our disposal. We counted the destroyed enemy tanks: seventeen.

Once we drew the tarpaulin shut over our truck, it became quite cosy in our little den. The uniforms were boiling hot, and it felt like a steam room. We wrapped ourselves in our blankets, teased and insulted each other, laughed together, and then, impossible though it might seem in retrospect, we managed to fall asleep while the vehicle rumbled along the bumpy roadway. Sometimes – well actually it happened very often – it came to an abrupt halt, or drove into a particularly nasty pothole, and we all went flying, together with our rucksacks, weapons and canisters. We simply packed everything back together, ourselves included, and went back to sleep.

This night came to an end. Morning was dawning. The clouds had broken up and the sky was clear. We had driven through the whole night and had reached the Greek frontier.

We threw our blankets off, rolled back the tarpaulin, sorted out the messy piles of luggage, put everything in its place, and were once more ready for war. Not a minute too soon. From the front, the sounds of launched tank grenades and rattling machine guns quickly travelled to where we were waiting. We were only able to move at a snail's pace.

Our Fieseler Storch had also returned, flying low over the grassland. Our column immediately recognised the whirring noise its engine made, and we could even make out the pilot and his co-pilot as we waved to each other. He flew in a loop over the lake, gaining in altitude as he approached the frontier. That's when the Greek Flak began to shoot at the reconnaissance aircraft and hit it. The plane came down in a flag of black smoke and crashed into the lake. We were furious.

The house of the Greek border guard that we reached a little while later lay in the midst of a beautiful small garden, filled with nice flowers and trees in bloom, and a large plaque with the Greek coat of arms adorning the front. But we couldn't go any further, as in front of us the road had been blown up and mined. It wasn't our job to clean up, so we turned around and drove along the narrow field path across the hilly terrain. Turning our vehicles around crushed the beautiful garden, turning its flowers and young trees in bloom into pulp.

The tanks had already spread out and, shielding each other from fire, we drove across the field. We also provided cover for the infantry fighting its way towards the fortifications and bunkers. This was the first time we witnessed flamethrowers in action.

Driving at lightning speed, we reached an incline and stopped where there was lower ground. That's where our field artillery was, all ready and positioned for firing. The gunners shoved the shells straight from the armoured tank into their guns. Open lock, close lock – bang. Open lock, out flew the cartridge, new one loaded, close lock – bang. It ran like clockwork.

The tanks inched forwards. We followed just as slowly; ours were, in fact, the first unarmed vehicles.

All of a sudden, we heard our machine-gunner yell out. He was clutching one of his arms. Blood was running down his hand and dripping to the ground. He had been shot right in his left elbow. We were devastated. What on earth was happening? Here we were, sitting peacefully in our vehicle, driving along, and, there, bang, you get hit. We put an emergency dressing on our comrade's arm, then had him transported by motorcycle to the first-aid station. For him this was the end of the war, one which in effect hadn't even properly begun. As for us, we all felt nauseous. We crouched behind the bushes. Not out of fear – no, no, just as a precautionary measure. If you were to receive a shot in the stomach, it was advisable that you empty your bowels beforehand, that's what we had been told. Suddenly, we felt very small. No longer were we sitting upright and arrogant on the top of our vehicles, as if we were nothing but curious onlookers in the spectators' gallery with the war unfolding beneath us. All we did now was peer furtively over the truck tailgate.

Infantrymen came down the mountain. Filthy, bruised, they dragged themselves down, and once they reached us they just collapsed on the road. Some had their arms and legs covered in bandages with blood seeping through.

***

We arrived in the Vardar valley. Every now and again we came across some Greek soldiers, who appeared from the oak thickets, holding their hands high. Close to a small village, we even met an entire company, all marching in orderly rows, the leader at the front. I must admit, it was a true example of good discipline. When we stopped them, asking if any of them hailed from Axiopolis, one man told us that it was his hometown. We ordered him to come with us on the truck and show us the Vardar bridge, near Axiopolis. In the meantime, we were sort of given to understand that our first camouflage operation was coming up: we were to occupy this strategically important bridge and save it from being blown up. When it dawned on the soldier that he had no choice but to come along with us, he was gripped by fear and began to shake all over. Would you believe it, he even started howling like a child? It was a disgusting sight, but I felt pity for him. He just couldn't understand why, of all people, he had been chosen to drive with us, whereas his comrades were permitted to be taken prisoner. We would have loved to just chuck him out of our truck.

Gradually the valley became broader and more open, making it possible for our trucks to overtake all the tanks along the road and reach the area down below. The further we advanced, the more excited we became. A strange feeling gripped hold of me, something I was to experience quite frequently in the course of this war. I felt it every time we were about to engage in a camouflage operation. It was a mixture of fear, expectation, hope and hunting fever. Nobody quite knew what would happen, and although I had tried to picture it thousands of times in my mind, the reality would be rather different. Would I be able to deal with this tension, strained to breaking point? Or would fear take hold of me? Covered in sweat, I felt paralysed. Dear God, let something happen to abort the mission at the last minute. It had happened several times in the past, so why not now? Why wouldn't one of the springs of our truck snap, or one of its axles? Every time the truck stopped, I breathed a sigh of relief, thinking that the operation would be abandoned. 'What a coward you are,' I would scold myself. 'Back home, why, even back at the base you played the hero, you showed off, citing stuff like zbV, bragging about being part of a special unit and so forth and now, when things are getting serious, you shit your pants.' I tried to calm myself, to keep my trembling hands and knees still.

My comrades were nervous too. Silently we fumbled with our weapons, checked the hand grenades, the ammunition belt and the MPi magazine. We laid out the Serb and Greek clothes, just so that we had something to do, and to keep us and our hands from shaking.

We had now reached the tanks in the vanguard, where a sergeant was standing upright in his cupola hatch. When we were alongside him, he looked at us in surprise.

'What are you doing here?' he asked. Second Lieutenant Grabert climbed up to him and explained what we were doing. With luck he will send us back, we were all probably thinking. They pored over a map. We couldn't hear what they were saying. The conversation didn't last long. Grabert saluted, then jumped down from the tank.

'Let's go, boys, it's our turn now!' he shouted to us. He mounted the truck and off we went, as the tank crew stared at us in total astonishment.

Close behind us came the second truck of our squad. We knew that they would remain behind to form the bridgehead on this side, while we in the first truck would reach the bridge, cross the river and secure the bridgehead on the other side. That was the way our operations had been planned, how we had practised them over and over. No orders were needed, each of us knew exactly what he had to do. What mattered most was to put as much distance between us and the first tanks as possible, allowing us to gain a lead of several kilometres. The enemy must have no clue about this manoeuvre, otherwise he would be ready to welcome us with open arms.

We came to a road and, thank goodness, we were no longer on an open field, where we might be spotted much more easily. We drove on at breakneck speed. Silently we sat on our benches. After a few kilometres, we stopped underneath in the shade of some trees. Our tanks behind, scheduled to drive on half an hour after our departure, had long ago lost sight of us. It was quiet around us, nobody in view; it was as though the war was a world away from where we were. We jumped down. The Serbian coats came flying down off the truck. Everyone caught hold of one, pulled it over his uniform, and put one of these local berets on his head while tucking our own mountain cap into our belt. One of our guys ripped off the front licence plate of our truck, while another one smeared dirt on the back plate so that no one could read it, and within minutes we had turned into just ordinary Serbian refugees, sitting on a nondescript truck. The Greek soldier we had with us just sat there next to the driver's seat, mouth agape, not believing his eyes. You could tell he no longer understood what was happening. We concealed our German weapons beneath the coats, just letting a few Serbian rifles we had gathered up somewhere along the way show. I decided, just in case I needed it, to put an egg hand grenade into my coat pocket.[6]

Now that there was no turning back, my earlier feelings of tension and worry were replaced by a grim decisiveness. Gone were all my fears. My nerves and muscles were strung tight, and my only focus was that cursed bridge. If we were ready to sell our skin, we were damned if we wouldn't do so at a very high price. My brain felt like mush, and everything around me seemed foggy and unclear, as if I had nothing to do with it – it was like a dream, unreal. My actions became automatic, unconscious, there is no thinking on my part.

We reached the top of a hill; below us and to our right we could see a broad river, which had to be the Vardar. So that's the route we had to follow in order to get to the bridge, and it couldn't be too far away.

Suddenly we saw some Greek soldiers standing in the middle of the road, blocking us. Wildly waving their rifles in the air, they refused to budge. We had to stop. Slowly, without causing any upheaval, I unlocked my MPi. The driver signalled the soldiers to get lost. I had no idea what language he was jabbering in, but it was of no importance since the Greeks didn't understand a word of Serb anyway, even if our driver did. Among all the shouting, I could only catch the word 'Germansky'. Were they about to discover us?

'Get lost, you dimwits,' I mouthed in their direction. 'Count yourselves lucky to even be alive.'

They did not give up easily and wanted to climb up onto our truck. They handed us up their rifles, which we of course gratefully accepted. Some soldiers actually managed to climb into the truck, sitting down beside us on the benches and speaking non-stop. Others simply stood on the footboard, and our ride continued. Everyone seemed to be happy. We, because we now had genuine Greeks on board, which only helped confirm our camouflage, and the others, because they had caught a last-minute ride and could get away. The disappointment which awaited them was, of course, awful. That's how we finally reached Polikastron, a small train station. The hamlet consisted of only a few low buildings along the road. Farmers ran around trying to catch some chickens. A few of their womenfolk hid behind windows and doors, throwing furtive glances at us. We just continued driving.

And there, all of a sudden, the bridge was before us. We had reached our destination. Our eyes remained fixed, committing every inch of the surroundings to memory. At right angles to where we were positioned, the road turned right, crossed the train tracks and went through a small forest and then over a bridge of some 200 metres, some marshland, finally ending up at the river. Every single detail became imprinted on our brain. What we saw were bunkers, trenches, and MG posts. Well, it would be our comrades arriving with the second truck who would have to deal with that.

***

78

More and more people wanted to get on our truck. 'Sorry , folks, we're full.' The Greeks who stood on our footboard gesticulated and shouted at their compatriots. That was fine by us, as it meant they freed up the road and we didn't have to do a thing. The soldiers sitting with us on the truck yelled at their comrades in the trenches, which obviously left them quite perplexed. All I understood was 'Germansky, Germansky'. A farcical situation, but in the end, it wasn't funny at all but bitterly serious.

Our drive continued at walking pace. At one point we got caught between an agitated crowd of people who had appeared on the road out of nowhere and were pushing with their bare hands some wooden wagons full of what seemed to be junk and rubbish. We were in the middle of the bridge. Our eyes, fixed to the front of us, glided over their heads, our eyes not meeting theirs. 'If we are discovered now, there will surely be a bloodbath,' we thought. And what we definitely didn't need at all was this other truck, which all of a sudden rumbled towards us from the other direction. It was full of soldiers. It was driving head-on towards the crowds. Men pushed past, wedged between the bridge railing and our vehicle. As if nobody were in the way, the truck moved along freely and approached us. The two vehicles stood facing each other, engine to engine, the bridge much too narrow for the two of us to pass. Nobody wanted to back up and nobody wanted to let the other one through. And between us were screaming civilians. Our driver firmly pressed the horn down without letting go while our Greek guys on board gesticulated and shouted like mad. Finally, the driver of the Greek truck went in reverse and moved back. We followed him closely and drew our weapons from underneath the coats. One of the Greek soldiers on our truck noticed our fumbling. He got hold of a gun and wanted to jump off. That was all we needed: now, a few seconds before we could reach the other end, this guy was going to mess it all up.

Pioneer Pfeifhofer was quick to react. He pulled the trigger of his 0.8 and mowed him down. The man fell backwards from the truck. Horrified civilians broke away and ran back. It was chaos.

We, sitting in the trucks, hardly reacted to this incident, and only later, when we revisited the events of the day, did it come up in conversation. We were completely focused on the end of the bridge where, all of a sudden, a reconnaissance vehicle had come into view. From its turret, two soldiers looked at the scene in bewilderment. They were wearing British steel helmets. Were they actually British? It was time for us to act. The first hand grenades were launched at the guardhouse of the bridge. We jumped from our truck and bellowed: 'Hands up!' Pointing our pistols, we ordered the crew to dismount. They put up their hands and descended from the tank.

They didn't understand what was happening. This was the first time we had come face to face with British soldiers and presumably the other way around as well.

At this point, just about everything was chaos. Everyone was running back and forth, away from everything and in all directions. Nobody knew what game was being played there. Civilians had vanished from the face of the earth. It was only we who acted, and we did so with purpose and skill. We actually welcomed the panic that had erupted. The bridgehead had been secured by the infantry, and soldiers had positioned their machine guns in the trenches. Together with my three pioneers, I ran up to the bridge. With wire cutters, we cut every wire we came across. While still running, we pulled our Serbian greatcoats off and chucked away the headgear. We grabbed hold of our own mountain caps from our belts and put them on so that we wouldn't kill each other. Once again, we were German soldiers.

I waded through the shallow waters, climbed up the dock, and ripped out all the cables and explosives that had been attached to the linkages. Everything happened at lightning speed, no orders were necessary, there was no room for hesitation, nor any attention given to the bullets whistling past our ears and ricocheting off the dock. We were on automatic, that was how we had been drilled. And we succeeded. Thanks to us, it was impossible for anyone to blow up the bridge.

We threw ourselves into the roadside ditch to take cover. Not a minute too soon, as bullets came raining down on us. It looked like the firing was coming from an incline some 300 metres high. Bullets splashed into the water behind us, some ricocheting, swishing through the air, a line of tiny dust clouds whirled along the road. With my heart pounding, I lay flat on my stomach in the mud, expecting to be hit. Then our machine guns started firing, which allowed us some breathing space.

But then we heard the gunners yelling: 'English tank ahead!' I raised my head and saw it for myself. At full speed, an armoured reconnaissance vehicle from Axiopolis tore down the road towards the bridge. He passed the gunners who lay hidden in the ditch while throwing hand grenades. The vehicle took no notice and continued.

'Concentrated charge – now!' shouted Grabert.[7] For God's sake, where was the charge? Yes, of course, it was back in the truck up there, and in this mad rush we had completely forgotten it. The reconnaissance vehicle reached the bridge and stopped. It couldn't continue, our truck was blocking its path. I was flat on the ground, hoping to be swallowed up.

'Concentrated charge – now, damn you!' yelled Grabert again. The vehicle attempted to pass, but his rear skidded into the ditch.

In a few swift movements I leaped onto the road and then jumped onto the truck to get the charge. With all the rucksacks, ammunition boxes, canisters, weapons and clothing piled up on top of each another, I just couldn't find it. Lying on my stomach, I searched desperately while my comrades shot at the reconnaisance vehicle, which was apparently still stuck in the ditch. I threw rucksacks and ammunition boxes onto the road, sweat pouring down my face and stinging my eyes. Where the hell was the charge? It had to be there somewhere, for God's sake – we had assembled it ourselves not long ago! Finally, I found it. Of course, it had to be at the far end and at the very bottom. I tore it out, pulled myself up a little bit to get a view of the reconnaissance vehicle – it was no more than ten metres away. I jumped off our truck and flung myself into the ditch. The vehicle was backing up. Grabert was lying on the other side of the road, shooting with his MPi and trying to hit the observation port. I gathered myself up and, running along the ditch after the reconnaissance vehicle, I tried slinging the charge under its belly. Too late – it merrily rolled off towards Axiopolis with only two wheels blown to bits.

For a while, there was only silence. An abrupt silence, one that suddenly blotted out the noise of past gunshots and war. It was eery. In moments like this, one felt disoriented, as if something was missing. We awaited the next burst of fire that would surely be fiercer and more focused than what had gone before. The likelihood that the enemy would roll up in armoured tanks at any moment concerned us.

Slowly, I raised my head and got myself into a kneeling position so I could look around. Here and there, a head appeared from behind a rock or out of a hole, we looked at each other, our eyes asking the questions.

'Stay under cover, boys,' shouted Second Lieutenant Grabert. 'Pay attention, it's going to start again.' We prepared our weapons; some of us jumped up and looked for better cover. We couldn't hear anything, not a shot, no engine sounds. It was an uneasy calm. What was the meaning of it? Was the enemy withdrawing, or would he go on his next assault? If they were clever, we thought, they would attack us with great force and we would be in trouble, seeing that all we had were weapons which were designed for close combat. There was little doubt in our minds that they would make mincemeat of us, and quickly at that. They must have surely noticed that we were just a few men who made a disproportionate amount of noise and fuss. The surprise card had been played, now it just depended who held the better trump card.

Hold on – what had happened to the other members of the crew whom we had taken out of the reconnaissance vehicle? I looked around and then spotted them sitting on the ground next to the brick guardhouse, leaning against the wall, calmly smoking cigarettes, as if they had nothing to do with the war. Only one of them seemed more nervous than the others. He anxiously puffed on his cigarette, restlessly shifting around until one of his comrades pushed him back to the ground and yelled at him. The others displayed this phlegmatic and casual sportsmanship, typical of the Brits – at least that's how I saw it at the time, and that's the way I understood it, maybe because my own feelings were much the same.

All they seemed to do was observe both us and the way we waged war, and I even detected some kind of wry smile on their faces.

Where on earth were our tanks? Why hadn't they arrived yet? We fired a white flare into the air: 'We are here', quickly followed by a red one, 'Hurry up, we need support'.

The immediate response we received was enemy fire, which forced us to the ground. I didn't dare raise my head but instead pressed my face into the earth. All I hoped for was that our machine-gunners had changed position and were now behind the trees, away from the road. They opened fire too. The sound of our own machine guns had a calming effect, these were short bursts, one quickly following the other; indeed, it was rather pleasant to hear.

But what was going on with those blasted tanks? Why weren't they arriving? White and red flares arced into the sky again. Surely, they must have seen them?

We knew our tanks were on the way even before we saw them, because of the shells, which suddenly whooshed by above us, crashing into the wall of the cemetery. The enemy fire stopped soon afterwards. The first German tank rolled over the Vardar bridge, which, as it turned out, was the only bridge that fell into German hands without suffering any damage, and that allowed our soldiers to advance unhindered further south.

We assembled at the bridge. Comrades from other bridgeheads joined us. Sitting at the side of the road, we wolfed down whatever we could get our hands on, after having thoroughly ransacked the British reconnaissance vehicle. We found plenty of biscuits, tinned fruit and corned beef, and Players cigarettes. We had to admit: these British led a good life. Of course, just about anything would have tasted better than our stale bread and liverwurst.

Now it was time for us to go over every part of our operation in great detail. Each of us had a story, his own personal experience.

We looked up and become aware of a slow-moving procession making its way from Axiopolis. At its head walked a man holding a long pole with a white blanket attached to it. He held it up ceremoniously in front of him, sometimes swaying it back and forth so that the white sheet could flutter a little bit on this windless afternoon. Next to him walked a clergyman, presumably the town priest. His long black cassock was torn and covered in dust, his grey beard nearly reached his waist. A tall, black, brimless hat covered his head. With both hands, he held a large crucifix. Some thirty men followed. Walking close behind the flag-bearer and priest, they huddled together, hesitant and nervous.

Once they had reached us, they really got started. Each one of them had something to say, all speaking at once and raising their voices. It was a mass of hands gesticulating in the air or folded in prayer, while a few monotonously repeated some litany. We couldn't understand a word, and laughing away, we nearly choked on our recently acquired corned beef.

Behind them came a few boys carrying crates full of raisins, sweets, chocolate and cigarettes all in white boxes. They had even remembered the wine. They uncorked the bottles, filled the glasses, and offered them to us with an inviting smile. Well, this was certainly a language we understood. A pleasant afternoon seemed to lie ahead of us.

The sun was about to disappear below the horizon when we finally set out. Soon we reached the advance party, which only had a few more kilometres to go before they reached Salonica. Rumour had it that the general was already in negotiations with the Greek authorities regarding the city's surrender. The next day we were to launch the invasion, so we remained with the advance party and waited. The term 'waiting' for us soldiers meant eating and sleeping, and we certainly indulged in both.

At dawn, we were ready to leave. Sitting up straight and proud in our Opel Blitz truck, we were all set to march into Salonica with great fanfare. But alas, the advance into Salonica was to take place without us.

Instead, we were ordered to get ready for another operation and capture another bridge, seeing that we were such experts at it. We were to be accompanied by a reinforced armoured reconnaissance vehicle. And so we set off once again.

The start of our journey was quite pleasant. The road to Salonica was wide and paved, and had none of the annoying potholes we'd endured before. Everywhere we passed we saw Greek clothing lying around: steel helmets, gas masks, coats and weapons. Roadside ditches were filled with carts that had been overturned and dead horses, their legs stiffly stretched in the air; their swollen stomachs glistened in the morning light.

Not long after, we left the road and turned south. Far away in the distance, with the sun rising, we could make out the snow-covered peak of Mount Olympus. Its summit soared majestically out of the mist as if hovering above the ground, it was truly surreal.

We had neither the time nor the inclination to admire this mountain steeped in legend, or to ponder Greek mythology and culture. All we could really see was enemy territory. Death was lurking around every corner, and this was foremost in our minds. At any moment, Zeus might cast his lightning bolts and destroy us. We were mortals. What on earth were we doing here, in the heart of Greece, at the foot of the divine throne? Had we turned into those Barbarians who desecrate the holy places, who defile and violate cultural heritage? Or was it the other way round? Was it us who were liberating the land of the Hellenes from the perfidious sons of Albion and carrying the torch of freedom to Athens?

You could look at it either way – it depended on where you were standing. Surely, the vantage point of the victors would be the right one.

We drove along a narrow field path without a soul in sight. A light morning mist covered the ground, and all we could hear was the croaking of frogs – it seemed to be coming from everywhere. Leading our force was the heavy armoured reconnaissance vehicle, with its commander standing erect in the open hatch. A reconnaissance truck followed within sight. They only moved forward at intervals. Following them was the Kübelwagen with the radio team and a platoon of Krad shooters; then came the English reconnaissance truck we had captured at the Vardar bridge, and which we of course took along with us, and then, bringing up the rear, was us with our two Opel Blitzes. Our movements resembled those of a millipede. The heavy reconnaissance tank drove ahead, then stopped, then waited for the light reconnaissance vehicle to catch up before it drove on again. Then the light vehicle waited for the Krad shooters, who then waited for us. And so, it could happen that one half of the reconnaissance troop was always on the move while the other half was able to offer them protective fire.

Slowly, the sun was rising and the fog had lifted. We now had better visibility and realised that we were approaching a small acacia forest. Suddenly, like a pheasant startled from its sleep, a British Spitfire appeared behind the trees. It rose into the sky, and then disappeared southwards. We were so surprised that we hardly had time to lift a finger. By the time we'd recovered, the plane had vanished.

What was this machine doing flying on its own? Was it on a reconnaissance mission, tasked to fly low over the forest, or had it just taken off? If the latter was the case, then there had to be an airport somewhere. Slowly, we crept towards the woodland to see whether more planes were there. The reconnaissance truck drove carefully between the trees while we circled the forest. The armoured bikers were on the left, with us on the right. But our precautions were unnecessary. We found nothing apart from some perforated gasoline barrels, some empty tins and cans, and some other rubbish. It looked as if the British had abandoned this quite puny airfield only the day before. Obviously, the Spitfire had just been a latecomer that managed to clear the field only last minute. We continued driving with our reconnaissance troop. The journey was awful, with us being tossed backwards and forwards, flung off our benches and back down again with a thump. We couldn't hold on to anything since we carried our weapons in our hands and had to guard them for dear life. It was pretty incredible what our trucks and our bones could tolerate.

This bumpy ride lasted for a good hour before our combat unit reached a wide river blocking our path. We had once again arrived at the Vardar. Surely this can't be true, I thought. Wasn't it enough that we'd dealt with the bridge near Axiopolis? No, of course it wasn't and it was once again up to us to capture yet another bridge – after all, as the saying goes: better safe than sorry. Or could it be that the bridge spanning the Greek Axios was different from the one crossing the Yugoslav Vardar? Surely it was the same river. Whatever this stupid river was called, there we were, and we had no choice but to look for the second bridge. At the front, tanks and gunners were getting on with their normal day's work, while all we turned out to be was an irritating group of bridge-obsessed soldiers resembling bloodhounds, clawing and scraping away with our noses close to the ground, in everyone's way. The mere scent of a bridge made us come running, offer ourselves up for special use, whether or not we were wanted. Sometimes, however, when the task seemed too daunting or difficult even for us to handle, we simply refused.

It was we, the Brandenburgers, who at this point took the lead. The reconnaissance truck and the Krad bikers remained behind, waited for some twenty minutes, then caught up with us and got us out of the mess we'd got ourselves into. Grabert was at the head, driving the captured British reconnaissance truck. On his head he wore a British steel helmet – that was it, in terms of his camouflage. We were in two Opel Blitz trucks following closely behind and we too were wearing British steel helmets as a disguise. From afar, we looked like real Brits, and we were pleased with that. All we needed was to be allowed to get as near to the bridge as possible. Nothing more. We had calculated that by the time anyone noticed our disguise, it was going to be too late – for them, that is …

We drove downriver. After a few kilometres, the terrain turned into a swamp, and our cars weren't able to continue. Bypassing the road to the left, we traversed fields and meadows until we reached a dam that formed the boundary to this flooded area. We ascended and drove for a short while before swinging right towards the river. That's when we saw the bridge. It was a robust iron construction but, thank Zeus, it had already been blown up. We stopped and waited for the reconnaissance truck and the Krad bikers, who were meant to replace us. A few minutes later, they came zooming towards us at such a speed you would think they were in some kind of a race. We had no choice but to turn around and drive to Salonica. We decided to leave behind the British reconnaissance truck because we had no further use for it. We just let it roll down and into the swamp. Our commander then wanted to test the tank grenades by detonating two of them in quick succession, until the British vehicle burnt like a flaming torch.

We passed some villages on our drive back, and every time we went through one of these small hamlets we experienced the same thing: people came running towards us, clapping their hands with joy and excitement. Girls threw paper flowers in our direction, the clergyman blessed us with his crucifix, and women dragged carpets out of their houses, spreading them in front of us for us to drive over. We then had to stop in the town centre where people had gathered, having lugged over crates of raisins, wine and bread, laying these various goods out over carts and tables. It looked like some kind of al fresco wedding.

At least that's how it was for us in Greece at that time. They welcomed us as friends. Unbelievably, that would change four years later: upon our return from Russia, we were to experience the very opposite. The very same peasants who had greeted us with such enthusiasm had turned into partisans, stabbing us in the back, ambushing us and luring us into traps. The flowers had turned into grenades, and the carpets once laid out to honour us became mines that would kill us. *Sic transit gloria mundi!*

What brought this change about? Was this spectacle in April 1941 nothing but a display of hypocrisy and artifice to make us, the victors, feel positively disposed towards them? Was their demonstration of submissiveness nothing but opportunism to save their own skin? Was the respect they so obviously showed us nothing but the result of fear, fear of our weapons and might? Probably. Or, looking back, could a modicum of admiration for us Germans be detected?

And why, later on, did we seem to have lost the little bit of approval bestowed on us back then and see that it had, instead, turned into hatred? I never understood. But one thing was certain: it wasn't us combat troops who were responsible for this change of heart. We active soldiers always and everywhere behaved without fault, and entirely correctly. But the occupying forces, the administrative personnel, those receiving orders from the Reich, all the people who came after us, who occupied and ran the country – they certainly embittered the indigenous population with their arrogance and appalling behaviour. The initial sympathy towards us turned into disappointment and eventually hatred. Nowhere, in no country, did the German leadership understand how to foster a good relationship with the population, something we always knew was so essential to cultivate from the very beginning. Instead, they had simply made enemies out of those who could have been loyal supporters.

We reached Salonica. Here, too, we were met with the same kind of spectacle as we had seen a few days earlier, where jubilant crowds waved and clapped as they walked towards us, welcoming the 'new masters'. We drove along the quay, with the blue sea to our right, and beautiful white villas to our left. The moment our car came to a halt, we were surrounded by masses of people who stood and stared at us, as if we had come from another planet. Our quarters were set up in the German Academy, right on the quayside. There were no beds, not even sacks of straw to lie on, and in general the place was barely furnished. This didn't bother us in the least. We were just glad to have a proper roof over our heads. From the building's balcony, we had a marvellous view of the entire seafront, and over to Mount Olympus. We spread our blankets onto the beautiful parquet, and within a few minutes we had organised our sleeping areas. We spent three full days in Salonica, and they were most enjoyable, wonderful days of sleep and rest.

— SEVEN —

The Vale of Tempe, Early Spring 1941

Salonica to Evangelimos

It was Easter Monday, no doubt a truly glorious day for millions of people. In Salonica the blue sea merged perfectly with the sky at the horizon, making it difficult to see where the water ended and the sky began. Gently the sunlight bathed the world in a warm glow of colour, showing off nature's full glory. All the trees were in bloom, and flowers were everywhere in abundance. A light breeze coming from the ocean wafted gorgeous fragrances through the air, the aroma of salt mixed with smells of different varieties of blossom filled our nostrils.

Standing on the balcony of our sleeping quarters alongside the seafront, I soaked up the natural beauty around me. A small boat debarked from the dock and crossed the harbour. Its white sail gleamed against the rising sun. Far away, way up high, the snow-covered seat of the gods loomed large. A picture of peace, so fitting for Easter Sunday. What an amazing day lay ahead of us!

The savviest of our group had made arrangements during the three days we had already spent here, and had planned a few rendezvous with some local Greek girls. I myself would never understand how they managed to engineer something like that. I certainly was never able to. My knowledge of sign-language didn't really go beyond rather clumsy and awkward gestures, and I couldn't remember a time when my charisma and personal charm were sufficient to catch the eye of one of those dollies.

We had brushed off our uniforms, polished our shoes and buffed up our belt buckles. We shaved properly, carefully combed our hair and cleaned our fingernails. We wanted to get ready for our evening out.

At 1000 hours the order 'Be ready for departure!' was bellowed out, and at 1200 hours the 5th and 6th Company were indeed ready to set off. We were, after all, at war, and this war would clearly not stop just because it was Easter Sunday. For a brief moment, however, we had completely forgotten about it.

Once again, we had to join the 2nd Panzer Division which, stuck somewhere below Olympus, wasn't able to move. The location was somewhere in front of the second line of defence which the Greeks had constructed in case the Metaxas Line failed. This line of bunkers, cleverly dug out to fit in with the terrain, hugging the coastline like a belt, reached well beyond the western valleys of the Olympus range. The line was primarily occupied by the British, as the Greek army had capitulated a little while ago.

The roads on which we travelled were dreadfully bumpy – not properly paved, but poorly covered in crushed stone, so that we were constantly being thrown from side to side inside our vehicle. All the bridges, even the smallest ones, had been blown up. In those instances where the engineers had managed to build some makeshift crossings prior to our arrival, our trucks crossed over the planks that had been put up, but only barely, and we had to hold on inside for dear life. When there wasn't a crossing for us to use, so-called *Schiebekommando*, 'push commandos', had been organised to give our vehicles the necessary shove, thus successfully forcing us across swamps and riverbeds that would otherwise have just swallowed us up. Once or twice we had to get out and continue on foot, helping comrades and vehicles back onto the road.

The sun was burning hot, there was no breeze to relieve the oppressive heat and the thick dust forced its way into our skin and covered the precious liverwurst which we always spread on our bread. Instead of a sumptuous layer of sausage, there was an annoyingly gritty sensation when we bit into the bread. Our throats were parched.

The truck halted yet again, the engine seemed to have given up and the carburettor needed cleaning. We had no option but to relinquish one of our Opel Blitzes and leave it behind, one of its axles broken. Our comrades redistributed themselves among the other vehicles. The other sub-unit would come along in the next few days and collect the defective vehicle.

By evening we had caught up with the 2nd Panzer Division. Their vehicles and tanks were spread out across the terrain and were well camouflaged. We stopped at a farmhouse and set up for the night, but unfortunately weren't able to have a campfire, as the light would have given us away. Early on that Easter Monday morning we had some visitors: three British planes roared over us at low altitude – we received bombs instead of the traditional Easter eggs – we rather resented this impolite gesture, to say the least.

We were meant to cross the river which lay a few kilometres ahead of us, but because the bridge had been completely destroyed, we had to wait until the engineers had built us a temporary crossing. To make good use of our waiting time, we went hunting. There was plenty of prey for us: lots of chickens and small black pigs, just right for the ideal Easter roast. When we had spotted the absolute perfect piglet, we got ourselves all ready, and set out to encircle and capture it. That was easier said than done, considering the agility of those little beasts. When the piglet noticed that it had become the focus of our attention, it simply ran off in a flash, with us scampering behind. What followed was a bizarre chase, taking us through hedges, bushes and fences; we were exhausted. In our zigzagging pursuit of this animal, one of us would every so often land empty-handed on his stomach after a misjudged dive. After a concerted effort, however, we finally succeeded in getting hold of the animal, and comrade Pfeifhofer finally had a chance to display his expertise as a butcher. Not long after, the piglet was merrily cooking on the roasting spit over a small open fire that was, in fact, a long infantry-type musket, a rifle from Napoleonic times which we'd picked up somewhere. Truth be told, we did have quite a large load of old junk collected in our truck.

Straight after lunch, and just as we were settling down for a quick nap, we heard the dreaded words: 'Get up – we're moving!' The engineers had done some good work. The bridge had obviously been sufficiently fixed for us to be able to cross. We reached the road that led straight down to the beach, where the sea forms a wide bay. Wouldn't it be wonderful to go for a swim, lie in the sunshine for a bit and leave the war behind us? Alas, such fantasies never became a reality. A deep ditch blocked our path, making it impossible to drive on. We had no choice but to push down hard on the pedals and speed through the shallow waters, thus avoiding the ditch and emerging again on the other side.

By the time we reached Katerini, yet another location where the advance force had got stuck yet again, it was nearly 1800 hours. Every road was under artillery fire but it was too late to go on the attack. We decided not to drive into Katerini, but instead divert into a nearby field so as not to obstruct the traffic on the road, and then wait for Second Lieutenant Grabert, who had travelled onwards to meet up with the commander of the advance group.

By the time he returned, darkness had settled. A few soldiers attached to the second group still had to go out for reconnaissance. We were allowed to sleep. I pulled a blanket over me, found a hollow in the field, threw myself into it and, using my steel helmet as a pillow, tried to sleep. Above me the stars were shining bright, the same stars that shone over my homeland. Tanks were continuously rumbling down the road, but they didn't bother me. My little hollow was my paradise. I could rest.

***

The following day, with the first rays of sunshine warming our stiff bodies, we set off once again. We drove up to the vanguard of the tank column which was attempting to go round Mount Olympus from the right-hand side in an effort to reach Elasson. There was a pass that would allow us to do that. After an hour's drive, we met up with the tanks, joined the advance troop and followed the slowly climbing road. Oaks gave way to alders and the higher up we drove, the denser the growth became, until we arrived in a cool and shady forest. Although pleasant, this was not a terrain conducive for tanks. They were only able to go single file, with no opportunity to overtake. Steering our trucks along the roadway packed with tanks, we advanced slowly and cautiously. Hours passed. The idyllic calm of this peaceful forest at the foot of Mount Olympus was interrupted only by the hum of engines and the rattle of tank tracks. The moment the first tanks emerged out of the protection of the trees and into the sunlit clearing, the spell broke.

We were suddenly hit by the noise of enemy gunfire blasting through the air, literally taking our breath away. Shells exploded out of the clear blue sky, one after the other. The British had clearly already dug themselves in and were waiting for us to leave the safety of the forest and come out into the open, allowing their artillery to blast us to bits – not what one would consider a friendly reception committee. We jumped from our vehicles and scampered like rabbits in search of a hole in which to hide.

The tank gunners, meanwhile, simply disappeared into their safety hatch to take cover, immediately closing the lid above their heads. In moments, this tranquil valley had turned into sheer hell. Sparks flew as bullets hit the ground, machine guns were fired indiscriminately and the explosions echoed far into the valleys. Mud splattered high into the air; pieces of wood and stone hailed down. Lucky was the man who found shelter in a muddy crater or a shell hole. We lay there exhausted, face down, our mouths wide open, hoping that what we had been told about these holes was true.[1]

Watching the trajectory of the grenades, we were in a good position to assess whether they would detonate far away or close to us. When the firing stopped briefly, we dashed back into the woods, where our tanks and vehicles stood waiting. Immediately we realised that a new volley of firing had started, hitting the trees, which then came crashing down to the ground, their branches smashing down above our heads. Between bursts of fire we managed to jump into our vehicles. But look who was there, calmly lying in the ditch and taking cover? Why, it was General Veiel! I recalled once again Guderian's phrase

'Tanks are led from the front' and this obviously explained his presence. He then ordered the withdrawal to Katerini.

We waited for the firing to stop, hopped into our vehicles and cleared out. But it didn't happen quite as fast as we had hoped, partly because the tanks weren't able to turn around in this tight space as quickly as our trucks could, and partly because there was no way any vehicle could overtake as the road was so narrow. The British had noticed our withdrawal and prepared for combat. Once again, the shells came down right and left. We lay flat and on top of one another in our trucks so that we were at least able to take cover from most of the shrapnel and chunks of wood that were flying around us. As we crawled underneath our benches, a young chap, Sepp Auckenthaler, with seemingly not a care in the world, stood upright at the back of our truck, his steel helmet pushed to the back of his head and his gun squeezed between his thighs. At the sight of the British bullets failing to hit their target, not touching even one of us, he burst out laughing, and couldn't stop himself. The charges exploded in between our vehicles, flinging stones and dirt in all directions, landing on the roofs of our vehicles. One detonated next to us, and the air pressure was such that our entire vehicle was flipped up onto two wheels – it was sheer luck that we didn't go flying out. Meanwhile, Sepp Auckenthaler continued to roar with laughter – surely it must've hurt his stomach to be laughing so hard. We just thanked our lucky stars to be able to escape this heavy barrage and finally arrive back in Katerini, safe and in one piece.

At lunchtime we managed to break through to the east of Mount Olympus. This saw us travelling along the beach, back down towards the south. The engineers had already cleared a path through the minefields and marked it with white ribbons. But behind it, vicious fighting continued unabated.

The Olympus range reached as far as the coast. Its foothills, much like a wall, stretched from west to east and ended with a steep cliff descending almost vertically into the sea. Nestling picturesquely on the top of the hill lay the ancient town of Salonica. Its impressive ruins reminded us of the times when the Byzantines occupied the entire northern part of Greece. Dense shrubland, mostly oak and alder, covered the entire hill, and in between, brilliantly camouflaged, the British had established a strong defensive line. The train tracks from Salonica to Athens led through a tunnel located right underneath the hill, but it had been completely blown up, so there was clearly no way to go through it.

Evening had fallen by the time we arrived at this natural stronghold. The 2nd Panzer Division had assembled on the plateau in front of it. The tanks were positioned in some of the fruit orchards, which stretched as far as the sea. The artillery was in position to target both the fort and the steep slope in front leading up to it, which was where the British had entrenched themselves. White puffs of explosives and black clouds of smoke rose in the sky.

We passed a first-aid station that was bustling with activity. Freshly wounded soldiers were continually being brought in by ambulances. The injured were being patched up in a mad rush, and there was no time for proper medical attention. We travelled along the train track until we reached the foot of the hill and couldn't move any further. We stopped in a small forest and camouflaged our vehicles.

An assault platoon was just returning. They had attempted, without success, to throw the British out of their positions and the men, understandably, were extremely tired, shuffling along no more than a few centimetres at a time and barely able to keep upright. Their faces, drawn by the efforts of combat, were covered in grime and dirt; clear streaks on their cheeks showed the sweat that had run down from their brows. Their steel helmets, shoved far back on their heads, served no purpose at that moment. These men were apathetic and worn out. Stumbling behind one another without any awareness of their surroundings, they had no idea what was happening to them, or even whom they were walking next to. You could only hear the clinking of the gas masks and flasks that hung from their rifle butts, accompanied by the crunch of their boots on the gravel paths. Nobody said a word. In the dusk, their faces looked grey and their eyes seemed sunk deep into their sockets. Their uniforms were filthy, torn and covered in blood. They wore their machine-gun belts, half-empty, around their necks, and they carried their weapons on their shoulders. Many of them were wounded, wearing blood-soaked bandages around their heads, arms and legs. Supported by their comrades, these soldiers hobbled along, defeated and downtrodden.

We just stared down at the ground, speechless. What we saw here before us was just a regular assault troop on its retreat, having achieved nothing – no glory, no distinction, just blows to their heads. And what would happen the next day, and the day after that? All they would do was move on to another assault, go into battle again, and fall. They would do this over and over again, and not a word of complaint would be uttered. They would be tightlipped, calm and collected, assuming all the while that this was the way it had to be. Those were our thoughts, despondent and resigned.

***

Night had fallen. The stars shone from the sky. The silvery moon lit the dark sea and cast shadows onto the surrounding landscape. Underscoring this peaceful nocturnal scene was the rhythmic sound of soft waves lapping on the beach. The firing had ceased for now. Only once in a while, a solitary grenade howled through the air, nothing but a nuisance. Some random shots coming from machine guns could be heard, a brief blast of fire, and then it was quiet again.

I was on guard duty. My comrades were asleep. I made my rounds, cautiously and slowly, with my MPi loaded and ready to fire. A cable-layer came by. The telephone lines had been broken and he was looking for the fault. His face and hands were all scratched up by the thorns and shrubs through which he had had to crawl in order to locate the problem. We exchanged some words of encouragement, then he went on his way, disappearing into the night. Once again, I was on my own.

I adored this time of day, the silence that came with being on guard duty, the stillness of the night, close to the enemy. It was my only opportunity to be alone with my thoughts – thoughts that invariably trailed off in the direction of my home country and my loved ones. What might they be up to at this very moment? Had they gone to the cinema, or were they gathered round the pub table along with the regulars, discussing the special news broadcasts of our campaign? I leaned against one of the vehicles and lit a cigarette. It was forbidden to smoke while on the job, and certainly while on guard duty. But, then again, who cared? Everyone was asleep and nobody would take any notice. I heard my comrades snoring heavily back in the vehicle, lost somewhere deep in their dreams. I looked up towards the enemy positions. That's where the British were, dug in behind their MGs, they too listening into the night. I was quite certain that they wouldn't catch any sleep. They would be apprehensive, frightened to see the rising sun, as it would once again spell the beginning of the deadly fight for survival.

What were the British actually doing in Greece? Did they really have any business here? But then again, did *we* have any business being here? Truth be told, neither of us had a reason. Apart from fighting each other on foreign soil, neither one of us could justify our presence in Greece. Would this war, too, spread all across the globe? Would there be another world war, in which we Germans would yet again be the ones to make an enemy of every other group of people inhabiting our earth? No, it might not come to that, it *wouldn't* come to that, the Führer would surely know how to avoid something like this! Or so I tried to reassure myself.

At 0200 hours, I woke the comrade who would replace me and immediately went to lie down myself to catch a few hours of sleep, finding a convenient spot underneath the truck. Artillery fire woke me. The battle around the Litochoro monastery had started up again, this time with full force; our artillery was shelling the British positions so they could then storm them. After our shock troops had fought their way through densely entangled bushes up the mountain slope, we heard heavy shooting.

Our group prepared to depart. We packed only what was absolutely necessary into our rucksacks, which we would have to carry ourselves from then on. We wrapped all the rest of the stuff into blankets and left it behind, stored in the vehicle. Who knew when the Opel Blitz would catch up with us? We slung our rifles over our shoulders and departed in orderly columns. Marching along the train tracks, we approached the tunnel that led through the mountain, a colossal rock that loomed before us. To the left, the waves broke at the bottom of the cliffs. We didn't hesitate. Entering the tunnel, we were soon engulfed by total darkness. Once in a while somebody's pocket light flickered; in the end, we didn't get very far. The tunnel had been blown up and was now filled with stones, rubble and soil, blocking the throughway entirely, leaving barely any gaps. As best we could, we climbed on top of this avalanche of stones, cautiously peering over it to get a view of the other end of the tunnel, but we couldn't see a thing. The further ahead we tried to stare, the darker it got, on our side we at least had a bit of the outside light filtering through. Still, one behind the other, we persisted, inching forwards, climbing over the rubble and hoping against hope that no British soldier would get in our way. Once we were on the other side, we advanced carefully, pressing our bodies firmly against the wall of the tunnel. But suddenly, our path was blocked by brickwork. Not only had they blown up the tunnel, but they had also closed it off with a brick wall. This was the end of the road for us! We turned back, and shortly thereafter stood outside again – back in the sun.

In the meantime, our comrades from the fifth unit had embarked on scaling the mountain in order to circumvent the fortress on the cliff.[2] We worked our way up and across the rocky slope which dropped steeply down to the sea. Because our guns were slung over our backs, we had our hands free. This allowed us at least to grip onto any bits of grass which were growing between the rocks and, clinging onto them, we crawled up, more on our knees than our feet, but we did it. Sometimes, a piece of rock dislodged by our boots would go sailing straight into the sea. In this way we scaled the mountain and circled the cliff. At the foot was a very wide bay area, and we could make out the train tracks zigzagging across it, then disappearing into the horizon. Looking around us, we saw a few houses surrounded by shady gardens and about a dozen large tents that had been erected between the olive trees. Far away, the smoke of a train travelling south rose into the sky. There was no trace of the enemy.

To our right, some German soldiers were already on their way down. We increased our pace, wanting desperately to reach the British tents before our comrades. This was our only focus. Our curiosity and speed were to be fully rewarded. What we found in these large tents were huge quantities of groceries, tinned meat, vegetables, fruit, butter, tinned milk, jam, ham, biscuits, cigarettes and whisky. Whatever a Landser could wish for, there it was, and plenty of it. By the look of it, the Tommies had also given thought to how they could best spend their leisure time away from home and had brought along all the equipment they needed to pursue their hobbies. We found tennis rackets, balls, nets, walking sticks and, yes, we even came across some golf clubs. This was all quite hard to take in for us simple folk. They had clearly made themselves comfortable in their new homes. The beds were clean and freshly made up, the blankets neatly folded. The only area that looked as if had been hit by a storm was the lounge, which by all accounts must have served as their barrack room: here, just about everything had been smashed to bits. Nothing so much as a medicine bottle had remained intact, all bandages were left unravelled. Nothing could be used. Walking into the sleeping quarters at the back, we came across a dozen injured men from New Zealand and Australia. There wasn't a trace of fear in their eyes, but I rather felt that they looked at us with something of a smile, some irony in their eyes. While my comrades continued to investigate the surroundings and the houses, I got talking to the wounded. Sadly, they weren't very talkative. I asked them what they thought about the war in Greece and, specifically, what they thought about the battle around the Litochoro fortress, and their reply in English was: 'It was a very nice match' [sic].

The soldiers attached to the advance troop, who had circled the fortress during the night, told us about their adventures. By dawn they had already reached the rear of the fortress and prepared themselves for the descent into the valley when they spotted a train which was ready to depart, with its engine puffing hot steam into the air. Continuing a bit further, they realised that the British troops were hastily loading the three wagons while their officers were enjoying a leisurely breakfast laid out for them underneath some acacia trees.

When our gunmen opened fire, they ran as fast as they could to the train, boarded it and disappeared at full speed. The remains of their breakfast were left on the table. Some soldiers, unaware of what had happened, ran out of their houses and tried to reach the train but failed. They had no choice but to surrender.

One of our gunmen joked, 'Well, we certainly enjoyed that leftover English breakfast, the tea was still warm!'

And with that, the battle of the Litochoro fortress ended. There was no way to contemplate a pursuit of the British without the help of vehicles, and they would certainly not arrive that day. It would take days to clear the tunnel and make the road accessible, and then the first vehicles to arrive would be the tanks.

Well, that was fine by us. We were in no rush. We had plenty to eat and drink, and a soft bed to sleep in. We had enough time to inspect all the stuff we had captured, but the only things we could really make use of were the British raincoats and their dust goggles. The night was uneventful and we slept deeply. There was just one dog that yapped incessantly. Suddenly we heard a shot – and that was that, as far as the yapping went.

Dark clouds had gathered in the sky, and a light, early morning mist hung over the bay. It was going to rain soon. Silently, and in a bad mood, as befits an early morning after such excitement, we started our ascent of the mountain. Halfway up, we came upon a road. This was the arranged meeting point with the tanks and from here, as per the plan, we were to join them and leave together, heading south. We sat down, snacked on the British biscuits we had bagged, and waited. We didn't much care if or when the tanks arrived. We had a knack for waiting; we had learned it well. Waiting during the war was something we particularly enjoyed, and we never grew tired or impatient doing it. It always gave us plenty of time to just hang around, but when it came to going into action or camouflage, that's when waiting took on quite a different meaning: we would get tense and anxious, desperate for the tanks to arrive and help us out. Time couldn't pass fast enough for us in those instances – but otherwise, waiting was a most treasured hobby.

We could feel raindrops, and we relished this first opportunity to put on the raincoats we had just captured. Soon it was bucketing down on us. At 0700 the tanks came rolling in. They were barely able to squeeze along the narrow roads, but finally managed by exercising some extreme caution. Either the path was too tight, or the tanks too wide. Only half of the left caterpillar track touched the ground. The outer edge was hanging in the air, dangling over the steep precipice.

The guys from the tanks were happy to see us. As we knew each other, we were aware of which skills each one of us could bring to the task at hand. In their eyes, we were the best infantry support one could hope for. As far as we were concerned, we were less keen to put these to the test. We were split up among the different tanks, with five to six men per tank. I, together with my group of engineers and Second Lieutenant Graber, was on the first tank. We fastened our rucksacks and off we went. Descending the mountain, we headed towards the plain. Why on earth had we been ordered to scale this mountain if it turned out that all we would end up doing would be to come back down, and at breakneck speed? We could just as well have waited down below. Well, that'll probably forever remain the mystery of strategic warfare, never to be comprehended by the likes of us simple Landsers! Meanwhile we were holding on to the turret, or whatever we could find, for dear life, using our hands, feet, teeth, anything really, just so we didn't fall off. I was afraid to look down – the sight of the vertical face of the cliff to which our tanks seemed to be glued made me dizzy. The path started crumbling beneath the heavy tracks; stones, debris and mud rolled down the slope. Leaning towards the mountain in a kneeling position, we were ready to jump off the minute the tank started to slip.

Finally, we reached the bottom of the valley and turned southwards along the train line. The tanks drove up the railway embankment and managed to keep one set of tracks inside the rails and the other set outside – this allowed us to move along quite swiftly. The leader of our tank, a second lieutenant, was standing in the open cupola directing us throughout the journey via his microphone and earphones that kept up the connection between us and the other tanks, which had fallen so far behind by now that we had lost sight of them. After about two kilometres, we left the embankment and crossed some rough terrain. The rain had stopped, but the fields were soggy and muddy. As we rattled along, clumps of soil and dirt were flung into our faces and nearly blocked our vision, because the tracks of the tanks dug deep into the marshland. However, truth be told, we far preferred this damp filth cooling our faces to the stinging and dry dust that had plagued us before. Once again, we arrived at the embankment, but this time we wanted to cross. However, the tank slipped down and got bogged down in the marshy ground. As much as we tried, it wouldn't budge, and we were well and truly stuck. We had no choice but to wait for the second tank to arrive and pull us out.

So that we wouldn't just be sitting around and do nothing – though we certainly wouldn't have minded that one bit – Second Lieutenant Grabert ordered us to march to the Tempe valley and scope out the stretch leading up to it, approximately four kilometres. The team of five of us departed. We left one guy back in the tank. He was to protect it, although that didn't make much sense, because in an attack he wouldn't have been capable of putting up a decent defence in time. The confidence the tank troops had in us Brandenburgers obviously knew no limits. We lined up and departed, with Second Lieutenant Grabert leading, and us obediently following behind. We kept our ears and eyes open, since we had been ordered to reconnoitre the area, but nothing happened. Of course, the closer we came to the Tempe valley, the more we were on the alert. The steep cliffs surrounding the beautiful wide bay area enclosed us to the south like a natural enclave. A narrow gorge of some ten kilometres in length and thirty to fifty metres wide left just enough room for the Pineios river to wind its way through, and a tiny road which in itself was not much more than a cart path. The single lane of train track went through tunnels. These had been constructed by using drilling and blasting and were built straight into the vertical cliff faces that rose along both sides of the gorge. That was really the only possible route to the south, and we absolutely had to pass through it.

Our main goal was to seize upon any opportunity which could provide us with cover. All the while protecting each other, we crept through the orchards, now in full bloom, and the fragrant acacia woods. Each time we arrived at a clearing, one man would leap across it, taking as few jumps as possible. We had to constantly keep in mind that at some point we might encounter the British rearguard or some other hostile reconnaissance troop, but fortunately we managed to arrive at the top of the gorge without any incidents. Looking around, we could see the train track disappearing into the tunnel a few hundred metres away. At this juncture, the footpath led to the other side of the valley, but the bridge over the Pineios had been blown up. Just a single, abandoned building stood by the side. Painted on its wall in large, faded letters was the word 'Rapsani'. We were curious as to where the village to which this train station must surely be connected was located, but we couldn't see anything; perhaps it was situated somewhere higher up the mountain.

Because of the destroyed bridge we couldn't cross the river, so we followed the train track to continue our reconnaissance. At some point, no doubt, we would come face to face with the enemy. The tunnel wasn't very long, and soon we were able to see the other end. Cautiously, sticking close to the walls, we made our way through the tunnel. It was followed by a second tunnel. We entered but didn't get very far as it had been blown up, which meant that we were blocked by a heap of rubble, spelling the end of our journey. We turned round. Once back at Rapsani station, we sat down and waited, hoping that the tanks would arrive shortly. A little while later, they rolled up, along with two motorcyclists. The decision was made not to penetrate further into the gorge, as this would have necessitated finding a causeway, but instead to check out the right-hand side of the mountain face and perhaps find a route which would allow the tanks to circumvent the gorge.

The tank lieutenant was just about to write the respective message to the leader of the advance troop for the motorcyclists to take back, when we heard the unmistakable noise of artillery fire. Instinctively, we threw ourselves to the ground, pressing our bodies hard against the earth; soon everything came crashing down on us, stones and fragments of wood and shrapnel flying through the air. The attack was brief, so perhaps the British artillery was just blasting away without focusing on an objective. Our two tanks turned around immediately, with us jumping on them. We knew what was at stake and left straight away.

The road wound gently up the mountain. We were well covered by the low acacia trees and the tall thickets of willow. Gradually the terrain became steeper, forcing us to take treacherous hairpin curves. Before crossing any open space, we stopped for a thorough inspection of the terrain. Anti-tank gunners could have been hiding just about anywhere. I was reminded of the second day of the war, when Serb tanks had rolled up the pass and were an easy target for our anti-tank gunners. Now it was our turn, and we found ourselves in the exact same situation. It wasn't pleasant being a moving target. I would much rather have been part of the infantry, where I could curl myself up into a ball and throw myself into a hole to pose a much smaller target than a tank. Suddenly, an aircraft appeared in the skies, just as it had back then in Serbia. Flying low, it nearly scraped the mountain ridges and, lo and behold, it had spotted us as well. It was a German reconnaissance aircraft and we waved our caps and handkerchiefs. It flew away above our heads, then performed a loop, returned, flying even lower than before and then, leaning into a last sharp curve, it dropped something. It was a message contained in a capsule that gave off yellow smoke. One of our men jumped off the tank and fetched the message, as it was easy enough to pinpoint where it had landed. It contained only a few words: 'Enemy approaching with many trucks, direction from Larissa to Tempe.' What were we to do? Should we turn round and descend back into the valley, where enemy fire was still a real possibility? Not able to turn round in the space available to us, we were forced to advance further.

It became ever steeper. Before each bend, we stopped and the two motor-cycles tore around the corner, climbing a further few hundred metres up. Once they were up there, our tank took the curve, followed shortly by the second tank. And so we slowly worked our way up the mountain. Anti-tank gunners could be lurking behind any of these dense patches of undergrowth, but eventually any thickets that could have provided us with cover, albeit minimal, had also petered out, and the slope, with its meandering path continuing upwards, was completely bare of trees. We took a moment to inspect our surroundings carefully before leaving our natural cover, but couldn't see anything suspicious, no tell-tale mounds of earth or other worrying signs. Instead, all we spotted were herds of sheep innocently grazing whatever there was to graze, guarded by a handful of shepherds who were eying us with curiosity. And there, right at the top of the mountain ridge, we made out the white buildings of a small village. That had to be Rapsani. It stuck to the slope like a swallow's nest. The landscape was calm and peaceful, just like the ones you could enjoy in our Alpine pastures back at home, up above the treeline. This is how it must have been for the past thousands of years. No war would have reached there and broken the tranquillity of that remote pasture. But on that day, it was torn apart by the noise of thundering engines and rattling tank tracks. These innocent shepherds must have wondered where on earth those black tanks came from. To them, they must have seemed like a pack of wolves unleashed from the dark gorge, bringing nothing but calamity and doom.

At full throttle, we sped up the mountain slope. We no longer cared if Tommy had entrenched himself up there somewhere and was waiting for us. We no longer had any cover, and speed was the only thing which could have potentially given us a chance. But nothing happened, and we reached the village unscathed.

The scene that we met was familiar. All the inhabitants had gathered in the village centre and greeted us with loud cheers and applause while showering us with flowers. Then they brought us baskets with wine, bread and eggs. It was a language we had come to understand quite well …

After these most welcome refreshments we continued with our recon-naissance mission. But the road we were on ended there in the village. Beyond that, there was only a narrow footpath, and for the tanks, this meant their final destination; the terrain was much too steep for them to carry on. So it was just us five Brandenburgers who continued.

Below and to our left, we saw a deep incision in the Tempe valley. From up there it had appeared to be nothing but a black line cutting right through the mountains. Now we could see that it divided the Olympus massif from Mount Ossa. The footpath we were trudging along descended slightly towards the valley, and we gathered that it must be leading us to the southern exit of the gorge. It meant that continuing on this road would be pointless. How could us five men even consider successfully attacking these enemy positions from the rear? Even the most daring Brandenburgers would have to admit that it would be likely to fail, despite the attractive prospect of the opposite outcome. Someone like Sergeant Hiller would surely have attempted it!

We sat down on the ground and enjoyed the panorama. Much as the mountaineer who climbs the summit might rest in a wildflower meadow to immerse himself in the tranquillity and beauty of the landscape, we five also delighted in the peace of the unspoilt nature surrounding us. Gone were the heavy grey clouds; once again, the sky had turned a dark blue. Some bees were busy dancing while the last rays of sun shone down, elongating our own shadows up the steep mountain slope. We chewed on some blades of grass and felt at peace with the world.

Suddenly, two men appeared on the path leading from the valley. Immediately we fell flat to the ground. Other men followed and we counted twelve of them. They were all bearing arms. Was it a British reconnaissance unit? We didn't let them out of our sight. They hadn't spotted us yet. Not suspecting anything untoward, they walked in our direction.

'We'll get hold of them,' whispered Second Lieutenant Grabert. We unlocked our weapons and took aim. 'Stay still – let them approach.' When they were about 100 metres away from us, Second Lieutenant Grabert whispered to me: 'Burst of fire – warning shot.' A short sharp shot came from my machine gun. The twelve men froze, then threw themselves to the ground. 'Hands up – come on,' shouted Second Lieutenant Grabert in English. And indeed, after only a few seconds they waved a gun in the air to which they had attached a white piece of cloth. 'Come on!' Grabert shouted again. They got up, one by one and, waving the white flag all the time, they climbed up the incline. But they weren't British, they were Greek. We lined them up, marched at either side of them and returned to the village. There, we let them go.

In the meantime, in the village square, the tanks had managed to turn around and stood ready for departure. We actually quite enjoyed spending time in this friendly village. We were in no rush to return to the valley. A 'hairdresser's salon' caught our attention. In fact, it turned out to be more of a barber shop than a coiffeur. A ramshackle room with a rickety chair standing in front of a clouded mirror – that was it. The barber offered to give us a shave, which in fact wasn't such a bad idea. Before going to war, we could certainly do with some sprucing up. Before we knew it, the good barber was busy lathering one of our men with shaving cream. Tenderly and full of feeling he then scraped off his beard and, after each sweeping motion, he carefully and in full view washed out his razor blade. He wanted us all to notice that he knew both his trade and hygiene, even though this was but a tiny and remote village. When each of us pressed ten drachma into his hand as a sign of our appreciation, he was beside himself with joy. Cleanly shaven and smelling like roses, we were ready to leave.

Accompanied by jubilant applause, off we drove. And that's when it happened. The first tank slid off the slanted cobbled road and ended up on its side against the wall of a house. People no longer cheered, but just stood around and gawped. Well, we would sort this out in no time. The second tank came along, thick steel ropes were attached within minutes, and the second tank then tried to drag the first one out of the position it was wedged in. The engine howled and the linked chains digging into the cobblestones sent sparks into all directions. Then a crash – the caterpillar tracks had snapped. At this point both tanks were stuck and us men, quite embarrassed, could do little but pull long faces. What should we do? We really had no idea.

The tank soldiers swiftly resigned themselves to the situation, realising that all they could do was wait for support to arrive. But what about us Brandenburgers, what were we supposed to do up there, in the knowledge that our comrades down in the Tempe gorge were probably preparing for an advance? While one might have assumed that we didn't much care what was happening far away from us and that we were content to remain in this peaceful village, that was far from the truth. Of course, this misfortune was certainly not our fault, but at the same time, we were acutely aware that a big battle lay ahead. We were concerned about our comrades, we wanted to be by their side, go into battle together and share the danger with them.

Bicycles! Could we find any bicycles somewhere? But there was not a single bike to be located in the entire village. It was already starting to get dark, and at precisely 2000 hours the British started firing in the gorge. We heard the bullets being fired and we heard their impact. The inhabitants had withdrawn into their homes, there was no light anywhere. It was only us standing outside, feeling quite lost. We were watching how down there in the valley the flames from artillery fire leaped into the air, when, all of a sudden, we heard the sound of a distant engine. Who might be coming up? The engine noise drew closer. It was the rifle squad Watzmann that had found its way to us, arriving by MTW.[3] It had received orders to circumvent the Tempe gorge and attack the British from the rear.

As soon as we met them, we bombarded them with questions, enquiring if they had any information regarding the Brandenburgers. 'Yes,' said the squad leader, 'a group of them are already down in the gorge, others are attempting to push through the valley via the Pineios and some assault boats are assisting them.'

'That's certainly a crackpot idea,' mumbled Grabert. 'We absolutely must go down there at once.'

'You can get down there with one of our MTWs,' responded the squad leader. 'We don't need them any more since we'll be continuing on foot. He continued assuring us that we would be able to depart in about half an hour; we would just have to wait for them to unload and turn round. That was easier said than done. Turning round in the narrow space and in pitch darkness was not a simple matter, and no one was more aware of that than us. It could take a long time for the whole manoeuvre to work. But that wasn't our problem. We were facing a different one. Our stomachs had begun to rumble. As soon as we had arrived we'd spotted the only restaurant in the square. That's where we five Brandenburgers were headed and little else seemed to matter any more. We searched for the innkeeper, found him, sat down at the table and ordered dinner. It consisted of scrambled eggs and green salad. We also made sure to take care of our parched throats and got through three bottles of red wine. We paid and returned to the entrance to the village. The drivers had successfully turned the MTWs around and we were all set to leave.

It was pitch dark. The luminous dial on my wristwatch pointed at 2300 hours. We couldn't turn on our headlights as it would give us away to a artillery observer or Brit who would have no doubt aimed and fired at us. Since 0800 hours, at precise half-hour intervals, they had been unleashing a volley of shots into the gorge.

Second Lieutenant Grabert stood erect next to the driver, who sat low down in his hatch, and was able to look out through the optics, just a narrow slit in the armour. But even in this position, Grabert could barely make out the road. Lance Corporal Egli therefore decided to move up to the front and help with directions. We advanced slowly through the dark night. We three Brandenburgers stretched out on the benches and were soon fast asleep. We had faith in Grabert and Egli. It didn't take long for our snoring to drown out the noise of the engines.

Midnight was far gone when we finally arrived at the station, right at the entrance of the gorge. Tanks and other vehicles were standing on the rail track and in the tunnel, but there was no sign of our men. We questioned the sentries – nobody knew anything. We ran back and forth, all the while shouting at the top of our voices: 'Brandenburgers, where are you?'

Finally, one man crept out from underneath a tank, then a second one, a third one followed. From underneath another tank Sergeant Modes came crawling out, one of those old soldiers left over from the First World War. He bore neither weapons nor belt and looked as he always did, tired and dishevelled. This man had never taken war seriously, and anything even vaguely connected with it seemed irrelevant to him. At least that was the impression he gave. He told us that they too had been down there in the gorge, but that when it grew dark and the artillery fire had set in, they preferred to withdraw because of the intolerable noise of the exploding shells.

I glanced at my watch. It was five minutes before 0200 hours. 'I think it might be advisable to get under cover. Get yourself underneath the tanks because in a few minutes it will start all over again!' said Sergeant Modes. 'The Hiller squad has not come back out of the tunnel, and we know nothing about what has happened to them,' he added, and with that, he disappeared underneath his tank.

'I think I'll go in and bring them back,' said Grabert, and before he had even ended his sentence, he had disappeared into the night. We returned to our MTW, crawled inside and lay ourselves onto the benches. At precisely 0200 a deluge of artillery rounds were fired but shortly thereafter the night fell still.

I slept for a long time. I awoke only at 0800 hours and peered out of the MTW which had been my home for the night. It was busy out there. At the river, the engineers were labouring hard to construct a wooden raft which would enable us to at least ferry the infantry across. Building the bridge would have to wait for a later date. Rubber dinghies were being prepared, and the tank squad searched for a ford so that the tanks could cross. Men stood waist-high in the water, stabbing the ground with some long steel beams. I finally left my cosy resting spot and joined my comrades, who were happily tucking into a hearty breakfast. I sat down beside them, and since it was food we were talking about, I easily held my own.

Refreshed and replenished, I set off to search for the tank where I had deposited my rucksack the day before, but I couldn't find it. I asked around until I finally learned that some tanks had followed the tracks into the tunnel. The tank I was after could well be among them. I had gathered, though, through speaking to my comrades in the reconnaissance troop, that they couldn't have got very far, as the second tunnel had been blown up. They couldn't have driven any further than maybe one or one and a half kilometres. I decided to go looking for my tank. Lance Corporals Egli and Tscherntsche joined me as they too had attached not only their rucksacks to the tank, but also their machine guns. The other comrades waited for the ferry to be completed so that they could be the first ones to cross over. We didn't have much time. This ferry needed to be ready very soon. In order for me to be able to move more freely, I put my steel helmet and machine gun in the roadside ditch and dashed into the tunnel. It didn't take us long to run through the entire length of it, and there they were. Our tanks stood right there – Egli and Tscherntsche quickly found their bags and their machine guns, but my rucksack wasn't there. I ran from one tank to another, but in vain, my rucksack was nowhere to be found.

To the left of the embankment, there was a steep slope down to the river, while to its right, the rocky face of the mountain rose straight up and very high. Using extremely tough steel cables, the tanks roped each other down the incline, one dragging the other, and once they had reached flat ground, they continued driving through the water, their engines hissing and fuming like mad. The road we wanted to reach lay on the other side of the river, concealed by trees and densely growing bushes. Perhaps my tank was over there? I ran back again and reached my comrades, men from our heavy weapons platoon, out of breath. 'Where are Egli and Tscherntsche?' I asked them. 'They have already crossed over,' replied Sergeant Modes. 'Where are my steel helmet and my machine gun?' I asked. 'Oh, that stuff? A corporal took them,' was the response.

There I was, all on my own and totally lost without my steel helmet or my machine gun, without my rucksack and without my squad. All I had on me was my pistol and two hand grenades.

'Why don't you stay with us?' suggested jolly Sergeant Modes. 'We'll wait for our trucks, and once the bridge is repaired, we'll follow them tomorrow. What would you be doing down in the gorge anyway, all by yourself and weaponless? And you certainly can't go anywhere unaccompanied. You'll get lost and fall into the hands of the British. So, come along, sit down, join us and wait. Those down there will definitely cope without you.'

Maybe the good man was right, I thought to myself. Wasting no time, I joined my comrades sitting in the cool shade and playing cards. But I just couldn't settle down. I sat there, staring in front of me. I couldn't concentrate on the words coming out of my comrades' mouths, and my thoughts were somewhere else entirely. Even though nothing about this situation was my fault, I still felt guilty. What an awful comrade I must be! Here I was, sitting around doing nothing, while my friends were engaged in battle. I would truly be considered a despicable unit leader if it was found out that I had left them to their own devices and to fight on their own; after all, my unit consisted of only three men. The question would surely be: 'Where was their leader hiding when the going got tough?' The answer? Ten kilometres behind them. It didn't bear thinking about, I couldn't take it any longer, I simply had to join them, I had to find them.

I jumped up, pulled my cap down on my head and ran as fast as I could, back through the tunnel; perhaps a tank would then take me further.

Damn, the tanks had disappeared by the time I got there. I just caught a glimpse of the last one driving up the bushy embankment on the other side of the river and onto the road. I returned through the tunnel, not knowing what to do next. How many times had I gone through that tunnel? Four times? Five times? And not once had I make any progress! Nothing made sense, it was all in vain! Damn tunnel. Outside once more, I spotted a tank about to drive into the water and cross the river. It seemed like a last opportunity! I ran down the embankment, waded through the water and followed the tank. The water came up as far as my belt, but that didn't stop me. I yelled up at the tank leader who stood erect in his turret, that he should please wait and take me with him, I absolutely had to get across. He turned towards me, saw that I was up to my stomach in water and stopped the tank. I trudged through the water, finally reached them, swung myself on board and crouched down behind the turret. He drove off and as far as I was concerned, I was happy that only half of me had got drenched.

But we hadn't reached the other side yet. In fact, we were only halfway across. And, would you believe it, the right-hand track got stuck in a hole, the tank turned on its side, the engine was puffing and steaming away and finally it died with all of us stranded, right in the middle of the river. The entire crew crawled out from inside the turret and crammed onto the turret, which was the only bit of the tank still above water. We were a sorry sight indeed and looked at each other in embarrassment.

This entire incident was of course observed by the others still on shore. We watched as the last tank took off, drove into the water and slowly approached us. It came up close, which allowed me to leap across. I slipped, and if the other tank leader hadn't caught me by my arm, I would have landed headfirst in the water. All we needed to complete this ridiculous spectacle was for the second tank to get stuck. But it went well, and we were able to cross and then drive up the sandy slope. At long last we were on dry land. First, I emptied the water from my shoes, then I went searching for my comrades.

I got onto the road and descended into the gorge on my own. The tank that had brought me over remained on the riverbank, with the crew working hard to drag out the other tank, which was still stuck. I couldn't wait; I simply had to find my comrades, and I had to do that as fast as possible.

Trees and densely growing bushes filled up the entire gorge, which wasn't any wider than some fifty metres, bordered on its left and right by sheer vertical cliffs that allowed only a small sliver of light to filter into the dark valley. Down the middle ran the Pineios river, frothing water thundering down the channel. The foliage was so dense that no rays of sun reached down to the ground. But for the sounds of the water, it was still. You couldn't hear the chirping of the birds nor the rustling of leaves.

I marched into the gorge, lost in thought. All of a sudden, I came across two of my comrades from our platoon sitting at the side of the road and ran towards them. One of them, Lance Corporal Deutschbein, was wounded. A bullet had hit his leg and he was bleeding profusely. The other comrade pressed hard onto the leg while applying a makeshift tourniquet. I handed them my first-aid kit.

'Where are the others?' I asked. 'What's happening up ahead of us?'

'It's hell on earth over there,' was the response. 'The British have established some very solid defensive positions, and because of their anti-tank units, our tanks don't even dare leave the gorge.'

'Where will I find my group?' I continued questioning them.

'Somewhere over there,' they told me.

'Is Second Lieutenant Grabert with them?'

'Yes, we did see him.'

'Well, so long, good luck,' I said and carried on.

I hadn't been walking more than ten minutes when two men from my squad came towards me. Between them they were dragging Sergeant Hiller, my unit leader, along the path, supporting him by his arms – a piece of shrapnel had penetrated the right side of his chest and blood was dripping out of the scant emergency dressing. I rushed up and helped ease the wounded man gently to the ground. His eyes were glassy and he could barely breathe, panting and heaving laboriously. He didn't utter a word, and only looked at me through a haze – I didn't know whether he recognised me, but I wouldn't have thought so. I didn't linger, as there really wasn't much for me to do there. I took Hiller's pistol and gun, which one of the others had carried slung over his shoulder, and moved on. I simply had to find and join my own unit. I couldn't bear being left behind while they were engaged in combat. I didn't feel any fear; my only focus was to be with them. This propelled me onwards. Lance Corporal Ankreuz, who had been with Hiller, accompanied me; the other man stayed with my wounded friend. They had to wait for the medics to arrive.

The gorge seemed to go on forever. The dense forest filling the entire valley seemed to swallow up any noise; we could only hear our boots crunching on the sandy path and the roaring of the river. Since I was once again in possession of a pistol, I no longer felt half as helpless as I had before. It was pleasantly cool in this shady forest, but maybe it just felt like that because of the wet clothing that still clung to me. Not a single bullet, no noise of battle disturbed the divine peace pervading this spooky gorge.

Suddenly, I saw two dead soldiers lying next to the road. 'Those are British,' said Ankreuz. 'Hofer got rid of them last night. We were on patrol and all of a sudden we encountered a British reconnaissance troop. Hofer was faster and fired at them from his hip using his machine gun, but then he himself was injured.'

I shot a quick glance at the bodies and continued in silence. Ankreuz followed me. Was this damned gorge never going to end? We had been marching for two hours already and still hadn't come out the other side.

Soon we were within earshot of the battle. We heard the rattling of machine guns and the pounding thuds of tank-destroyer cannons. We knew our comrades couldn't be far away. The gorge took a turn to the left and gradually became wider. The shooting became heavier, but I still couldn't see anybody. We hurried on. And that's when I saw Sergeant Glänzel from our heavy artillery platoon, some twenty metres ahead of me, hiding behind a rock while the rest of the platoon had set themselves up in position.

Approaching the sergeant, I asked: 'Sergeant, where can I find the 6th Company?' He hadn't heard me come up to him and seemed shocked at seeing me. Looking at me dumbfounded, he pulled at my sleeve and pushed me down to the ground behind a rock.

'Have you actually gone mad?' he bellowed. 'What on earth are you doing just standing around, you idiot? You'll be sure to get whacked on the head if you continue walking along all upright and such.'

'Yes, Sergeant, sir,' I responded as we are supposed to. 'Where is the 6th Company?' I asked again.

'They're way in front, you'll never be able to find them. I think that they're somewhere up the slope. They're attacking the British trenches, the slope is full of them,' he answered.

'And the tanks?' I wanted to know.

'They're positioned somewhere here in the bushes. They don't dare come out of the gorge yet, the British have well-camouflaged defence positions.'

'I absolutely have to reach my platoon,' I said finally.

'Well, good luck then,' he answered, 'but be careful and stay under cover; Tommy has made quite sure to close in on this area.'

'Understood, Sergeant,' I said and got up. I ran along the right-hand side of the river and alongside the embankment to make some headway. I was more cautious now and took care to remain ducked and under cover. The gorge gradually became wider, finally opening into a broad valley. Trees became sparser, and so did my opportunities to take cover. However, protected by the riverside bushes, I made quite a bit of progress. I noticed two German tanks driving slowly along the road, firing shots up the slope. That was obviously where the enemy positions must be.

At long last I stumbled across comrades of the third troop. They advanced only slowly, one by one, each soldier dashing forwards then instantly diving into cover – just as we had been taught to do in the Allgäu. As one sniper ran forwards, all on his own, the other machine-gunner would protect him with covering fire, then came the next sniper, and so forth. I joined them and, surrounded once again by familiar faces, I felt better about myself.

'Where's the 6th Company?' I asked the first comrade I could get hold of.

'Up there on the slope,' I was told.

'Is Second Lieutenant Grabert among them as well?' I continued.

'I did see him, but where he is at this moment, I really couldn't say,' he replied, and was gone with the next move forwards.

Out of the dense willow thicket two more German tanks appeared. Slowly they advanced. They too were firing cannons while targeting some object on the hillside, but as I looked closer at what they were targeting, I couldn't make out anything special. The British positions were fabulously camouflaged. Neither could I see any sign of the attacking comrades. Bushes blocked the view. But there was no doubt that quite a bit was going on up there. I heard bursts of fire that came from pistols and machine guns, and hand grenades exploding and smashing into the ground. The smoke rising into the sky indicated the direction I should be taking. Then white signal flares appeared over our heads, which usually meant: 'We're here'. Obviously, the tanks needed to be alerted as to the precise position of their comrades. The scrub gradually thinned out and so did the embankment, no longer providing useful cover. We ran after the tanks, trying to keep up with their speed and hoping they would protect us during our advance. I reached the second tank, grabbed onto the rear and trotted alongside. Immediately we were fired at. The bullets whistled past over our heads and smashed into the ground, sending small puffs of dust into the air, ricocheting sideways or colliding with the thick armour plating of the tanks. In retrospect, relying on the tanks' protection wasn't such a splendid idea.

Then came a scream: 'Full cover – the first tank is on fire!' As one, we leaped from the tank and into the ditch. I lay as flat as I could. The first tank was ablaze. A sniper jumped out onto the turret, but immediately fell back, with one leg, held by nothing but skin and fabric scraps, dangling back and forth. A second man appeared in the hatch but was instantly taken out by a burst of fire and collapsed without a further sound. His arms sank to the ground – lifeless. Flames shot out of the turret. Where the hell were these anti-tank gunners? They must be somewhere up the slope, well camouflaged and with a clear view of their targets.

We stormed up the incline. 'Jump up from cover, run a few steps – lie flat. Repeat.' We kept murmuring this to ourselves. Firing a few shots with our pistols, we moved onwards. The second tank protected us with covering fire and we could feel the shells flying past over our heads. In front of us lay a ditch; we jumped in and onto … some dead British soldiers.

We didn't pause and climbed upwards, marched onwards, leaped over rocks and rubble, ran, lay flat. Repeat. My tongue was stuck to the roof of my mouth; I was sweating and perspiration streamed down my face, burning my eyes. Breathing was difficult and painful. Beside me, my comrades were panting, but managing to keep up. Jump up from cover, run a few steps, take cover again. Repeat. I couldn't run any more. I lay there exhausted. 'And what'll happen if they'll get you?' There wasn't time to think. I scrambled up. Jump up from cover, run a few steps, take cover again. Repeat.

Goodness, where were we actually running to? We could make out the enemy positions dug into the dense undergrowth of the slope only once we were practically on top of them, and then there was another ditch. We fired some shots and ran, fired a few more and ran again.

There – the British were surrendering. Waving white fabric cloths in the air and hands raised, they climbed out of their trenches. Without uttering a single word, we jumped in. With no voices left to scream, gasping for air, we gave way to our overwhelming exhaustion. If it had come to close-combat fighting, Tommy would have had easy game; we had nothing left inside us.

My friend Kisswetter handed me his flask, which I greedily put to my burning lips to drink some left-over tepid tea. Oh, what blissful and divine libation! We felt re-energised.

As for the British, we just sent them back into the valley, surely there would be someone to welcome them. They carried with them their wounded comrades. Then, left on our own in the trenches, we took a look around the area. It was strewn with weapons, helmets, coats, ammunition and tinned food. But none of us had any interest – we had a funny feeling that the battle wasn't over just yet.

After a brief rest, we crawled out of the trenches and climbed towards the ridge, which pointed diagonally down towards the valley. Down there our tank was still smouldering, while the other one had returned and stood in the bushes near us. In front of us lay a narrow valley, followed by yet another mountain slope similar to the one we had just stormed. Lying close to each other, Kisswetter, Harich and I, with only our heads peeking out, noticed on the slope opposite some trenches, one above the other, but they seemed beyond the range of our pistols. We would need our machine guns for those. It was clear to us that we couldn't advance any further along this route but had to approach them from another side and perform a flanking manoeuvre.

We crawled back, leaving only Harich lying there – he was dead. He had a round hole in the middle of his forehead with a thin river of blood trickling down to the ground, staining it bright red. He had crumpled up, without a sound, and we hadn't even noticed. He was only seventeen years old, born in Banat, an ethnic German, just like us. He was the Benjamin of our company – and the first one of our men to be killed. Killed in action for his people, Führer and homeland – for which homeland? For which Führer? But those were not questions we asked ourselves at the time. He had been a German soldier, a comrade who had dedicated his life to the same ideals and the same goals as we did. At the time, all of us, regardless of our homeland, fought for the same people, for the same fatherland, and for the same Greater Germany in which all of us wanted to live in peace. This Greater German Reich, a centuries-old dream of ours, always just out of reach – this is what we were now fighting for, together, brothers in arms.

Second Lieutenant Grabert came down the slope, as did Egli and Tschentsche, carrying their machine guns. Together we returned to the valley. Smoke was billowing from the tank; the tank gunner, burnt to a crisp, hung out of the hatch and – would you believe it? – this was exactly the tank where my rucksack was. Of course, it too was burnt, nothing more than a piece of fabric with smoke still coming out of it.

Cautiously, we edged along the trenches towards Tempe, a small village some 500 metres in front of us. Behind us, tanks started emerging from the gorge. The machine-gunners positioned themselves alongside the road and provided us with protective fire. We made good headway with these guys following a bit behind us. A little further on, some thirty metres away, a tall stone wall marked an area filled with white gravestones. This must be Tempe's cemetery. Some bushes grew at the corner of the wall, and, lo and behold, we could see a gun peeking out.

'Look over there, Tschampetro,' said Grabert. 'Over there, just to the left, alongside the graveyard's wall … looks like that's where the anti-tank gunners have dug in.'

'I can see that,' I replied, 'but there doesn't seem to be anyone there. I bet you they've all scarpered – there's no movement at all.'

'Well, let's wait and see,' responded Grabert. We stayed put at the side of the road and waited until the machine-gunners showed up. That's when we realised that the gun barrel was moving, slowly veering in our direction.

'Take cover!' shouted Second Lieutenant Grabert. Quick as a flash, we rolled down into the ditch. 'Machine-gunners, covering fire, now,' ordered Grabert. 'The others, follow me.'

Thank God the ditch alongside the road was deep enough that we could remain unnoticed by the enemy if we kept totally flat to the ground. What we needed to do was approach them from a concealed position, attacking them from the flank, or better still from behind, but approaching them head-on would never have been possible. One behind the other, we crept along the ditch, mindful not to lift either our heads or our backsides, and we actually succeeded getting past the anti-tank units without being noticed. Although they now were behind us, we still had to get closer to be able to wipe them out. In order to do that, we had to first cross the road and reach the wall of the cemetery.

'Cross the road, get close up to the wall,' ordered Grabert. We leaped up all at the same time and dashed across the road in just a few swift movements. We dropped to the ground and, fast as a lizard, we reached the wall. We needed to catch our breath for a few moments. I took my glasses off to get the sweat and filth off, but rubbing the lenses between my thumb and finger, I only managed to spread the dirt, which wasn't of much help. Only once I had polished the

1. *Sterzing in the 1920s.*

2. *Reifenstein Castle near Sterzing. Secret assemblies took place here during the 'illegal times'.*

3. *Groups of girls gathering at secret assemblies on remote mountain meadows.*

4. *Songs, sport and folk dances were enjoyed at the so-called 'cultural camps'.*

5. *Students of the Hegelhaus, 1939/40. South Tyroleans were the first to be offered courses leading to the Matura.*

6. *A training camp for the 8th Company Lehrbataillon zbV 'Brandenburg' in the Pfeffermühle, Wertach, Allgäu. Originally this was a camp for the Reich's labour service.*

7. In the camp at Petrič (Bulgaria), examining the Greek uniforms. The comrade wearing a fatigue jacket has just received a Greek kitbag containing a rolled-up blanket. The foreign uniforms supplied by the OK (Oberkommando) were never used, as they were brand new. During an operation we used to remove the uniforms of captured soldiers and wear them on top of our own uniforms.

8. The Vardar bridge near Axiopolis (Greece). This was the only bridge crossing the Vardar which was taken by the Germans undamaged, during the Grabert camouflage mission. Grabert was honoured with the Knight's Cross. For the author it was his baptism of fire and he was decorated with the Iron Cross, Second Class.

9. *German tanks cross the Pineios river, just near the Vale of Tempe. The Gebirgsjäger at the far left of the tank is the author.*

10. *The advance has come to a halt. 'Brandenburgers to the front!' We overtake the armoured vanguard.*

11. *En route on the Marathon road. Only a few more kilometres to reach Athens.*

12. *Brandenburgers in Bulgarian uniform.*

13. *The flag with the swastika on top of the Acropolis. We hoisted it on Sunday 27 April 1941 at 9.30 in the morning.*

14. *In the camp at Petrič. The 8th Company has reported for duty.*

15. *The Brandenburgers attending the victory parade in Athens, 3 May 1941. In the front row, from left to right: Lieutenant Grabert, Oberjäger Slama, Private Burrer, Private Hass, Private de Giampietro.*

16. *The bridge over the Düna in Dünaburg, Lithuania. The city is on fire, but the bridge remains intact. It was captured and secured at dawn on 26 June 1941 in a camouflage operation by the half-company Knaak of the 8th Company 'Brandenburg'.*

17. *The remains of a captured vehicle in which the Brandenburgers, dressed in Russian uniform had crossed the bridge in Dünaburg. Hit by a PaK, it overturned and fell over the embankment.*

18. *Lieutenant Grabert.*

19. *Lieutenant Grabert and Second Lieutenant Hüller.*

20. *The graves of Grabert and Hüller at the bridge before Bataisk.*

21. At dawn on 25 July 1942 the first half-company of the 8th Company 'Brandenburg' stormed the bridge before Bataisk, near Rostov, under the leadership of Captain Siegfried Grabert.

22. Gathering of the dead and wounded after the battle.

23. *The bridge of Maikop in the Caucasus after the battle. There are still some dead left on the ground.*

24. *The first tanks cross the undamaged bridge in Maikop.*

25. The grave of Second Lieutenant Ernst Prochaska and his men who fell at the bridge of *Maikop on 19 August 1942 (Fritz Schmied, Sepp Shöfer, Hans Gruber, Max Galuf, Willy, Fritz Renz). Second Lieutenant Prochaska was awarded the Iron Cross posthumously.*

26. *The men remember the death of their comrades at the open graves (author, with glasses, is fourth from the right).*

27. Lieutenant Wolfram Knaak outside Dünaburg. He was wounded in the right arm during the operation in Kedainiai. One day later he fell at Dünaburg.

28. *Grave of Lieutenant Wolfram Knaak – and Privates Karl Heinz Röseler, Karl Innerhofer and Anton Stauder and Senior Rifleman Matthias Plattner, at the crossroads at Dünaburg.*

lenses with a bit of grass could I make them somewhat more transparent. At least I no longer had to constantly peer over the top of my glasses.

'Three men crawl ahead and smoke the hell out of the anti-tank positions,' ordered Grabert, once he had caught his breath. Immediately, three men crept alongside the small wall towards the bushes where the gunners were positioned. Grabert and I were pressed to the wall, holding our breath. Would our men be able to get close enough to throw their hand grenades or would they themselves get it in the neck? Any minute now, they would be there.

'Go, Tschampetro,' whispered Grabert, without turning towards me. 'We'll give you some covering fire.'

We jumped up together, firing our pistols over the wall and across the bushes, emptying half of our cartridge. Then we immediately crouched down. That was exactly when our comrades leaped up and thrust their hand grenades into the positions. There were three near-simultaneous detonations.

'Get going!' yelled Grabert, ducking along the small wall towards the comrades. I jumped over the wall into the cemetery and ran in the direction of the enemy position, all the time shooting from my hip holster. A Tommy leaped out from his hiding place and staggered across. With both hands he was holding his stomach, ripped open with all his intestines hanging out. The sight of a man running across the cemetery and holding his guts in his hands stopped me in my tracks. After a few metres of just staggering back and forth, the man spun round and then fell head-first onto a gravestone. Behind the man's hiding place, we found another three dead Tommies.

The tanks were now able to approach without any further obstacles stopping them. They drove past us and continued unhindered through Tempe, with us following. The valley broadened, allowing us a better view of our surroundings. On the other side of the river, we could still see intermittent white flares going up, signalling that the Gebirgsjäger, who had traversed the mountains from the right, were now descending into the valley. At the entrance of the valley we sat down underneath some shady trees and rested for a little while, joined soon afterwards by the reserve snipers who had supported the tanks in their assault. They too had suffered losses, some dead and wounded. There were five of us Brandenburgers, including Grabert. The others had got lost in the bushes and had become separated from us. We couldn't wait for them and moved on with the tanks. In squad line formation on either side of the tanks, which proceeded at a slow pace, we saw them shoot at everything in sight. They fired at every wall and every bush behind which they suspected a hidden enemy soldier and scoured the top of the trees for concealed firing equipment with their machine guns. The moment we were anywhere close to the front tank, its turret rotated menacingly towards us and we had to take cover and pray. Once, a stationary freight train on the tracks caught their eye, and they practically showered it with heavy machine-gun and cannon fire, even though we couldn't spot anything suspicious; but better safe than sorry, they probably thought. After that fusillade, the tanks had an unencumbered vision over the field and felt able to spread out. We could hardly keep up, and eventually fell behind. Seeing that the battle had not yet reached its final stages, we had to remain cautious. The British, prepared to stage serious resistance, lay hidden everywhere.

There, a few metres in front of us, a British corporal leaped up and tried to flee, but his attempt was too late and we caught him. There were quite a few British whom we plucked out from these bushes. Obediently, they all shuffled into captivity. For them, the battle was lost, over and done with, so they simply accepted their fate. How bad could captivity be?

In those times, both sides still fought a war with a keen awareness of what was fair sportsmanship. 'It was a very nice match.' Never shall I forget that expression. We had won this round, but next time the game might be theirs. None of us bore them any hatred, certainly not us, and it seemed to me that they felt the same. It was a 'competition' between two equally matched partners, and sometimes one side got the upper hand, and sometimes the other side did. Perhaps, at the time, I idealised the war, probably down to my youth and lack of experience, so my enthusiasm might today be considered naivety. This attitude towards war as a competitive sport would change dramatically later on in Russia. There, from day one, we would learn what it really meant to be fanatical, to hate, and to wage a brutal war of survival for the sake of a regime that wished to live on forever, and whose relentless struggle turned the Russian campaign into all-out war.

It was damned hot. The sun was burning down from a blue sky in which there wasn't a single cloud to be seen and sweat was streaming down our faces. Our thirst became unbearable. We found some tins and thought it was British beer. Piercing holes into the cans we put them to our lips, but, oh hell, it turned out to be sweet condensed milk. In disgust and anger at the Tommies, we chucked the tins into the bushes.

The tanks picked up speed, with the countryside wide open in front of them without obstructions. We decided to climb up onto one of the heavy tanks in order to keep up. We lay down flat behind the turret, holding tight as best we could so as not to be flung off onto the stony ground, or become a visible target. When the tank came to a halt, we slipped down for cover. Once it started up again, we returned to our turret position. This went on for quite a while, until a deep ditch blocked the road. We jumped off the tank, which then drove into the ditch but slipped, and with that the three fog grenades fixed to the rear of the tank came loose. Immediately, a waft of dense, brown smoke and fog rose into the air, enveloping the tank in thick cloud. The tank soldiers, who all of a sudden couldn't see a thing and had to assume that they had been hit, climbed out of the hull and ran away. One of them, dressed in a British khaki shirt and sand-coloured combat field pants, emerged suddenly from that cloud and was immediately fired at. In a flash, he disappeared back into the cloud.

The fog eventually dispersed and at long last the tank driver managed to get his vehicle out of the ditch all on his own. We mounted it again and now the driver stood upright in his turret, his Iron Cross gleaming in the evening sunlight. The tanks had come into their element, finally having a fleeing enemy they could chase. With measured precision, the flares targeted the British truck column, which was on its way towards Larissa. Then, suddenly, the air was filled with a roaring noise. Stukas came flying through the air and bombarded the British, forcing their retreat. Penetrating the Tempe valley had turned into a war game of cat and mouse. East Thessaly had now been cleared of the enemy.

From the right, the first Gebirgsjäger were preparing for their descent. They had been pushed down the mountains and had swum across the Pineios, which saw them being caught by British artillery fire and caused many of them to drown. These Jäger then joined us in marching towards Evangelimos, a small hamlet on the left side of the lush valley. We were sitting on the tank, and they were running alongside us.

One of the Oberjäger shouted up to us, quite rightly thinking that we were exposed and an obvious target. 'Get down here,' he said, 'you are only putting yourselves at risk. Just now they were shooting down at us from the top of a tank.' We ducked a bit lower but stayed put. Suddenly there was an cry, and the man who had only minutes ago given us this warning sank to his knees, hit in the chest. He died in the arms of his comrades.

At that, we heeded the warning, jumped from the tank, and scuttled around for cover. Fierce shelling came from the direction of Evangelimos and the mountains behind. Bullets came whistling past our ears, smashing into the ground. Ricochets whirled in the air. Undeterred by the noise and disregarding the shooting, two storks remained sitting in their nest right on top of the church tower of Evangelimos, offering in the midst of the battlefield a serene image of peace.

We remained under cover, waiting for the firing to die down. We weren't able to respond as the distance was beyond the range of our pistols. Jumping into the hole next to me, an Oberjäger joined us. Swearing, he fumbled with his pistol, but it was stuck and wouldn't load. He had taken it apart but obviously couldn't reassemble it and so then asked me, in the purest South Tyrolean dialect, to help him put that piece of crap together, assuming that I must also be familiar with that kind of stuff. Unfortunately, I wasn't able to help him. The weapon had become wet when he waded through the river, and water and sand had got into every crevice.

After several attempts at fixing it and answering him in our dialect, I told him that he might as well chuck the thing. The Oberjäger was pleasantly surprised that I too came from the South Tyrol, and so we continued chatting in our familiar dialect.

'Yes, indeed,' I answered, 'I come from Sterzing.'

'I am a true Bozen guy,' he said. We exchanged a warm handshake and off he went. The Gebirgsjäger stormed Evangelimos and cleared the mountain area behind it. We five Brandenburgers remained in the hamlet, as we wanted to wait for our comrades to arrive. We made ourselves at home – an art we had become quite good at, and not many could surpass us in that respect. With an expert eye, we chose the most beautiful houses and hung posters on their doors that said in big letters: 'Occupied by the OKW'.[4]

Now that we had set up home, we went about organising ourselves. This too was a skill mastered by only a few. What it required was good instinct, a fair bit of cheekiness, speedy action and plenty of audacity. We had quite a few men among us who were endowed with such qualities, and each one was proud of his virtuosity. These chaps would be able to find the most unbelievable, the most unexpected objects anywhere, but the best thing about it was that the items were extremely useful to us and contributed significantly to making life in the countryside tolerable.

Not a single civilian was left in this hamlet – they had all fled. We chanced upon a good supply of eggs, bread, wine, sugar, tea and jam. For now, that was quite enough. When our comrades arrived a few hours later, they were warmly welcomed, and an opulent supper awaited them. My group also arrived, exhausted and worn out. They brought sad news with them: comrade Pfeifhofer, a man from my engineering troop, had been killed in action. Right in front of the Tempe valley, a bullet had hit him in the stomach and put a quick end to his glowing youth. One of the bravest and most daring of our comrades had fallen. The news of his death hit me hard – I had come to really like this rough-edged, upright and honest guy.

It was 6 o'clock in the evening. We had lost sight of the tanks and could only see a faint dust cloud far away, slowly winding its way up the mountain, disappearing in the distance, but still followed by the gleaming traces of grenades fired from enemy tanks. Black clouds of smoke marked the escape route of the British.

For us Brandenburgers, today's battle had come to an end. We drew some water out of a cistern, pulled off our sweaty and dirty uniforms, and scrubbed ourselves thoroughly. It was sheer heaven to get that filth washed off our bodies, after such a truly awful day. We then went into the houses, brought out all the quilts, pillows and duvets we could put our hands on and spread them out in our room. Our soft beds were ready. Dead tired, we fell into a deep sleep. The poster on the door that read 'Occupied by the OKW' protected us from any disturbance during the night.

After a good breakfast, we searched the houses again, this time looking for fresh laundry, as nothing else really interested us. I felt like a thief, the way we just pushed into the houses, broke open locked doors, cupboards and neatly packed suitcases, carelessly rummaging through everything and picking out fresh shirts, underpants and socks. But, truth be told, it was ever thus: ever since soldiers first fought in wars, this is how it has always been, and that is surely how it always will be among us humans. The Greeks, the Romans, the Huns and the mercenaries – all of them behaved in this manner: the whole world over, the victorious Landser takes what he needs. We had soon worked this one out.

All morning, the Gebirgsjäger brought in wounded soldiers who, sadly, could only be given the most basic care. Transport to the field hospitals was impossible due to the bridge over the Pineios, right at the entrance of the gorge, still not having been repaired, which meant that the *Sankas* couldn't come and fetch them.[5] We too were waiting for our trucks. But we weren't in any rush, we had plenty of time. We heard the droning noise of the Ju 87 across the sky, the trucks of the air, so to speak. White flares ascended from the mountains encircling the valley, and boxes attached to small parachutes, came floating down from the planes and performed a curious dance through the air. They were delivering extra food supplies and ammunition for the Gebirgsjäger.

We busied ourselves with some carpentry work and made simple crosses for our fallen comrades. I made the one which I wanted to place on the grave of my friend and burnt onto a small piece of timber the inscription: 'Obsch. Pfeifhofer, field post 03271, killed in action for Greater Germany.' That afternoon, together with my comrades, I returned to the gorge to place the cross on the grave of Pfeifhofer.

On the way, we found a British two-seater vehicle. It was a small, open, yet armoured vehicle. Its steel plate showed two round holes indicating that it had been hit and finished off by a Panzerbüchse.[6] One dead British soldier was still lying inside. We lifted out the rigid corpse, lay it on the ground and covered it with stones, placing the dead man's steel helmet on top.

The seat and the floor of the vehicle were smeared in blood, but since the motor still seemed to be working, we assumed that we would have no problem operating the vehicle, even though it was British. We mounted it, with one of us at the steering wheel, and drove off. That's when things went wrong. The vehicle hurtled forwards and one comrade went flying from the rear of the tank and onto the ground, landing on his back. Swearing, he jumped up and ran after us. But we had come to a halt. We changed drivers, but the next one couldn't manage any better, and so we speedily zigzagged down the narrow path, with the oncoming Landsers jumping aside and having themselves a good old laugh at our expense. Of course, the inevitable happened, and we landed in the ditch. The motor had died. So, we continued on foot, which was a much safer and quicker way to get us to our destination.

The grave was on a gentle incline, in the middle of a green meadow. We hammered the cross into the ground and hung his steel helmet on top. Then I addressed my companions: 'Comrades, let us remember him.' We lined up, took off our caps and stood there for a few minutes in silence.

I took a step forwards and spoke, my words coming out hoarse: 'Comrade Pfeifhofer, your true, open and honest heart has stopped beating. You were obedient, yet still followed your instincts. Listening to your inner voice, you left South Tyrol, your home and family, and volunteered to fight for the freedom of our people. Faithful and keeping to your oath, you have offered up your life for the Führer, the people and your fatherland, without a moment's hesitation. Now you are at rest, far from your beloved home country and in foreign lands. But you are not dead; you continue to live on within our hearts. We consider it our duty, and this is what we swear to you at your grave: to follow in your footsteps and fight until we have won the final victory, or be killed in the field of honour. Adieu, Comrade Pfeifhofer, Adieu.'

We returned to Evangelimos in silence.

— EIGHT —

Athens, Spring 1941

The 6th Mountain Division was marching towards Larissa. The comrades were exhausted; they weren't so much marching as more dragging themselves along the dusty roads and paths, stumbling over stones and holes beneath a scorching hot sun. It required a huge effort to put one foot in front of the other – the division must by then have already clocked up several thousand kilometres, crossing numerous byways through rain and snow – and though it was only April, the heat was nearly unbearable. They had marched through the gorges and the peaks of the Rhodope mountain range, right across the Balkan peninsula, and were now struggling to tackle the endless paths of Greece. Nothing seemed to matter other than marching, marching onwards and upwards, marching down the slopes and up to the peaks, a march that didn't seem to have a foreseeable ending.

Trailing behind them trudged the heavily laden pack animals, along with the foot soldiers, who would often grab on to their tails to be pulled along. Rifles slung across their torsos, they carried the machine guns that pressed down hard on their shoulders, weighing them down. Ammunition boxes in their hands, grenade launchers on their backs, they disappeared into a cloud of dust whirled up by the endless column of vehicles relentlessly passing by.

Looking at those men, I felt a mixture of embarrassment and awe; comparing them and their gigantic physical achievements with our good selves, comfortably seated on our trucks and cursing the very prospect of having to travel on foot for even one lousy kilometre, I was humbled. At least our drivers were considerate enough to slow down and reduce their speed when they were about to overtake the marching columns, so as not to raise any dust and not further aggravate the marching infantry, who were already plenty annoyed at the vehicles passing them.

Our trucks had arrived during the night, ready to leave Evangelimos the following morning. Immediately, we found ourselves wedged among vehicles of all kinds and were only gradually able to overtake the endless supply convoys. British tanks lay strewn to the right and left of the road, and trucks and guns which had been blown apart and burnt out gave evidence to a battle lost. The air pressure caused by exploding Stuka bombs alone must have often forced them far across the fields.

We reached Larissa at around lunchtime. The city had suffered a lot during that year. In March, it had been hit by an earthquake and shortly thereafter was ravaged by bombing raids by our air force. Barely a single house remained undamaged, entire streets had been torn apart – whether the cause was the earthquake or the bombs was of little importance. Blackened chimneys rose to the sky, streets had collapsed into rubble, destroyed houses created tall heaps of debris and ashes, shop shutters were bent and broken – there was devastation everywhere.

We left the city and looked around for a place to pitch our tents. We came upon an abandoned British army ration supply depot. Neatly stacked crates filled with tins awaited us: corned beef, ham, fruit, vegetables and cigarettes. We helped ourselves to as much as we could fit in our truck. This was a pleasant surprise for our cooks and foragers! They organised the vehicles earmarked for British booty, packing them up to the very top, but they had to work quickly and efficiently to get away with their prize before the quartermasters from other troops could get their hands on it. For months, even in Russia, our daily menu consisted of nothing but rice with corned beef, and by the end, we couldn't stand the smell of it. Not far away, we also chanced upon a British fuel dump – well, what more could our hearts desire? We immediately set about filling all our cans with fuel and oil. At long last, we could enjoy fuel and food in ample quantities and no longer had to rely on further supply deliveries, which tended to take their time in getting to us. We were especially blessed on that day in that our motorcyclist troop, who always went ahead to explore the terrain for the optimal locations for our tents, had returned to inform us that they had found an abandoned British camp. Immediately we set off and, lo and behold, just moments later we saw an orderly row of some twenty twelve-man tents, in which we found what for us at the time seemed like treasures: British khaki shirts, colonial-style shorts and tropical helmets – all brand-new stuff. It only seemed right that we should appropriate these items in the name of the OKW, and we certainly didn't need much convincing to regard this requisitioning as simply a useful aid for our undercover missions.

We had figured out quite quickly that the lightweight tropical shirts were much more pleasant to wear than our hot and thick grey uniforms. And thus, it slowly but surely came about that the one or two soldiers who had decided to wear these British khaki uniforms the minute we had found them were soon joined by half of the company. We sewed the national insignia, the rank insignia and the collar patches onto the light brown shirts and tucked the field-grey jackets away in our rucksacks. We were probably the first German soldiers to do so – outside the Afrika Korps, who already wore khaki uniforms. It was no wonder that some other battalions made fun of us at first, though this quickly turned into envy. One thing was certain: we caused a stir everywhere we went. Even later on in Athens, the Wehrmacht's patrol posts would recognise us by that uniform, and it resulted in a few nasty incidents.

By 23 April, our stay in Larissa drew to a close. Once again, it was time to head off to the front line. The tanks had already crossed the western parts of Thessaly and had moved beyond Farsala. They had overcome the Phurka Pass before reaching Lamia. Still ahead of us lay the challenge of conquering what was probably the last British defence line. Tommy had chosen to dig himself in at the Purnaraki Pass and at Thermopylae. Marching along the advance route, which took us over the Phurka Pass, we came across the now-familiar scene: a sheer endless column of heavy trucks struggling up the pass; huge bomb craters and destroyed British tanks and vehicles as far as the eye could see. Greek soldiers were busy working along the roadside. Once, in the middle of the road, we came across a bomb crater into which they had tossed a British tank, which they then had covered with some stones and wooden beams. We crossed over it and marched onwards, reaching Lamia in the evening.

The castle at Lamia, situated on a hill and dating back to the Middle Ages, reminded us of Litochoron. Immediately upon our arrival we searched for a camping spot and found one on a beautiful meadow, surrounded by fig trees and cacti, and that's where we pitched our British tents.

Our artillery, positioned right next to our tents, continued with its shelling throughout the night. We spent two days here. What would a Landser be expected to do when he found himself on stand-by? Above all, he would look for anything and everything edible. It wasn't that we were actually hungry. No, it wasn't that. Never during the war did we suffer hunger pangs. That didn't stop us, however, from always wanting a decent meal. The farmers, with whom we communicated by hand gestures and a few Greek phrases we had learned during our stay, understood our wish for eggs but refused to hand them over to us, stubbornly insisting they didn't have any. Apparently, the British had stolen all their chickens. Well, look at that – Tommy obviously didn't just make do with the eggs: he had made off with the hens that laid them! Gradually, however, once we showed the farmers our drachmas, indicating that that we were quite prepared to spend them, they became less suspicious and even started trusting us. So much so that a farmer invited us into his house, where his wife cooked us an amazing meal, *Schmarren*, without skimping on eggs or butter.[1] A large pot of creamy goat's milk topped it all and I felt as if I was in some rich pasture in South Tyrol.

It was 26 April by the time we finally left. We crossed the gorgeous Purnaraki Pass, which had been stormed by our comrades of the Waffen-SS the day before, and by the time we reached Thebes it was pitch dark. We couldn't see any signs of the glory and magnificence that had once made this city the stuff of legends and myths. We found a hut – it was filthy – and lay down to sleep, not allowing the scuttling of rats or mice to disturb us. But throughout the night, we kept being woken violently from our dreams by the detonation of bombs. The British were blowing up the bridges and roads leading to Athens.

We got up at 0400 in the morning and left. Our group had been ordered to find any route that would take us to Athens, as large sections of the main road had become inaccessible. That was certainly a reconnaissance mission tailor-made for us.

We split from our troop and criss-crossed the countryside. Being left completely to our own devices brought a certain degree of danger, but also some considerable advantages: we were extremely mobile because of our trucks, we were able to or indeed were forced to improvise, we didn't have to put up with being stuck in a stinking column with the other vehicles, and there was nobody looking over our shoulders to check whether our behaviour complied with the HDV.[2] Relying on our good luck and in high spirits, we drove out into the silver-grey morning, visibly excited.

The sun was rising slowly on the horizon, heralding a hot day. The large leaves on the fig trees, still wet from the morning dew, glistened in the first sunlight like Christmas decorations. Cacti grew along the side of the roads, and the dark green of the olive trees promised healthy pickings.

We no longer gave the British any thought. They wouldn't be able to do us any more harm, and they certainly didn't have the means to stop us in our tracks. Most likely, they had fled a long time ago in order to board the last ship leaving Piraeus. We rather enjoyed this lonesome adventure and were glad to have been able to get away from the boring cavalcade.

We reached the sea at the Euripus Strait. '*Thalatta! Thalatta!*' Singing these words, our hearts rejoiced.[3]

A veil of mist hung over the water, allowing us to make out only faintly the outline of the island of Euboea. Small white sailing boats rocked on the water;

fishermen, not allowing the war to get into their way, were hard at work. What was it to them if we Barbarians – the Germans and the British – banged our heads against each other?

We came across a very heavily armoured reconnaissance car section of the Waffen-SS, and all of a sudden, we felt rather small. They were supported by armoured reconnaissance vehicles, motorcycle riflemen, whose sidecars carried their machine guns, and radio cars, with their long antennas constantly swaying back and forth. The crew sat proudly aloft with guns held between their legs, their uniform shirts buttoned right to the top and their steel helmets buckled, underneath which their eyes looked sternly out ahead of them, their faces wearing an expression of utmost seriousness.

Compared to them, we were a scruffy bunch. Our fighting force consisted of two filthy Opel Blitz cars whose licence plates had either gone missing or were completely illegible. We wore English khaki shirts, an unfamiliar attire at the time, and many of us wore those British tropical helmets. Not a single one of us carried a weapon in our hands – these same hands were busy smearing liverwurst onto our bread at breakfast. After all, this meal was important to people like us; for all we cared, our weapons could just as well be left on the side of the road. Nothing about us would have reminded you of the German discipline and snappiness, nothing at all. Not surprisingly, others looked at us with disdain in their eyes and with a smirk on their faces. It didn't bother us, seeing as we preferred spending time with our liverwurst. Truth be told, we had received the exact same orders as they had; they too had to investigate the best route to Athens, but obviously went about it in a different manner.

After a brief meeting, we separated and, because they had decided to take the direct path to the south and thus move straight on to Athens, we decided to turn west and reach our destination via detours. We were soon on our own once again. In front of us lay a suspicious-looking group of poplar and cedar trees. We had finished breakfast by then and had gathered our weapons. Cautiously, we drove up to the small wood.

Of course, it only stood to reason that we would at some point encounter the British rearguard, who had been left behind for one reason or another. We were aware of that, and there were certainly plenty of clues suggesting that this in fact might well happen. Abandoned trenches and lots of discarded war materiel indicated that the enemy was close. Every single bridge, however small, had been blown up, forcing us time and again to descend from our vehicles and push them through dry riverbeds.

The rail crossings had, of course, also all been destroyed. This forced us to get onto embankments and drive along the train tracks. They were going in the right direction – where else would the tracks lead us other than to Athens? After several kilometres of bumping over railway sleepers, causing considerable wear and tear to the springs and axles of our trusty vehicles, we once again chanced upon a road and were finally able to come down. Here, once more, we saw countless mine craters as well as anti-tank mines that, because they had been lain in haste, were poorly covered. We of course immediately recognised them for what they were and drove around them.

Finally, after roaming through the area and feeling lost for quite a while, we found a wide road, blessedly smoothly paved in cement. We thought that it must surely lead to Athens, which couldn't be far away. We put our foot on the accelerator and sped through the countryside. To the right and left grew fragrant fruit orchards, and poplar and cypress trees formed a long and shady avenue. Huge agaves and cacti dominated this gorgeous natural scenery and, behind the vast gardens, we caught sight of gleaming white villas.

We couldn't bear to remain seated on the benches of our vehicles, so stood up and looked ahead over the cab to try to make out what lay in front. No other vehicle was in sight. Could it really be that we would turn out to be the first German soldiers to reach Athens? We could hardly believe our eyes, but yes, there, in the middle of the road, stood a blonde girl dressed in the BdM uniform, waving to us.[4] We started yodelling, we were so happy. More and more girls gathered along the street; they blocked our cars, cheered and threw flowers onto the vehicles. We finally stopped the cars.

'At long last, here you are, we've been waiting for you so long, but now, all is well and, guess what, the British set sail early this morning.' Everyone was shouting at once. We couldn't contain ourselves for all the excitement and joy. We were being embraced and kissed and showered with flowers. From the windows of the house where the German delegation to Greece had appeared, the swastika flag had been raised. Steaming hot tea along with biscuits were served up, and everyone had tears in their eyes. I think we Brandenburgers were no exception.

Suddenly, motorcyclists came zooming down the avenue. They too were stopped, offered refreshments, admired from all sides and embraced.

'Get going, guys, get back to your seats,' ordered Grabert in a soft voice and with a friendly but unmistakably serious wink. We immediately understood and reacted just as fast. Instantly we were back on our vehicles, off and away. Under no circumstances were the motorcyclists to get ahead of us. We wanted to be the first German soldiers to arrive in Athens. We drove as fast as our sorely tested Opel Blitz vehicles allowed us, then we saw a signpost: three kilometres to Athens.

As we sat on our benches, our eyes were glued to the road ahead. Then, at the end of it, the outlines of the Acropolis emerged, with its white stone pillars starkly contrasting with the deep blue sky. Our final destination, given to us exactly three weeks ago, was now securely within our reach. We drove through the deserted streets of Athens, with the Acropolis still looming over us. The blinds of all the shops we passed were pulled down, window shutters were closed and the tables and chairs in front of coffee shops were empty. The city had sunk into a deadly calm; it was eerie, unfamiliar and disconcerting.

We drove up the winding road to where the Acropolis stood, jumped out from our cars while the driver pulled the swastika flag from under his seat. it wasn't the German Reichskriegsfahne, no, just a simple swastika flag like the one we tie onto the bonnet of our motor vehicles to mark them clearly as one of our own. Clutching the pole in our hands, we ran – yes, we literally ran – through the sacred temple and jumped over the toppled pillars of bygone glory, our hobnailed boots showing little respect for their holiness. We sprinted, as we could clearly see the motorcyclists driving up the hill behind us, and we certainly didn't want to have them beating us to it. We reached the flagpole on the northern flank of the Acropolis, where the red, white and blue flag of the British was still in place. We dismantled it and quickly fastened to the mast our creased and crumpled flag before lining up and placing our hands to our caps. Second Lieutenant Grabert issued the order: 'Hoist the flag.' Slowly, ceremoniously, the swastika flag rose up the pole, flying atop the Acropolis, high above the city and visible to all.

At that very moment the motorcycle riflemen arrived with their flag tucked under their arms.

'Too late, comrades, too late by just a few moments.'

But, whatever, we were all happy, as together we had made it, and we were all equally overcome by the magnitude of what was happening to us at that hour. We embraced each other, threw our caps into the air, jubilant. The battle had been won, the enemy had been eradicated from the Balkans and our homeland liberated from impending danger.

That's at least how it appeared to us.

The month we then spent in Athens, and which marked the end of the invasion of the Balkans, was probably the most beautiful month we experienced during the entire war. In Phaleron, a suburb of Athens, we moved into confiscated villas and enjoyed a balmy springtime. The air was filled with the fragrance of the thousands of flowers that bloomed in abundance in the villa gardens, displaying the splendour of Greek flora. Every day we went down to the nearby beach to swim, and the warm sun shining from a clear blue sky tanned our bodies. Late in the afternoons, we would drive into Athens and stroll through the streets.

All the units had been ordered to leave the city, and soldiers were only allowed to visit on Sundays and Thursdays. Only those of us who belonged to Grabert's group were given a special red permit as acknowledgement for being the first German troops to have reached Athens, and this allowed us to visit it every single day. We certainly took good advantage of this privilege, even though these regular nocturnal forays didn't always go so smoothly. What with us wearing the British khaki uniforms, we always caused something of a sensation, and our company received daily reports regarding this matter from

The author's special permit to enter Athens, stating rank, name, unit. stamped by the city headquarters.

the Wehrmachtsstreifendienst.[5] We enjoyed excursions to Cape Sunion and Corinth, participated in the victory parade in Athens and devoured masses of strawberries with cream, a delicacy which we'd missed for quite a while.

We had no illusions that the war would end any time soon. We weren't a bit surprised, therefore, when we were suddenly ordered to embark on an airborne invasion of Crete by parachuting down to seize the last remaining Greek island from British hands. In the end the attack on Crete went ahead without us because the parachute detachment requested that we join them only for their third campaign, insisting on undertaking the first two campaigns on their own. But our superior, having none of that, wanted to have it his way: either we participated in the first campaign or not at all. For us Landsers, quite frankly, even the last campaign would have come too early for our liking.

Then, a rumour suddenly made the rounds, saying that we would be relocated to somewhere in the Middle East, to Syria or Persia: we were to make our way through the desert and operate behind the backs of the British, whom Rommel would chase out of Egypt. That way, the British would have the Afrika Korps to contend with on one side, and behind them would be the Brandenburgers. But that, too, came to nothing, thank God. But what did come at the end of May was the order to return home. Nobody among us could have imagined a more wonderful order to be issued, and when we departed from Athens, our mood was suitably relaxed and happy.

We returned via the same route as our advance. On Whitsunday, we arrived in Belgrade. We camped outside the city but drove into the centre of town that very afternoon just so that we could have a look around. There we were in our trucks, driving along the streets quite aimlessly as we had no leader, and nobody among us had ever been to Belgrade. Eventually, we turned into a side street, hoping to park our vehicles for a while and have a walk. Much to our surprise, we realised that we had stopped in front of a bordello, and we concluded that this could only be due to our truck drivers' sixth sense. When it came to large cities they tended to hit upon just the right spots.

Our group probably best symbolised the Brandenburger character. The number of our vehicles had doubled, as we had with us confiscated vehicles of every sort, colour and make. Starting with the elegant limousine, we had everything from trucks of every size to regular buses, and our motorcycle messengers had even captured some Norton motorbikes and some Harley Davidsons. Everyone who had a driving licence at the time also had to drive a vehicle. The bumpy roads in the Balkans had caused a lot of wear and tear, so by the end, many a captured vehicle had packed up and had to be left behind, just abandoned on the road.

Passing through Budapest, we finally reached the German frontier. We could hardly believe it, but the moment we set foot on German soil, it started raining. For months we had gone without feeling so much as a drop of rain, we hadn't spotted a single cloud in the sky, and there, the minute we found ourselves in Germany, it was raining, and what with us still wearing our khaki uniforms, we were of course freezing cold. We had to roll down the tarpaulins of our trucks, and the chirpy mood that had filled us not so long ago disappeared all of a sudden. We didn't return to our home covered in glory, as we had imagined. Instead we were a nameless, insignificant Wehrmacht group that was slowly driving along the empty roads of Burgenland villages, with no girls blowing us kisses, nobody waving flags or laying carpets on the streets, and no sounds of cheering filling the air. Towards evening, we reached Oberwaltersdorf, a forgotten village in Lower Austria, where we set up camp in the barns of a country estate.

— NINE —

The Invasion of Russia, Summer 1941

East Prussia

Our stay in Oberwaltersdorf lasted only a short while; it couldn't have been more than ten or twelve days. Even though this sleepy village didn't offer much in the way of attractions for young and adventurous soldiers thirsting for action, we were nevertheless quite happy to be back in the homeland we had left behind half a year earlier.

My goodness, what hadn't happened in those few months! We had actually carried out a genuine invasion and conquered the entire Balkans. A few among us had even been decorated with the Iron Cross, and all of us had returned home victorious. But there were not many occasions where we had the chance to show off with stories of our escapades or acts of heroism. There was much to do, and we were very busy.

Our company was being totally reorganised, with new forces being added. The division of our company into commandos had proven successful and was being carried forwards. Nominally, a commando worked more or less in the same way as a normal infantry platoon, except that it was much larger in terms of numbers and was armed and equipped differently. A Brandenburger 'commando' was an autonomous fighting unit, and as such was generally attached to an advance troop, under which it served *zur besonderen Verwendung*, 'for special purposes'. That's why our company was never deployed as a closed company per se; at most they would enlist only half of the company and specifically earmark it for a particular operation. Once we were at the front, we hardly ever had contact with any of the other commandos, and thus barely knew anything about each other.

Since each commando could only rely on itself during its deployment, and since it potentially operated for days, deep in enemy territory and without any support whatsoever, it went without saying that each commando leader was intent on accepting into his unit only the best soldiers and securing nothing but the finest weaponry and the highest-quality equipment. When it came to how they made their selection of their men, it was much more about each soldier's determination to fight, about his courage, perseverance, capability to improvise and to think creatively on the spot, rather than about traditional military drill and bullheadedness. For that matter, we were never what one would traditionally define as a group of perfect and conventionally trained soldiers, but rather a bunch of feisty lads who hated nothing more than drills and barrack life. But it wasn't only the leader of our commando who was keen to have the best men in his unit: each one of us regular soldiers was motivated by those same desires. We too would always prefer to have a solid, reliable, courageous and resourceful leader at our head instead of a timid one, or somebody indecisive or stubborn, as not only was the success of each operation dependent on him, but indeed our lives, and actually our deaths as well, depended on that person and his decisions.

The very real possibility that a failed camouflage operation could spell death for the entire commando always stood foremost in our minds. We had no reason to hope that the enemy would show us mercy. None whatsoever. We didn't have the right to be taken as prisoners of war as we stood outside international military law, and we all knew this.[1] Should we fall into the hands of the enemy, we wouldn't even be entitled to be shot. They would hang us without giving it another thought.

Naturally, squads and platoons, each one defined by its distinct character and indeed unique type of leader, started forming within our company, which resulted in growing rivalry between the different operations. The final decision as to whether or not a particular operation be executed depended solely on its leader. While he could never be forced by anybody to carry out an operation which he might have considered to be futile, *he*, on the other hand, did have that power over others and was thus in a position to suggest to the leader of the advance detachment that certain operations be either carried out or not.

Siegfried Grabert, who in the meantime had been promoted to lieutenant, was the undoubted master of the company. It was a true privilege to be assigned to his operations; in fact it was practically considered an award. While we respected Grabert deeply, even revered him, we did not feel the same about any of his NCOs.

I had always been part of the Grabert unit. I thought I practically belonged to him and felt at home there. My disappointment was therefore huge when I was transferred to a different commando, for reasons inexplicable to me at the time; I was hurt, and felt bitter and rejected.

At that time, a new officer had joined us, and we all felt rather uncomfortable with him around. He was a man who, as far as we were concerned, didn't fit into our group at all. We rejected him because he was entirely different to us. He was tall, had a haggard look, was extremely strict and had an abrupt manner when he spoke in his northern German accent. He wore a monocle, his features were angular, and his uniform was unadorned by any medals: his name was Lieutenant Knaak.[2]

Of all the commandos I could have been transferred to, it was my lot to be assigned to the Knaak commando.

When I was quite young, I had crafted for myself a bit of a personal philosophy that could be summarised: 'Who knows what good might come of it?' This mantra supported me throughout my life. I imagined my journey through life as swimming in a torrential river. Just before the river branched into two distributaries, I would deliberate which one I would tackle: would I choose to go left or right? Once I had decided that I would swim down the distributary leading to the right, I would muster all my energy to get to that side. But if the current proved too strong for me, and if all the kicking and pushing of my legs was in vain, and if my left arm seemed to be the stronger one, then I wouldn't regret abandoning the right distributary but would immediately turn my attention to the left-hand one: 'Who knows what good might come if it?'

That is how I quickly came to terms with my transfer. It was made easier by me then realising that some of my old friends were also being transferred to this new unit. But it wasn't the elite of the 8th Company – that was still the Grabert operation. We were now what one might describe as 'seconds'.

At the time in Oberwaltersdorf, I had no clue of what lay ahead. I accepted my lot, crying with one eye and laughing with the other. Crying, because I had to leave behind many of the comrades I had made during our invasion of Greece; laughing, because I expected the Knaak operations would be less wild than the Grabert ones.

Much to our surprise, it was going to be under Lieutenant Knaak that we would carry out the most audacious operations in the glorious history of the Brandenburgers! They turned out to be the classic and typical operations that characterised the Brandenburger way of waging war, which then became a model for the entire company and contributed considerably to the expansion, development and glory of this young division.

We received new weaponry, brand-new Opel Blitz trucks delivered straight from the factory. Each group received new uniforms and different sorts of entirely new equipment.

We didn't quite understand why all these efforts were being made on our behalf. We made wild guesses about all kinds of places where we would perhaps be deployed. The most extravagant rumours about our new missions began to circulate. But nobody among us soldiers knew anything specific. You'd even hear gossip about a war against Russia, but nobody took this very seriously; hadn't Germany just recently signed a non-aggression pact with Russia?

It wasn't actually war against Russia which was looming, but something quite different. Our Oberkommando had planned a genius chess move. Russia would allow us to march through its territory, which would take us, via some detours, across the Caucasus and into Iran; we would, so to speak, form the other jaw of the pincers that Rommel used for his campaign into Egypt and beyond, far into Africa. This would have resulted in us launching a surprise rear attack on the British, who were fleeing the Afrika Korps. Even when we were in Baden bei Wien, waiting to board a goods train to travel north to East Prussia, this rumour was still alive. That was precisely the inspirational bit of the entire plan! This stranglehold was envisioned – as per rumour – to be a wide sweeping move with the aim of tightening our grip on the enemy and firmly holding him between our hands, and the spreading of this rumour was intended to deceive the British spies. Only once we were deep into Russia, far away from any curious eyes, would we turn towards the south and turn back on ourselves.

We detrained in Königsberg and continued by road towards the east. We were in a good mood, making jokes and laughing. What on earth could go wrong, here in the most north-eastern corner of the German Reich? We looked forward to our journey to Russia and imagined the looks on the faces of the British when they saw us lot emerging from the Caucasus and coming from behind, while they had imagined us being somewhere else entirely.

We passed through the lovely town of Tilsit. Cheering people, raising their hands joyously in welcome, lined the streets everywhere, and we were quite taken by how pretty the young girls of that area were: tall, slim, blue eyes and blonde hair, each one was more attractive than the one before. What a lovely surprise.

'By golly, this is where we'll spend our next holiday,' I said enthusiastically to my friend Willy, nudging him with my elbow and feeling quite enlivened by all the beauty around me. The further we got, the more army units we came across. Vehicles of all kinds and tanks of all sizes stood well camouflaged in forests and villages, while their crews were busy completing their various tasks, and motorcyclists dashed through the area doing their job.

What were these troops doing here? Well, it looked as if they were going to travel with us through Russia.

The pine forest through which we drove became ever denser and darker. Tanks and guns were everywhere, though they were so well concealed you could hardly make them out. There was something fishy in the air; something, we felt, just didn't seem quite right.

All of a sudden, it struck us. All these troops, all these vehicles assembled around us, could mean only one thing: war with Russia.

In an instant, the joyfulness we had felt before was gone and quashed, along with our songs and our laughter. In silence we sat in our vehicles, brooding. The endless forest through which we were travelling was full to the brim with tanks and vehicles of all kinds, light and heavy artillery – again, all excellently camouflaged.

Darkness had descended and we drove without our lights on, only able to guess what was going on around us. We had arrived in the staging area of an enormous army. No campfire and no light penetrated the darkness. The sky, moreover, was covered by black clouds, and a light drizzle was coating our uniforms. We made a stop somewhere in the woods, and now that all the engines had been turned off, the absence of any sound along with the total darkness surrounding us seemed sinister and scary.

Uncertainty mixed with feelings of doubt gnawed at our nerves, weighing our spirits down. A hitherto unknown sense of fear and helplessness crept into our souls, and our bones felt so heavy that our muscles seemed paralysed. The order for absolute silence was given for a second time, but it was hardly necessary, as nobody felt like talking. Any noise had to be avoided at all costs. Meanwhile, the only thing we could see were the messengers scurrying through the night without even whispering so much as a word to anybody. A heavy stillness descended upon us. We tried to prepare ourselves for the night, but frankly, nobody could even think of sleep. Each of us was lost in his own thoughts. What on earth would there even have been for us to talk about?

Maybe it would all start happening the very next day. A new chapter in history would dawn, and we were going to be part of it – right in the front row, just as it had been in the Balkans.

Questions were whirling around my head: will it be another Blitzkrieg, as we have waged before? Will it be our last one? How many of us will be killed in action, never to see our homeland again? What will the Russians be like? What is their combat style?

Thousands of such questions crowded our minds. We kept telling ourselves: 'Nobody can stand up to the German Wehrmacht. Once our Führer gives the order, we will wrestle the enemy to the ground, as we have done before. We will prevent his attack on our homeland, leaving devastation in our wake; we will pre-empt him and beat him on his own turf. Nobody will be able to harm you lovely girls from the Tilsit. We will protect you fair lasses! Have faith in us – that's what we are here for, after all. Fear not – no foreign soldier shall ever put his foot down on German soil.'

The night was interminable. We gathered in small groups, nobody dared speak. Once in a while, in a hushed tone, we would tell each other something of little importance just to calm our nerves. We were rummaging around in our bags, checked our weapons and our ammunition. One last warm meal was being silently distributed, and I'll never know how our cooks ever managed this feat, what with it being pitch dark all around us. We ate without really tasting. Our throats were tight like tourniquets, every bite seemed to get stuck halfway down. We could literally hear our hearts, beating fast.

The strange and indescribable feeling that always came over me before an operation was there once again. It was that same nerve-wracking anticipation of the unknown horror and fear; the fear that came with the realisation that life hung on a single, thin thread, so thin that it made us feel weak at the knees. The anxieties kept increasing, eventually becoming despair; my hands turned ice cold and clammy, and beads of sweat appeared on my forehead.

I sought strength in anything I could, wracking my brain for something to hold onto, but this time I could find nothing, and couldn't think of anything to alleviate the stress; my head was filled by a constant buzzing. I tried to encourage myself by remembering events or loved ones which might calm me, but failed. The slogans trumpeted by the people, by the Führer and the homeland suddenly sounded empty. I wanted to crawl into a hole and hide myself away. The stillness became ever more eerie and unbearable. If there is no going back, then why isn't it starting already? With midnight gone, 22 June 1941 was dawning. Soon the sun would rise.

'*Fertigmachen*', came the order – whispers of 'Make ready' were being passed from one vehicle to the other.

We sat up. We fastened our steel helmets; our hand grenades were tucked into our belts. With trembling hands I clutched my MPi. We stared in front of us in silence. The die had been cast, and, realising that, I became curiously calm, and finally both my optimism and my confidence that good fortune was on my side returned. Gone was my fear. My previous despondency gave way to decisiveness, my despair turned into courage. Once again, my heart was beating entirely normally.

Then, all of a sudden, as if some ghost had orchestrated it, bursts of fire erupted everywhere. They came crashing down, seemingly all at the same time, spewing from the muzzles of thousands of guns, while the first shells burst above our heads. Within an instant, the forest had become alive. Our comrades revved their motors and grabbed their camouflage; orders were being bellowed out everywhere. The wood was filled with the rumble of gunfire and explosions. The thin crescent of the moon paled with the dawn of the morning. The German Wehrmacht had reported for duty, and once again the war machine was rolling on. The clock read 0315.

Josvainiai, Lithuania

0500 hours, 22 June: We found ourselves driving down a dusty road, east of Ariogala in Lithuania.

'Lieutenant Knaak to the front line,' we heard the order while standing in the convoy. We knew what that meant. It was our turn now. The first operation of the invasion stood before us.

We had been with the vanguard attachment of the 8th Tank Division ever since the previous morning. The forest at the border had soon been crossed, and before us lay large cornfields, criss-crossed by woody patches and deep marshy hollows. Enemy positions were seized in quick succession, albeit causing the 290th Infantry Division to suffer heavy losses. We had not been deployed.

Right from day one of this war it had become quite obvious that the Russians were going to be a totally different sort of enemy from the British, at least as far as how *we* had experienced the British – say in Greece. The Russians allowed the vanguard tanks to roll past them while they hid in the woods and cornfields waiting for the unarmoured cargo vehicles to pull up and only then would they attack. Thus, our first casualties were not among the vanguard of our company, but from the ones in the rear, the field-kitchen and so forth. The snipers shot from up above the trees or from very cleverly dug one-man holes. We had to wipe out every single one of the enemy's nests.

Those one-man holes, which we first got to see in Russia, were a hellish sort of trap. They were round holes, usually with just enough room for one man to stand upright in, and they were spread all across the terrain.[3] Unlike those one would find in trenches, these holes were not connected to one another.

Individual and separate holes thus afforded their occupiers excellent shelter from artillery fire. A grenade would have had to explode practically above the soldier's head for it to kill him; the holes also offered perfect protection from any stray shrapnel. They even allowed soldiers to be sheltered from tanks on attack missions. The rifleman, invisible in his hole, could almost be driven over by a tank and could then finish off the crew from behind with a single concentrated charge. To actually kill the rifleman, the tank would have had to turn around precisely above his hole, thereby crushing and grinding him down into the ground; this method was practised time and time again throughout the war and on both sides. However, the rifleman did *not* have the ability to crawl out from his hole easily. If he did manage to jump out, nobody could provide him with cover, and he stood no chance whatsoever. His death was certain. Generally, the Russians were well aware of that and thus tended to remain in their holes until their last breath.

It was often quite tricky to spot such holes in the terrain. One usually only saw the head of the rifleman appearing above the parapet, and only for just a few moments. Their helmets would be so well camouflaged that they could only be made out if one also happened to spot the muzzle. These holes made us realise what a uncompromising and determined enemy we were dealing with, and how different the course of this campaign was going to be. No British soldier would ever think of occupying such one-man holes.

The first prisoners passed our convoy. We took off their steel helmets and berets as well as their military tunics, all of which we required for our operations. We needed to chuck out the Russian uniforms that had been neatly packed and delivered by the OKH, as they were useless to us, being brand-new, clean and pressed.[4] Had we worn those later on, we would have been sure to draw attention to ourselves immediately. What we needed was dirty, sweaty uniforms, the ones that an Ivan would wear in battle. A little later, we were also in possession of two trucks, some really old and rickety Ford models. They had no benches in the cargo area, and the side panels were very low. On the back hung the licence plate, its painted number now discoloured. We loaded the sweaty uniforms onto the captured vehicles and towed them along between our Opel Blitz cars.

Up until then, we had made good progress. By the evening of the first day we had already reached Ariogala, some eighty kilometres deep in enemy territory. In no time at all, the 290th Infantry Division had captured the large viaduct leading across the Duby valley, near Ariogala.

The second day of the war was hot and humid, a merciless sun beating down on us. The tanks whirled up an enormous cloud of dust that settled on our stationary convoy, burning our skin and eyes. That was when Lieutenant Knaak returned to us. 'Dismount, form a semi-circle,' he ordered. We descended from our vehicles and grouped around him.

On the hood of his open-topped army car he spread a map of the area, studying it carefully with his monocle firmly pressed to his left eye. We stood around in silence and waited. Suddenly he looked up, stretched himself to his full height, and the words he then spoke in a light but very clear voice cut through the air like a knife: 'We shall capture and take control of the Josvainiai bridge.'

As if he had given away too much, he immediately fell silent and looked each of us in the eye. Was he trying to gauge our reaction? Whether we would tremble in fear or jump in the air for joy? We stood there, nobody uttered a word, and I doubt that he could figure out what we were thinking just by looking at us. What else were we supposed to do? Probably all of us were afraid, but to show our fear would have been unbecoming, degrading and cowardly, while surely it would have also seemed quite opportunistic to pretend we looked forward to the impending operation.

With his hand, he beckoned us to come closer, saying, 'The target is situated at a distance of some eighteen to twenty kilometres from here. There is a junction 300 metres before one gets to the bridge, and this is where we'll take the left-hand road. It turns at a right angle and then descends in a steep incline to the bridge. On the other side of the bridge is the village of Josvainiai, or whatever that Russian dump is called.'

He stopped, removed the monocle from his eye, and bent down low to study the map once more. Then he turned to us and continued: 'Group Langenhahn traverses the bridge and forms a bridgehead. The engineers disable the bridge and secure the target. The MG troop and two men advance to Josvainiai to secure the entrance to the village. Heavily armed grenade launchers descend onto the riverbank and position themselves there. The Pils group remains at the crossroad and secures the area surrounding it. All clear? Any questions? If not – prepare for operation. Semi-camouflage, we're off in fifteen minutes.'

We knew what we had to do: cross the bridge, disable it, secure the surrounding area until the tanks arrived. It sounded simple enough; there were no ifs or buts, yet it somehow seemed unreal, it felt as if it had already all happened and lay way in the past.

'Go,' ordered Knaak, 'on the double!'

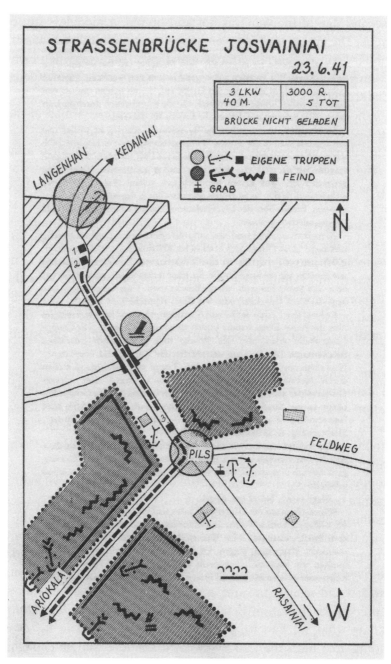

The roadbridge at Josvainiai, 23 June 1941. The notes in the box state that the bridge is not rigged. Left side: 3 trucks, 40 men; right side: 3000 Russians, 5 dead. The circles indicate German troops and enemy troops and the gravemarker.

We turned on our heels, gathered our weapons and ammunition which were kept in the Opel Blitz cars, and stowed them in the three captured vehicles. I felt sick to my stomach as I got into this lorry. As there were no benches, we just sat there, squeezed together on the floor of the cargo area, some of us kneeling, others sitting on ammunition boxes. We had crammed as many egg hand grenades into our pockets as we could, making me feel as if I myself were a concentrated charge. There were even some grenades just lying on the floor, ready to be grabbed whenever we needed one. I had supplied myself with plenty of hand grenades, as when it came to close-combat fighting, I considered them more effective than a rifle. And anyway, ever since I had been assigned to the Knaak company, I was no longer in possession of an MPi. It was different from when I was with Grabert; he wouldn't just follow army guidelines and would ensure that his lot were equipped to the hilt for close-combat fighting.

I never really much liked the rifle, feeling that it was too heavy for me, too long and too unwieldy. Also, when it actually came to close-combat fighting, the firepower and firing sequence were completely unsatisfactory. At the first opportunity that came my way, and without asking or waiting for an order, I exchanged the rifle for an MPi. I just did it. But at that moment, I was saddled with having to deal with the rifle – that's all there was to it. For that matter, it was the only time I would ever embark on an operation armed with a rifle.

We set off and drove past the tanks, which had by then caught up with us on our right. The crew were waving at us, but all we could do was respond with a grim smile. We reached the front vehicles of the advance detachment, where an army captain was leaning out of the open cupola of the first tank, so we stopped once more, with Knaak shouting across: 'Follow us soon, but don't kill us off.' The captain raised his hand in a greeting and shouted back: 'Good luck, we'll soon be following you.'

We pulled ahead from the tank vanguard, knowing that they would only start moving after half an hour. Left to our own devices, we could only trust in God! But this wasn't a time to pray, it was a time to act.

Taking leave of the armoured units was always a tricky moment, especially if it had to happen in broad daylight and on the move. We could have easily been spotted and located by an enemy observation unit. Had that been the case, we would have been nabbed in an instant. And yet, we had to run the risk.

We passed through a small forest without seeing a soul. Soon, we had lost sight of the tanks, the only sign of them being a brown plume of smoke lingering in the white sky. After having driven for three kilometres, we arrived at one of the countless dips criss-crossing the wide expanse. The road took us down one side and up the other. This type of situation was brilliant for our purposes. We stopped in the bottom of the dip. That was the moment we had to act fast. First, we got into those stinking and sweaty Russian tunics, which were most unsuitable for our purposes: they were buttoned up, and we had to pull them over our heads to put them on. That fact alone would always delay a rapid discarding of the camouflage and make things quite problematic – first, as you couldn't remove the uniform quickly, and second, it required both hands to do so, which necessitated putting down one's weapon.

We put on the brown steel helmets, tucking our caps into the belt. We hid our German weapons as best we could. This is what was then called 'semi-camouflage'. Only one man in full camouflage per vehicle was considered necessary, and this entailed also wearing Russian trousers and boots, as he might have needed to step out of the vehicle. Mostly, the full disguise consisted of a Russian officer's uniform. The fully camouflaged soldier would sit in the cab next to the driver and was tasked, should the truck be held up, with negotiating with the Russians and distracting them from the rest of us, sitting up in the rear of the truck. Our group contained Baltic Germans or V-men, who spoke Russian.[5] One of these men even went so far as to wrap a bandage around his head, smearing it with blood. To pretend to have been wounded was always effective, we felt. In a few minutes, the camouflage was complete, so much so that we didn't recognise each other.

We were set to continue on our drive when all of a sudden, high up in the sky, an aeroplane appeared. We peered up, wondering whether it was a Russian or German plane. The pilot performed a loop and then kept flying lower and lower. It was German Jäger, a Messerschmitt, thank goodness. But damn, we were dressed in Russian uniforms, and standing next to us were Russian trucks. How would he ever know that we were German? He will definitely shoot us dead, is what we thought. If he had caught even one of our three vehicles, our entire operation would have failed. We would never have fitted in just two cars. Watching closely, we saw him dive down to our right. We waved and shouted – but to no avail. His BK came crashing down, while we scuttled for cover.[6] Its tracer soared high above and passed us, smashed down into the marshy terrain, just missing the road by a few inches. The Jäger roared past us, disappearing from sight.

'He will reappear, I am certain of it,' shouted Knaak. 'Prepare the orange smoke signal.'[7] Before he could even finish shouting his order, we had already spotted the Jäger. He approached us from the left, again in a nose dive, and one of us released the smoke flare but it dropped in the field next to the road. Still, a plume of orange smoke did go up and the Jäger, recognising it, yanked his plane up and disappeared into the clouds. With a hissing sound, the flare extinguished in the mud, and we breathed a sigh of relief. Our only concern then was that the Russians, who couldn't be far away, hadn't observed this spectacle. They would certainly have put two and two together.

'Listen up,' ordered Knaak, 'we're moving forwards.' I mounted the second car. Tightly squeezed against each other, we crouched in the cargo area. Just our upper bodies showed above the side planks. Knaak was kneeling down beside me, peering over the driver's cab to see what was ahead. He looked fabulous, all kitted out in a Russian military tunic and with a brown steel helmet on his head.

'Lieutenant, sir, do the Russians also wear monocles?' I asked him. 'Damn!' he exclaimed, removing his monocle. We had descended into the dip as Germans, yet moments later we emerged as Russians. Nothing was moving, no enemy was in sight. That was a good thing, and our tanks were able to advance at a decent speed. After a few kilometres driving through meadows and farmland, we saw a cornfield ahead. The road led right through it, dividing it into two parts, with both sides seeming to go on forever. We approached the field at full speed, with no Russian to be seen anywhere. We carefully scanned the area, scrutinising everything and anything around us, as we were convinced that Ivan must be lying in hiding somewhere around here. Or had he withdrawn behind the bridge and blown it up? Were we too late?

We reached the cornfield – and that's when we finally spotted them. From up above, in our vehicles we were able to look down into the fields where they were sitting huddled together in their positions. They were everywhere, cowering between the tall ears of corn growing to the right and left of the road. We were able to establish where the mortar positions were, where the MG nests were, and as we surveyed the area we even spotted two anti-tank gun positions. Damn, we thought, these could really make it hard for our tanks and might obstruct them, which was not something we wanted. There was nothing we could do at that point; we had to advance to the bridge. The tanks would have to fend for themselves – that's just how it was going to have to be, we concluded.

We pushed down on the gas and zoomed off. We saw more and more Russians, the cornfields on either side of the road were full of them. We could see the green-brown steel helmets everywhere and realised that we were now deep in their midst. We waved to them, they waved back – mercifully not recognising us. Thank God for that, as otherwise we wouldn't have stood a chance. There must have been thousands of them in that cornfield.

The field ended abruptly and we approached the crossroads. To the left, at a right angle, a road led down towards a wide dip. That's where the bridge lay. It went across a small river, whose banks were steep and high. If the bridge was blown up, the engineers would have to build a crossing, we reflected. The tanks, we knew, would no doubt find their own way, but that would most definitely be coupled with losing time, whereas the directive given from the leaders emphasised speed, and speed alone.

To the right, there was another road, which continued across an empty field and whose end we could not see. And then there was a third road at the junction, leading straight ahead. It was quite narrow, more of a field path, in fact. Some houses and sheds were located at a distance around it; beyond the dip, a bit ahead, we saw a village. Russian soldiers were standing around everywhere. From a small incline overlooking the junction we spotted some MG bunkers, in front of which sat Russian soldiers, all of them smoking. We waved to them, since this had held us in good stead in the past. We hoped they wouldn't stop us. Tension was high, barely tolerable – we weren't allowed to stop, we had to keep going. We swung to our left and drove the 300 metres down to the bridge. The last vehicle with the Pils group on board remained at the junction. They pretended their vehicle had broken down, and some Russians approached them – it was all going according to plan. The Baltic comrade, fully camouflaged, got out and spoke to them. I had no idea what story he was dishing up to them, but all he had to do was gain enough time for us to reach the other end of the bridge. That only took us a few minutes, but they were crucial ones. The 'fire magic' had to be started on both sides of the river at the same time, as surprising the enemy seemed our only chance of success – and the only way of coming away from this alive.[8]

I didn't look back; my full attention was focused on the bridge, which we were steadily approaching. As a trained engineer, I only had eyes for this target, and frankly, nothing else really needed to interest me at that time. I had been charged with cutting any ignition leads I came across at the presumably rigged bridge pier, and only once an explosion had been avoided would we join the defence. Until then, the only duty the rifle company was tasked with was to keep the enemy at a distance from us.

We rolled across the bridge. Here, too, Russians were dotted everywhere. Then, a sudden burst of fire erupted from a German MPi, right at the crossroads. The fire magic had started. We drew our weapons and loosed off several bursts of fire. Frozen with fear, the Russians stared at us incredulously, not able to grasp why they had been attacked by their own comrades. Their surprise only lasted for an instant before they slumped in a heap, dead.

Hand grenades were thrown, exploding around us. This gave us a moment to breathe. We leaped from the trucks, jammed our guns into our hips, fired, and scuttled for cover, all practically simultaneously. I tore off the Russian steel helmet and put on my cap, while my friend Willy, MG rifleman no. 1, was lying next to me in the dusty road, looking for bits of his MG, which had been scattered when he jumped off the vehicle. Obviously he hadn't locked it properly, which meant that the actual lock had arced through the air, together with the spring, then fallen into the mud along with the barrel. Damn, we really could have done without that. At the very moment when we desperately needed to rely on our weapons, the first MG failed. I had no time to help him; shots were raining down all around us. I reached the bridge pier, searched for the explosives, hunted for the ignition cable – but I found nothing! My other three men couldn't find anything either. So, it turned out that the bridge wasn't rigged. I was furious. There they were, committing us Brandenburgers to a mission with an unrigged bridge!

In the meantime, the shooting had stopped on our side, and no Russians could be seen anywhere. Any among them who were still alive must have fled. But on the other side, where the crossroads was, the firing continued. Hand grenades were exploding and I heard short bursts of our MG fire alternating with the slower ones fired by the Russians. It seemed that our comrades were in distress, and our side was still engaged in the shelling too. I threw myself to the ground, realising that – oh damn – I was still wearing the Russian tunic. I tried to pull it off and over my head but got myself all tangled up, and the pulling didn't help get rid of this idiotic uniform, which couldn't simply be unbuttoned like a normal one. Finally, the tunic just ended up sitting around my neck, partially covering me in one twisted mess and, of course, I couldn't see a thing. I kept on ripping and tearing at it, finally ridding myself of it. Poor unfortunate Willy had meanwhile gathered all the pieces of his MG. 'Pioneer troop and MG, come here at once,' yelled the lieutenant. 'We have to return to the junction; the Pils group seems to be having problems.' While giving the order, he slid down the steep embankment to the river, with my three men following him. We immediately saw that it would have been much too dangerous to run back across the bridge, seeing as it was totally exposed and we could have been shot at from all sides.

'Sepp, help me,' shouted my comrade with the MG. 'Hold my gun for a moment, I have to piss into the barrel as it is full of sand'. I stared at him in disbelief but took the MG out of his hand. He then unbuttoned his trousers and – well, let's just say he did actually manage to wash the barrel clean, after which he calmly assembled his MG, inserted the drum magazine, and got it ready for firing.

At the run, we followed Knaak, who had by then already crossed the river and climbed the the steep bank on the other side. My three men were with him.

The river wasn't deep; judging from the muddy and slippery riverbanks, we saw how it swelled with the rain. We hurried through the river with the water reaching up to our hips and, once across, we scaled the other side. We couldn't hear any battle sounds from the junction any more, only a few random shots. Once we had reached the top, we cautiously raised our heads above the embankment and stared down at a cornfield which began some two metres in front of us. On the right-hand side, the slope dropped down steeply to the road that ran from the bridge up to the junction. There we spotted Knaak and the three comrades, working their way forwards with only a few swift movements.

'Where are all the Russians we saw when we drove down here?' we asked ourselves. Had they fled, or were they still hiding in this cornfield in front of us? We cocked our ears, but heard no rustling, no fleeing footsteps, only the wind rustled through the corn. I got my bayonet ready, the first and only time I did something like this during the entire war.[9] I would have given a lot to have had an MPi on me.

Ducking low, shoulder to shoulder, we entered the cornfield. Willy, with his MG fastened to his hip, guarded the right, while I guarded the left, ever at the ready to take a stab. Every so often, we got onto some muddy paths that crossed the field, but our vision was so terrible we could barely see more than a metre ahead of us. We could have fallen on the enemy at any given moment, and so it really became a case of whoever was fastest would survive. Another horrible thought crossed our minds: what if they had heard us approaching, had let us pass, and were about to jump on us from behind in order to finish us off either with a shovel or a knife? Nobody would have noticed it, and nobody would have found our bodies until the next harvest time. We didn't dare raise our heads above the tops of the corn. Every so often, we stopped and listened, but perhaps it was more out of fear than for strategic reasons. Sweat streamed down our faces. We didn't utter a word, and only communicated with our eyes. It had become totally still around us; there wasn't a shot to be heard, nor an order given.

What did that mean? Surely, we thought, the Russians must have recovered from their first fright. What would they be doing next? Had they figured out that all we were was a ridiculous bunch of some forty men, dispersed over an area of one kilometre? Were they preparing for a counteroffensive? Where were our tanks?

Finally, we reached the other side of the cornfield and found ourselves at the junction. I was glad that at long last this field was behind me. The Pils group had done good work. Their surprise assault had done the trick. We had successfully taken both the MG nests and the Russian positions at the junction. Those Russians who had survived had fled, while we only suffered two losses and a few lightly wounded soldiers. We then adopted the hedgehog defence tactic to secure the junction. We had lost interest in the bridge, which couldn't be blown up. What was important to us at that moment was to put up a defence while waiting for the German tanks to arrive. What we feared most was that the Russians would return and attack us, seeing as we had spotted hundreds of them sitting in the vast cornfield during our approach. If they were being forced out by our tanks, surely, we figured, they would come flooding back and then get us once and for all.

We organised ourselves and positioned two MGs in such a way that they could cover the road leading to Ariogala on which we had come, as well as the cornfields bordering it. My friend Willy and I were deployed to secure the long straight road which forked off the junction leading to Raseiniai. The heavy mortar was positioned at the bridge, while the snipers lay all around, safely under cover. The Langenhahn group had marched through the village of Josvainiai and then moved south. As for us twenty-five or so men, well, we were sitting at the junction and at the back of hundreds of Russians.

Both the danger and our support could only come from the west. Thus, that's where our full attention was focused. I got myself into a ditch next to the road, prepared my shooting pad, and dismantled my bayonet. The only thing that protected me was a cornerstone. I had an excellent view far to the south. As the road leading to Raseiniai and through flat and open ground was as straight as a die, it provided us with a clear field of fire. On the other side of the road lay my friend with his MG, and, hidden behind a shed, he was thus able to change position rapidly if needed, with a field of fire to the west and far south. All he had to do to change positions was to move to the other side of the shed. With him were machine-gunners no. 2 and 3, carrying with them their ammunition boxes. The minutes ticked by and nothing happened. All remained quiet. No sign of the Russians. But the question which occupied us most was where the hell our tanks had got stuck. The half-hour which they had given us as a head-start had long since passed.

Gradually we grew suspicious of how quiet, even eerie, it was. Could it be that the Russians, hidden by the corn, were sneaking up on us to then suddenly go on the assault? Ah, those tanks, were they scared? Why weren't they coming? All these worries weighed heavily on us.

Then, suddenly, coming from the south, we saw a cloud of dust, followed by engine sound. Tanks? No, the noise we heard was different. Anxiously, we waited to see what might be coming up the road. Willy, behind his MG, nodded to me. The noise came closer and there, finally, we saw motorcyclists approaching us without a care in the world, and so we quickly concluded that they must be Russian.

'Enemy motorbikes advancing from the south, approaching us!' I shouted as loudly as I could.

'Fire at will!' yelled Knaak from somewhere.

I glanced back over the road to the MG. My friend was ready and prepared to fire. The motorcyclists came closer, and when they were 200 metres away we opened fire. Those at the front fell from their bikes, those behind them slipped and tumbled into the ditch, while the others turned on their rear wheel and disappeared. In a few moments it was all over. The dead and the shattered bikes were left behind. Calmness returned once again.

No sign of our tanks. No sign either of the Russians still hiding in the cornfield.

The lieutenant then decided to dispatch a messenger to the tanks. He was charged to deliver the urgent directive that they speed up. The messenger didn't get very far, and never reached the tanks. Later on, we found him, shot dead, in a ditch.

The minutes crawled by, and our unrest grew. We cursed our cowardly comrades in the tanks. An hour and a half had gone by – it felt like an eternity.

At long last – my watch showed the time of 19:44 – we heard the thunderous noise of tank cannons, saw them light up the sky, and heard the rattling of machine guns. A cloud of dust rose in the west and came closer. We had to pay attention, as we knew that this was the precise moment the Russians would appear on the scene. And indeed, we were proven right: the first ones emerged from the cornfields and ran straight towards us.

We opened fire; some fell, others ran back into the corn. It was a wild mess, with Russians fleeing in all directions, and us firing at them from all sides.

The first tank appeared. Jubilant, we ran towards it, cursing the crew at the same time.

'Apologies for being late,' said the tank driver, 'but we had to remove some PaK positions before heading off to come here.' The lieutenant then ordered the tanks to cross the bridge immediately. By that time, the infantry had also arrived, and thoroughly combed the terrain. We assembled at the junction, with the Langenhahn group joining us half an hour later. This was the end of our first operation.

The first day, full of adventures and excitement, drew to a close. We sat on the embankment, close to the junction, like swallows on a telephone wire; we smoked and reviewed what had happened. Meanwhile, below us, the advance detachment kept on rolling towards the east. Some random shots still reverberated through the night, but we didn't much care – for us, the work was finished.

Suddenly, one of our comrades flinched and tumbled down the embankment. A shot had hit him right in his neck, and he was dead on the spot. No time was wasted, and a troop was put together, tasked to comb the terrain. But we returned from our search none the wiser. It had probably been a chance hit, an errant bullet, particularly bad luck.

In the meantime, some comrades had already dug a grave at the junction. Four bodies next to each other and wrapped in tarpaulin were lying there in the pit. A field priest had also arrived.

'I'll go and look for some planks to make a cross,' said a comrade, and he climbed up the embankment and approached a house that stood in a small orchard. We heard another shot, and this comrade too fell down, dead. We were seized by an indescribably fury.

'There must be a sniper holed up over there, we'll smoke that swine out,' we said. We got hold of our weapons, circled the house, and threw hand grenades through the window. 'He's up there, up in the loft,' shouted a comrade. 'I got a clear view of him in the dormer window.' A volley of fire put an end to the nightmare. Just like in a Western, the Russian soldier fell from the dormer window.

We buried the fifth comrade.

Kedainiai, Lithuania

It was midnight by the time we were granted some respite. We had laid our fifth comrade to rest, had constructed a simple wooden cross and had written their Feldpost numbers on it. The field kitchen had arrived, along with our vehicle and, in spite of the late hour, we received a warm supper.

In the meantime, the infantry had occupied the village of Josvainiai, while the tanks continued with their advance. We entered the village, looking for a place to spend the night and found some space in the village school. Nobody felt like talking, we were all dead tired and just longed to sleep. We cleaned our weapons in silence and reloaded the rifles we had emptied during the day. Then we took off our shoes, lay down on the ground, wrapped ourselves in a blanket and we were gone … asleep within seconds. The men assigned to our luggage wagon were on guard duty.

After two hours, we were woken. 'Get up, you lumps, we're off again,' shouted the sergeant attached to the motorised troop and who had been on guard duty that night. 'Move, get up, get ready, you're off on a mission.' That was Oberjäger Pils barking at us. They had to yell at every single one of us, drag us out of our sleep and shake us, just to get us to wake up. It was pitch dark in the room. Finally, some torches were flicked on, helping us to gather our stuff. We were angry, still half-asleep, and swore at everything and everyone.

Then Lieutenant Knaak entered the room. 'Listen up, everybody,' he ordered, already leaning over a table with his torch hanging from his neck as he spread out a map. We gathered around him and the map and tried to focus, our eyes still bleary.

'Here is Josvainiai,' he explained, pointing his finger at some spot on the map, but we actually couldn't give a damn. 'The tanks pushed forwards yesterday by some two kilometres and are now situated here.' His finger moved across the map. He then went on to explain that the distance between the spearhead of the tanks and Kedainiai was ten kilometres. The bridge which was our target lay in the middle of the town. Thus, we wouldn't have too much leeway, and everything would have to happen during the night. We were to capture the bridge at dawn. The Pils group, which was my engineering group, and the flamethrower, were tasked to join Knaak and be the first to cross the bridge and then form the bridgehead. Meanwhile, Oberjäger Langenhahn was to form a bridgehead on the other side, together with the rest of our company. Since the air force reconnaissance had informed us of the approach of Russian tanks, we decided to take both our anti-tank rifles along as well as concentrated charges, just in case. We were told that we would get further orders when in position. 'All's clear,' said Knaak. 'We'll depart in five minutes.'

We left the building that had given us two hours' shelter and were on the road once again. Wistfully glancing back at our Opel Blitz cars, we mounted those damned captured trucks that smelled of oil, filth and death, especially when one had an empty stomach. Once again, we donned the Russian kit.

Without switching on our headlights, we drove through the grim darkness. Tanks, which we could only make out by their shape, stood on and next to the road, shoved into the fields. The guards probably couldn't believe their eyes when all of a sudden, Russian trucks with Russian soldiers on board were passing by them. Before they could even so much as catch their breath, we had already disappeared into the dark. Soon, and once again, we were alone in no man's land.

I was on the first truck. I had organised for myself a Russian revolver, fitted with a drum magazine, and felt grateful to have been able to switch to this weapon and not have to rely on my rifle. As we were expecting hand-to-hand combat on the road, I considered myself better equipped like this. I knelt down on the floor of the cargo area and, leaning on the roof of the driver's cab, was able to see ahead of us. Next to me, Lieutenant Knaak was crouching down, and beside him stood a rifleman who, with his MG positioned on the roof, would be ready to shoot at a moment's notice.

Knaak was in a surprisingly cheerful mood. He wore a constant grin on his face, one cheek pulsating with a nervous tic. Or did it just seem like this to me? Abruptly he turned around, saying: 'Boys, if all this works, we'll have completed three missions by the end of today!'

I stopped breathing.

'Yes, Lieutenant,' I knew that my lips were forming these words, but didn't quite comprehend what I was agreeing to.

What was it we were hoping for: that everything would go okay, so that we could complete another three operations, or should we have wished that it all would go wrong and that at best all we could manage was one operation?

It began at dawn. In the east, some patchy pink stripes appeared in the sky. Without incident, we reached the houses on the outskirts of Kedainiai, still wrapped in deep slumber. No lights shone anywhere, nobody was out. Who could even imagine that the Germans were right there at their doorstep? Well, that was fine by us.

We were driving along a broad road when, all of a sudden, a truck emerged from between the houses and, coming from the right, turned into the main road, plonking itself right in front of our column. It was the same type of vehicle as the one we sat in, and also boarded by Russian soldiers, but these were genuine ones.

'Not bad,' I remember saying to Knaak. 'They'll now lead us to the bridge, and we'll just pretend that we're part of their group.'

Looking at me sideways, Knaak just smirked. 'Flamethrowers, prepare,' he whispered. His cheek muscles started twitching again. The two men in charge of the flamethrower crawled forwards, training the gun on the Russian truck which was just a few metres in front of us.

'Stay calm,' Knaak said in a low voice to the flamethrower operator. 'First we have to secure the bridge, then we'll blow them up.'

We travelled for a while: in front of us was the Russian truck carrying the unsuspecting soldiers who quite literally had death sitting on their tail. But then, suddenly, they veered off the main road, turned and disappeared between the houses, just as suddenly as they had appeared a few minutes earlier. We didn't pursue them, as our objective was the bridge, which we knew must be situated ahead of us.

Gradually it began to get light, and we were still wandering around in the town. We worried what would happen if we didn't find the bridge. We couldn't just turn around and drive back! We came to a junction and stopped. The co-driver got out to consult with Knaak.

'Lieutenant, sir,' he asked, 'where to now? Left, or straight ahead?'

'Shit,' muttered Knaak, leaning down to the man to tell him that soon it would be light, and that we would absolutely have to find the damned bridge, otherwise the whole mission would have been for nothing. 'Let's turn left.' I saw that the co-driver was wearing a Russian officer's uniform. He stood on the footboard, and we continued driving on.

We turned left and advanced down a long narrow road. Then, suddenly, we were at the Nevėžis river. It was around 100 metres wide and was bordered on both sides by ten-metre-high quay walls. Several small streams meandered their way along the bottom of the sludgy bed, which was much too deep and too wide and – without any water – appeared desolate. Perhaps it would be filled by springtime, after the snow had melted and the ice in the mountains had thawed. Finally, we found what we had been looking for from the start. Some 300 metres downriver lay a wooden bridge. We turned and approached it from the right. In the grey light of dawn, we saw two guards. They were standing in the middle of the road, blocking the entrance to the bridge, holding their guns, ready to shoot. Our co-driver, in his Russian uniform, jumped down from the footboard and screamed at the two soldiers in Russian. The poor devils stood to attention and saluted. We didn't pay them any more attention and simply crossed the bridge.

When we were halfway across, a machine gun started firing behind us. It was just a short burst. I turned and saw the two guards drop to the ground. In the same moment, some of our comrades from the two cargo trucks who had been following us leaped onto the road. At full throttle, we sped across

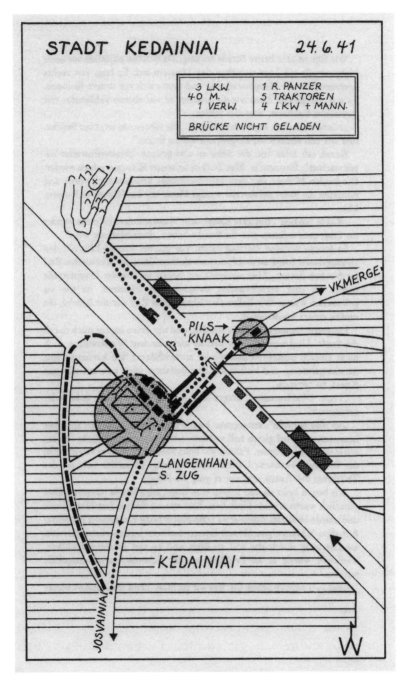

Kedainiai, 24 June 1941. The notes in the box state that the bridge is not rigged. Left side: 3 trucks, 40 men, 1 admin. Right side: 1 Russian tank, 5 tractors, 4 trucks + crew.

the bridge and carried on for a bit between the houses on the other side and up the hill, when the truck came to a sudden stop.

We jumped out and ensured everything around us was safe. Within seconds, we rid ourselves of the Russian uniforms and put on our mountain caps. No orders were needed, each of us knew exactly what he had to do. I ran to the bridge, searching for explosives and wires. Turned out that this bridge hadn't been rigged either!

We pressed ourselves against the walls of the house and checked that everything we needed was in place to defend our bridgehead. This took us no time at all. But there was no movement. It was ominously still. Other than the short burst of fire which had finished off the guards at the bridge, there had been no shots. What did that mean? Could we assume that the Russians had disappeared? We felt almost disappointed that everything had gone so smoothly. If our tanks had arrived at that moment, our first operation would have been done and dusted.

That's when we heard engines. Peering around the corner of the houses, we saw four Russian trucks full of soldiers approaching our river. There they were, dutifully sitting on their benches with guns tightly tucked between their legs. Obviously they wanted to cross the bridge, but seemed to have no idea of what was going on.

We let them come closer, and only then did we hit them with a barrage of bullets. We shot like crazy. The first truck was instantly ablaze, the second one slipped and, tumbling over the quay wall, finally crashed into the river. Bodies were flung into the air. The two trucks at the back simply stopped and the Russians leaped out and vanished into the houses.

We heard a shout: 'Enemy tanks from the right!' Immediately, standing just next to the houses, we ducked. Approaching from the right, rolling down the quay, a Russian tank was about to cross the bridge.

'Concentrated charge, now!' somebody yelled, repeating it twice more. Well, where the hell was it? Everyone kept shouting for it, yet nobody seemed to be able to put their hands on it, and there I was, absolutely beside myself. I was the one who was responsible for it, and yet I kept forgetting where I had put it. 'Surely it must be on our captured truck,' I told myself. and ran up the hill to the truck. 'Hand me that ammunition box!' I heard Knaak yell. I jumped off the vehicle, grabbed the concentrated charge bundle and frantically sped back.

'It's burning!' cried my comrades in jubilation, and then I too saw the tank, cloaked in a cloud of smoke, yet still driving and turning towards the bridge.

The comrade now in possession of the ammunition box fired relentlessly. Watching the tracer, I could see how the bullets ricocheted off the armouring. Seriously, was this stuff really meant to be ammunition? It was acting more like a door knocker, in my opinion. It would have required a miraculous stroke of luck for it to crack a tank.

By then, the tank was already halfway across the bridge. That's where the driver stopped, turned his cupola, evidently searching for his target. And that was precisely the moment when the flames came shooting out of the tank.

'For God's sake,' we thought, 'just get off that bridge.' But would you believe it, he didn't budge, the idiot – he wouldn't continue driving, and by remaining there he almost set the entire bridge on fire.

As if he had heard our prayers, he then actually did get moving, and even got off the bridge at the far end, still enveloped in smoke and flames; our comrades on the other side finished him off.

Calm settled in once again. Time seemed to stand still. The minutes spent waiting seemed like an eternity. Where the hell were the tanks? 'You just can't rely on them,' we thought, and were disappointed at being left stranded like this. Wouldn't they press ahead regardless in order to come to our rescue? How were we expected to secure the bridge if more Russian tanks came along? By that point, the enemy must surely have caught on to what had been happening at the bridge. And what chance would we stand if the infantry assaulted us in full force?

Night had turned into day. The sun was shining on the rooftops of Kedainiai. Everything was still. There was a deathly silence. Had the Russians fled?

Then the sounds of a distant battle reached us. That would surely be our advance detachment, we thought. Shells came crashing down into the quay and onto the houses behind which we had taken cover. Yes, go ahead, shoot us all dead, you tank imbeciles.

Finally, two German tanks appeared from between the houses on the other side. We immediately sent some white flares into the air, then motorbikes thundered over the bridge, followed by infantry.

We had held the bridge for over two and a half hours before the backup arrived. We only suffered one lightly injured man, who happened to be Lieutenant Knaak. A shot had grazed his lower right arm, nothing too serious. There we were: in the space of ten hours, we had carried out two camouflage operations and secured two bridges. The Manstein Tank Division could thus push forwards towards Dünaburg without delay.[10]

On that same day, Lieutenant Knaak received the Iron Cross, First Class.

Dünaburg, Latvia

It was dawn on 26 June 1941 when we started driving with the vanguard of the 8th Tank Division on the highway leading from Kovno to Dünaburg, then in an almost straight line towards Leningrad. For four days we were part of that vanguard, the first unarmoured vehicles prepared for 'special use'. Since the beginning of the war, we had travelled over 300 kilometres. We had managed to overcome all obstacles in our way, had traversed all sorts of terrain, and had met all kinds of challenges.

What happened to the left or right to us didn't much bother us Landsers. Why would we give a hoot if other divisions advanced just as fast as us? We had our own problems to deal with, so the others, in our minds, should look after theirs. Just keep going, don't allow anyone or anything to stop us, always be on the move; those were the only things important to us.

As long as the advance troops were making headway, everything was fine. Never let the enemy rest, continually stay on his heels, don't give him an opening to organise his defence. For us Brandenburgers, the task was to stick to the enemy – better still, penetrate his retreat and thus create confusion and panic behind his lines.

What could a lance corporal know about the larger situation, about operational targets and strategic chess moves? He actually wasn't especially interested. He was pretty much a nonentity, much too insignificant a soldier and too preoccupied with simply getting through each day – in fact with surviving from one hour to the next – to be bothered about the grand plan. If only it could continue like this – or speed up, for that matter – then the war would be over sooner. This was his only concern. He really didn't give a damn where this great advance was heading.

Thus it didn't impress us soldiers much when we heard about Dünaburg, and how important this city was in terms of our continued advance. What was it to us? In order to conquer cities, we had tanks and the infantry, and surely it was up to those troops to do the job? Our ears only pricked up when the conversation turned to two bridges, which were apparently enormous. One was a road bridge, the other one a railway bridge that spanned the huge and awesome Düna river. Those were the bridges we were tasked to seize.

'Brandenburgers to the front!' We had to forge ahead, take the bridge in a surprise attack and secure it until the tanks arrived. That was it. Nothing else, we got no further information. We Brandenburgers, known for our clandestine operations, were left in the dark![11]

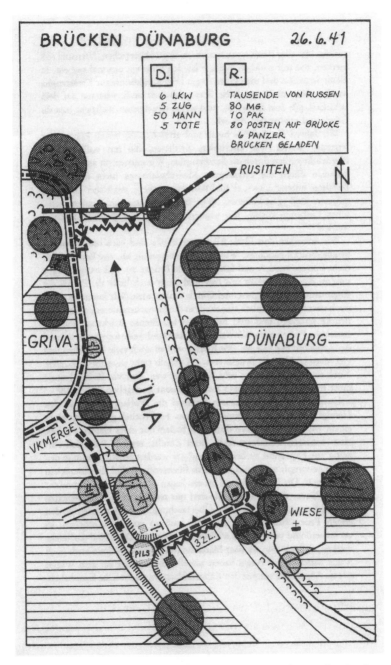

The bridges at Dünaburg, 26 June 1941. D = Germans (6 trucks, 5 platoons, 50 men, 5 dead). R = Russians (thousands of Russians, 80 machine guns, 10 anti-tank guns, 80 guards on the bridge, 6 tanks), bridges rigged.

***

It was time. The tank vanguard drove up along the right and stopped.

'Change to the trucks!' came the order, short and sharp. 'Shit, and shit again!' Out came the Russian tunics, which we pulled on as fast as we could, followed by the Russian steel helmets. This time round, the entire group of fifty men had joined the operation. We didn't have enough Russian uniforms for the whole crew. Some of us quickly threw tarpaulins over the trucks, under which hid a bunch of our comrades in German uniform. The tank people who stood around watching couldn't believe their eyes and laughed heartily upon seeing our 'masquerade'.[12] We sure weren't in the mood for any 'masquerade': we were well aware that a sort of suicide mission lay ahead of us. We had a good sense that what we were facing was going to be utter hell, and that what we would require was a huge amount of good luck to get us through the whole affair alive and in one piece.

After a short briefing, we departed, leaving the tanks behind. They would catch up with us within the next few minutes, or so they assured us. We could only hope that this was true.

It was 0630, and we had eight kilometres to travel to Dünaburg. The road, which was more of an avenue, sloped upwards. After two kilometres, we had reached the top of the incline and looked down on Dünaburg.

The rising sun blinded us so that we couldn't quite make out the size of the city, which was also shrouded in the morning mist. But what we did get to see was enough to make us realise the complexity of our mission. We had no time to contemplate the situation or indeed to hesitate. The operation was already underway and we had to carry it through to the end, whatever the outcome might be.

All we could focus on was the enormous river winding its way through the maze of houses. Although the view was hazy and vague, we did spot the two bridges which we had been ordered to seize. Down below, on the right-hand side and upriver, was a huge iron construction that turned out to be the road bridge, which rested on three tall concrete piers. Downriver, we saw the railway bridge, just as large as the first one, and at that very moment a train with its puffing steam engine was just passing over it.

Oh, how dearly I wanted simply to turn around and find a place to hide. In spite of the morning breeze blowing gently into our faces, fear made me break out in a cold sweat. I tried to calm myself, gather my courage, but my heart was beating like crazy. I looked over to my comrades for reassurance, but their faces too were white as sheets, their hands were also trembling and their eyes were flicking round nervously. I tried as best I could to pull myself together. Nobody should know what I felt like inside. I took a few deep breaths. In this type of situation, one is not permitted to show any anxiety, as that would invariably end in disaster. May the chips fall as they might, I thought, let's believe in good fortune, let me do my best; it might all go pear-shaped, but maybe I'd strike lucky once again, and would live to see the end of this war.

We drove up the incline and reached the first houses of the suburb of Griva. We overtook the civilians who were rushing through the streets on their horse-drawn carts, spilling over with various goods. We had to stop often, as we couldn't get past the chaotic mass of frantic people. The co-drivers of our trucks, Baltic Germans in Russian uniform, screamed and gesticulated. We passed some Russian infantry units and waved to them. That'll be fun, we thought to ourselves.

We reached the river. Our eyes were carefully scanning the road bridge to our right. We made a ninety-degree right turn, with our four captured trucks following each other closely, and drove towards the bridge. That's when the last vehicle in our convoy detached itself from us and turned left. He was going to capture the railway bridge – 'Good luck to our comrades,' we thought. As for us, we were hardly making any headway and were practically wedged in the throng of people pouring down to the river. We seemed to have landed right in the middle of the enemy's retreat. Posts flying red Russian flags urged civilians and soldiers to make haste. The Russians were obviously keen to save as many people and materials across the bridge as they could. That was probably the reason it was still standing. The Germans were still eight kilometres away, but the Russians didn't have much time. The bridge could be blown up any minute, and then what?

With trembling hands, we clutched our weapons and fumbled with the hand grenades; tension grew by the second. All we hoped for was that we wouldn't snap under the pressure. It would only take the smallest mistake, the tiniest carelessness, or of course just some bad luck, to have the powder keg explode before it was supposed to. And then we would be finished – ground down to nothing, stomped into the muddy earth as if a herd of escaping buffalos had suddenly panicked and trampled us. We knew that the initiative had to remain with us – at all times and throughout the entire mission. Never were we to let go of that basic principle. For our attack to be successful, it relied entirely on the element of surprise. For that reason, the first volley of fire had to come from us, and it had to be as powerful as possible, unleashing total confusion and devastation in its wake. The enemy musn't notice that all we were was a small bunch of lads who were, furthermore, scared to the core. Indeed, the reality was that all of us sitting in that vehicle were frightened to death; our teeth were chattering and our knees shaking. Nothing would tear us out of this paralysis other than the first shot, the first explosion, and what would follow would be a life-and-death battle.

Russian soldiers clung onto our vehicles, asking us things we didn't understand, so we just pointed behind our backs and shouted: 'Germansky, Germansky'. That word most definitely had put the fear of God into many of Europe's nations. Packed trams, with people hanging off the footboards like overhanging grapes, drove alongside us. Light artillery, pulled by horses, marched towards the bridge. Soldiers thronged between our cars. The one goal in our minds was to keep going and not stop or lose contact with each other.

Finally, the first of our trucks reached the bridge. Soldiers gathered there were fumbling with their red flags and, together with policemen, directed both us and the civilians across the bridge, shouting and gesturing. Our car weaved its way through the mass of soldiers. The second vehicle also turned off and headed towards the bridge. A bridge guard screamed at him, intending to stop him. The driver responded by pushing his foot down onto the gas, which of course sent the guard into an absolute fury. He yelled at the top of his voice, tore his machine pistol from his shoulder strap and fired a few shots.[13] That's was when our third truck pulled up. While we were driving, we threw some hand grenades over into the crowds, then jumped off and, with our guns and pistols, sprayed bullets blindly into the people around us. The Russians tumbled over each other; some managed to jump out of the way to seek shelter somewhere, others were killed on the spot by our hand grenades.

In the wild panic that had erupted around us, we had to be extremely mindful not to shoot each other. We pulled on our mountain caps, but there was no time to take off our Russian tunics. Well, so be it: both friend and foe would recognise us. In the end, did it really matter who it was who shot you?

The vehicle in front was continuing across the bridge, which now seemed to stretch on forever. From the car window soldiers were throwing hand grenades, and within seconds the road was littered with the dead and the wounded. I sped off to the bridge with my two men, pulled the wire cutters out from our belts and cut through every single wire in sight. MG fire from all sides was the immediate enemy reaction, and bullets whizzed around us, hitting the iron bridge railing and then ricocheting back over our heads. All we heard was their hissing noise. A comrade next to me got hit. He stood there for a second, dazed by the shot, then collapsed in a heap on the ground.

I wasn't sure how many wires I had cut – my only hope was that the right ones were among them. Then I spotted, right up in the air, another wire spanning the distance between the bridge abutment and the top window of a house that stood at the riverside and rose some three storeys high above the bridge. I suspected that the detonator might be hidden up there. It was impossible to climb up the girders supporting the bridge, I wouldn't have been able to get even close to anywhere useful.

We were in the midst of heavy shelling. Surely the Russians had gone mad, as in reality our group was quite small. Whom were they targeting, for God's sake? It was a deafening cacophony of noise, of shooting and orders being yelled back and forth, screams from the wounded, the blast of explosives mixed with the rattling of machine-gun fire. Then, across the high embankment, I spotted rows of long trenches that had been dug, one on top of another. That's where the crazy MG and PaK fire targeting us was coming from! How were our comrades coping on the other side? They seemed to be stuck in far greater shit than we were.

I turned around and climbed down the bridge. I saw dead people everywhere and heard the groaning of the wounded who were lying in enormous pools of blood. Were these Russians or our men? I didn't really take it all in. I tore off my Russian tunic, thinking that if I did get caught, I'd prefer to fall as a German; the alternative was that I could quite likely end up being buried with Russians in the same grave.

All of a sudden, I heard yelling that sounded something like 'Urrah, urrah!' which struck a chill in me right to my bones. This was the first time I heard it. That wild scream got right under my skin and though I would hear it often later on throughout the war, I was never ever able to get used to it and it stayed with me forever.

There they were, storming the bridge, arms linked together as if they were one solid block. Indeed, even 'shotgun women' were among them, poking their bayonets in front of them like spears, and heading straight towards us.[14] How many were there? A hundred, two hundred, five hundred?

The entire road along the river was literally full of them. They kept coming closer, screaming continuously. That's when we deployed our machine guns and simply mowed them down. Each bullet must have hit at least one of them, what with all of them sticking so close to each other. The first row of them fell to the ground, the ones behind stumbled over them and were left lying there. The machine guns were still going strong, continually; surely the barrel must have glowed with the heat. I too was shooting until my magazine was empty, after which I simply chucked it as far as I could towards the attacking Russians. I let myself drop into a ditch by the road and landed on top of some wounded guy. He screamed in German, and only then did I realise that he was a comrade. Next to him was his MPi. I grabbed it, tore the rounds out of his belt pouch and tucked all but one of them – which I loaded into my MPi – into my pocket, after which I crawled back onto the road and recommenced my shooting.

The awful 'urrah' noise subsided. There were heaps of dead bodies strewn across the road.

Heavy-calibre guns then smashed into our bridgehead. I got off the road, and rolled down the embankment, which dropped a good fifteen metres to the river. There below me was the house to which the wire I had detected before was attached.

Lying on my side and slipping down the steep embankment, I plummeted off a barrier wall and slid down the last two metres, but had meanwhile glimpsed two Russians who disappeared into the house. The MPi fell from my hand, the hand grenade slipped out of my belt and I feverishly gathered it all back up without rising from my lying position. A comrade then came flying down the hill and landed right next to me. Together we dashed to the house and threw ourselves against the wall, hoping that it would give us some protection. We had no time to relax. I threw a hand grenade through a window on the ground floor, just next to the entrance door. After it detonated, we rushed into the house and found ourselves in a stairway. I pushed open a door with my foot, simultaneously letting loose a burst of fire. The hand grenade had caused huge devastation in this narrow space. Chairs were toppled, a desk was blown apart, and heaps of files and documents lay scattered everywhere. A picture of Stalin hung askew on a wall – just like in a cheap film.

Behind the door in a corner cowered a Russian, hugging his knees and with his head stuck in between them. He was trembling all over and his eyes stared at me, horrified. Blood came trickling down his sunken cheek and his crossed arms were also smeared with blood and dirt. His mouth stuttered something incomprehensible, though it was obvious he was begging for his life. I just turned away and left him to his fear.

My comrade stormed up the staircase, pressed himself to the wall, fired some shots and then leaped up some more stairs. I followed on his heels and we reached the top floor, where a Russian stood, holding his hands up in surrender. One could read in his face, which was drained of all colour, what the horrors of war had already done to him. A second Russian was in the room. He was furiously fussing with a piece of equipment, pressing frantically down on a lever. Once he saw us, he too raised his arms. I knew instantly that he had been fumbling around with an ignition box. I jumped across, pulled out all the wires and swiped the machine from the table. It was all pointless anyway, as the bridge could no longer be blown up. We had obviously cut the correct wire back when we had sliced through all the cables.

We hoped that the other side was as successful as us and had managed to cut all the wiring system in time. Or would the bridge still blow up at the last minute?

We looked out of the window. Below us lay the bridge – and there, on the other side, the German tanks came rolling in. Alongside them came the infantry, who stormed across to neutralise the defence, and with that, our mission had been completed.

From the first shot up until the arrival of the tanks, the entire operation had lasted no more than twenty minutes. But, my Lord, those had been some unbelievable twenty minutes, and with them had come an unprecedented carnage.

Shoving the captured Russians in front of us, we descended to the bridge. There, totally exhausted, we sank to the ground and – apathetic and detached – we watched the riflemen file past us.

A sergeant came by us, looked us up and down and bellowed, 'What on earth have you been doing? You must belong to a penal colony to be behaving in this way!'

We looked at him with dismay. My comrade slowly got up and placed his MPi on the ground. He didn't say a work, but walked up to the sergeant and slapped him quite violently across the face. Wisely, the sergeant scrammed. Only then did we notice that my comrade was still wearing the Russian tunic.

Finally, Corporal Pils approached us, accompanied by two comrades who were asking where the others were. We asked them in return what had happened over there, on the other side. 'Everyone has been wounded or killed,' said Pils, 'including Lieutenant Knaak. A bullet penetrated his steel helmet.' We sat down in the ditch. My tongue was stuck to the roof of my mouth. None of us could utter a word. What could we have said?

On the other side, across the bridge, the violence of the battle had still not abated. There was still artillery fire within the city; German and Russian, all mixed together. More and more tanks were crossing our bridge.

Some of our people had returned and eventually joined up with our group. I counted fifteen of us; that was all that remained of Knaak's task force. Out of fifty men, fifteen had survived the hell of Dünaburg. Five had died there and then, thirty had been wounded, some of them seriously, and many more died later on in the military field hospital.

***

We had a sad task ahead of us. We had to cross the bridge one more time to bury our dead. The bridge was still under fire. The Russians were doing their best to destroy it with the help of their artillery, but, despite them, we were determined to make the crossing. Every so often we had to climb over dead bodies. Suddenly, one of the supposedly dead corpses jumped up, swung itself over the railing and plummeted into the Düna . Terrified, we just stood there, immobilised, incapable of doing anything. What kind of human beings were these? Why would somebody pretend to be dead for hours, have tanks and foot soldiers pass by him, and then try to save his life by jumping into the Düna? This act of desperation filled us all with respect and admiration, but also demonstrated what these enemies of ours were truly made of. No British soldier would ever have done something like that!

We buried our dead in a communal grave. Knaak was surrounded by his men. Lovingly, we constructed a cross on which we wrote:

Here fell for Greater Germany
Lieutenant Knaak, who stormed the bridges of Düna, along with
his men: Corporal Karl Heinz Röseler, Corporal Karl Innerhofer,
Corporal Anton Stauder, Senior Rifleman Matthias Plattner. They
fell in the morning of 26 June 1941
Feldpostnummer 03271

Only later did we find out that in fact there had been three ignition cables installed for the purpose of blowing the bridge. We had managed to sever all three cables and thus prevented its destruction.

Thanks to the rapid intervention of the 8th Tank Division, our operation at the Düna bridges had been a total victory, even though the element of surprise hadn't been fully successful. We Brandenburgers certainly could not have held the bridge for a further ten minutes.

We paid dearly for this mission, sacrificing many. Our half-company had practically been wiped out, but we had accomplished a great victory nonetheless. We had forced the crossing over the Düna, which was of vital importance to the rapid advance into Leningrad.

That same afternoon, Field Marshal von Manstein arrived and took the opportunity to commend us, personally shaking our hands in thanks for the operation accomplished. After that, he sent us back to our homeland.[15]

TEN

Bad Vöslau and Oberjoch im Allgäu, Early 1942

The fifteen survivors of Einsatzkommando Knaak returned to Bad Vöslau six days after the invasion of Russia. We received a hero's welcome, were duly admired and treated with the greatest respect. For lodgings, we were assigned a villa that was located in the middle of a beautiful park where we were allowed to rest. Exempt from all duties, we only had the one obligation, which was to give the odd talk to replacement companies and inform them about our past missions. Indeed, we were desperately in need of that break. Our young and untrained nerves had been sorely tested by the camouflage operations and when we arrived we were close to breaking point.

So much so, that we actually had a hard time switching and adjusting to this new environment. For example, when my friend Willy and I returned late from the cinema or coffee house and walked through the dark park towards our villa, both of us, without saying anything, would draw our pistols, ensure that all was safe on both sides, and only then would we walk through what appeared to us as a sinister alleyway. I firmly believe that we would most definitely have fired had we so much as heard a comrade kiss his girl behind a tree. We suspected danger at every corner. Only gradually, and only once we were back with our families would the tension ease and the world appear beautiful once more.

During the following war years, there were to be many occasions when we were given the opportunity to get used to such emotional pressure, but at that time, it was all new ground for us.

With winter at our doorstep, and with the offensive thus being forced to grind to a halt, our units were returning from Russia. Many of our best friends and comrades had fallen or lay wounded, sick or with their limbs amputated in the military hospitals.

So, here we were, in the Oberjoch near the Allgäu, preparing for the forthcoming summer offensive, which was to take us into the Caucasus.

The focus of our army life at this time was to make the most of our holiday.[1] Our camp, situated near the edge of the forest at Oberjoch, was covered in a deep layer of snow. It had snowed so heavily that the barrack roofs were fully hidden under a blanket of white, leaving only the black chimneys visible, their smoke rising up to the sky, day and night. To connect the various lodgings we had dug out passage ways, and the tall banks of snow on either side measured up to two metres. We had also been given the backbreaking task of clearing the snow from the square in the middle, around which the barracks, previously owned by the RAD camp, were situated.[2] The idea was that our company would use that space to report for duty. The area was too small and unsuitable for drill exercises; that shortcoming suited us just fine.

The barracks on the northern side of the camp were located slightly higher up on a gentle incline and contained the officers' quarters, the orderly offices and the sick bay. The west side comprised the washrooms and showers, where we were able to have our twice-weekly hot baths, while the south and east sides held the unit's accommodation. A small block built in a traditional style at the entrance to the camp was reserved for the guards.

We would spend some quiet and restful days in that idyllic and romantic camp.

Why were we so privileged? During the first few months of the Russian campaign, we had completed our task to a more or less satisfactory degree, chalking up some significant results and having some successes, but by the same token we had suffered some serious setbacks. When the German advance had then come to a standstill and found itself on the defensive, our company had been pulled out and moved back to the homeland so that it could regroup and refresh. We were too important a part of the operations to be treated like the others.

The fact that our company had stood out in these first missions of the campaign offered further proof, should it have been necessary, that we were a unit entitled to some significant advantages. While other units were still being exposed to the harsh Russian winter, fighting difficult battles on a daily, even hourly basis, we had been given a break. And while our comrades were committing to actions which without a doubt surpassed our operations in so many ways (for example in toughness or duration, deprivation and sacrifice), *we* got to enjoy some peace and quiet in some of Germany's most beautiful countryside. Uniquely, we were granted time away from the heavy demands of the battlefield. We were told to relax. No Landser could ever have even dreamed of such luxury. Of course, when we were indeed called to an assignment, it was usually a suicide mission, where nothing could be done by halves: it was either victory or death. How often did we have to cope with the bitter news that not a single comrade had returned from a special mission! Neither did we have the benefit of numbers on our side; when it came to our operations, we were usually just a small group facing an enemy who far outnumbered us.

The enemy would never find out how strong or how weak we were before an operation, and more often than not he overestimated our actual size. Also, most of our attacks happened on the move, while the enemy was busy withdrawing – an important detail, and one usually of considerable disadvantage to the enemy. For us, on the other hand, surprise worked in our favour; it also heightened our fighting morale, an important factor in warfare. This, together with the concentrated firepower we had at our disposal, certainly gave us the edge.

Our actual performance on the battleground mostly lasted just a few seconds, and never more than a few days, whereupon tanks and infantry units would step in. The Brandenburger missions were self-contained operations with a clear beginning and a clear end. Because our actions targeted above all strategically important locations, we soon earned ourselves the reputation of being a reckless, fearless and cunning lot.

We were given all the advantages which, whether justified or not, a special unit always tends to benefit from. For example, while we would travel in our trucks, others had to walk, and while we were allowed to have a nap, the others were ordered to engage in a hedgehog defence around the tanks; all we had to do was wait until the advance started up again, and only then would we be called in. We never had to live in actual army barracks with their unpleasant HDV drills, but instead were put up in hotels or, as during this particular winter, in the very lovely camp of Oberjoch. And furthermore, we went on holiday, even when the entire Wehrmacht was forbidden to do so.

All these advantages that we delighted in, a simple Landser could only wish for. It was thus quite understandable that many comrades welcomed being enlisted and then applied to be moved over to our unit. In fact, the process wasn't even that difficult. All it took was for our commando to request that consideration be given to specifically named applicants, and immediately the respective soldier would be transferred to us, regardless of which part of the troop he might have belonged to before that. What happened in my group was that the core crew belonging to Graber, consisting of Germans from the Sudetenland, the Baltic states and Swabia, all urged their friends to enlist with them. Their goal was to be surrounded by friends, but also to strengthen their own position within the company. This put us South Tyroleans, by nature a somewhat withdrawn and more ponderous bunch, at a slight disadvantage, and as a result we would get pushed into the background. When, for instance, it was our turn for promotion, some new corporal would emerge from left field, take over, and before you knew it he would be appointed sergeant. It was much more difficult for us to make a name for ourselves and climb the military ladder.

There was a particular lad from our group who had seen the situation for what it was early on, and he just wouldn't have it. He reported to Grabert, informing him that he would no longer meekly accept being ignored and overlooked time and again. He seriously objected to this type of practice, and he insisted that it was now his turn to be promoted Gruppenführer and sergeant. He would not allow himself to be fobbed off yet again. He threatened that if his requests weren't given serious consideration, he would use his political contacts, contacts that led all the way up to Gauleiter Hofer.[3] This was indeed a brave step to take but also laid bare the reality of the politics at the time: since the party stood above all else, the party was all-powerful, and with the help of the party one could achieve anything and everything. If one was clever at working the system and navigating the political maze, success was certain. Grabert was a man who didn't want any fuss. He wasn't going to get involved with the party and all that would entail, just because of one single corporal's wild ambitions. So he got rid of this unpleasant lodger and, without further ado, sent him packing, to war school.[4] After several months the corporal returned as a second lieutenant, but was immediately transferred to the Arctic Ocean.

Our time at Oberjoch passed much too quickly. We lazed the days away. In the mornings and when it was nice weather we would organise fencing exercises, maybe take our skis along and have fun on the nearby slopes, or hold downhill races on the Einstein. Once in a while we amused ourselves by storming dummy bunkers or blowing up lanes, hidden behind wire contraptions. At lunchtime we would lounge in the balmy spring sun, lying on wooden benches to get a bit of a tan. The signalmen had installed an outdoor radio station and, switching to the Request Concert which was most entertaining, they would turn the music up as high as it could go.[5] When the weather was bad we stayed in our rooms and only ventured outside for our weapons and uniform inspection. In the evenings we traipsed in single file to Oberjoch, went to the Hotel Löwen and had a beer.

There was a BdM camp located in Sonthofen. Lieutenant Grabert had managed to convince the head of the camp that the girls should attend a social evening at the Oberjoch. There they came, crammed into four trucks, and it really did turn out to be a fun event.[6] We had organised a few skits which we performed, and in between we sang our Tyrolean songs. Beer flowed in abundance. By midnight the magic was over and the girls returned to Sonthofen. Grabert had been pressured to make absolutely sure that all the girls were returned on time and 'undamaged'. On the following Sunday, quite a few of us applied for special permission to visit the Sonthofen.

This is how the winter months passed in the most agreeable of ways. The recruits who had joined us to fill the gaps in our ranks caused by our losses were a thoroughly upright and fine bunch of boys who very quickly got to know what we were about, and we all got on very well.

On 1 April I was promoted to sergeant. Prior to my appointment, Hiller, who had meanwhile been promoted to second lieutenant, had made me crawl on my hands and knees through the camp at midnight. It was a well-known humiliation, but one we didn't mind in the least.

For a while we had been so far removed from all that was happening out there that we were able to forget about the war completely. Quietly, to ourselves, we were hoping that the war too would forget us. But that wasn't to be. In the middle of April 1942, the dream came to an end. We were being transferred to Neuhaus in the Triesting valley, and then, at the beginning of July, we would be going east again.

— ELEVEN —

Russia, Summer 1942

Rostov to Bataisk

The initiative lay once again with the Wehrmacht, and after several harsh winter months, the advance towards the inhospitable expanse of Russia had got rolling again. We had been subordinated to Heeresgruppe A, under Field Marshal List, and tasked with conquering the Caucasus.[1]

A group of sad girls with tears in their eyes waved us goodbye, and our transport left on the 2 July at 4.30 p.m. from Vienna's Ostbahnhof. We were in good spirits and thirsty for action. At the top of our voices, we sang: '*Muss i denn, muss i denn zum Städtele hinaus*'.[2] The lengthy stay in the mountains had allowed the horrors of the war to fade into the past, and they had all but disappeared from our minds.

We travelled through the Hungarian Puszta and reached Szolnok and Debrecen in Romania.[3] On 5 July we arrived in Dorna Watra, and in order to cross the Carpathian mountains, our transport was divided into two groups. Puffing along a single rail track, our train worked itself up the passes. From Campulung onwards we were able to pick up the pace and descended towards the beautiful and fertile plains of Bukovina. People dressed in colourful traditional costumes stood at the train stations we passed and waved to us. Over their white woollen trousers they wore long shirts reaching right down to their shoes, and on top of these gowns they wore long, black, sleeveless vests, lined with fur. Only a very few men and women wore civilian clothing. Girls wore heavy make-up that announced their profession. In the evening, when it turned dark and we longed for our homeland and for those we loved, I used to climb up onto a truck with some comrades and sit in the driver's cab. There, huddled close together, we would look down onto the landscape that was slowly being swallowed up by the night.

Sometimes, one of us would talk about his girl, his family or his hometown; just like that, just because he felt like it, while the others listened in silence. I really loved these tranquil and peaceful moments, and indeed needed them like others might need their daily bread. These hours always seemed to fill me with renewed strength and courage. Of course, we all had the same troubles and the same desires at the time, the same needs and the same dreams. Just to be able to talk about such things with a friend helped to ease them, or at least didn't make them seem so daunting.

It was only in Jassy that we finally got to hear some information from the front again. We were told that the assaults were progressing speedily and that the enemy was withdrawing just about everywhere. We grew impatient, it couldn't go fast enough for us; we also longed to be given another opportunity where we could prove ourselves useful at the front. We crossed the Pruth behind Jassy.

We then travelled through the monotonous and drab countryside of Bessarabia, which was only broken up by some hills, otherwise it was sheer dreariness. I saw nothing at all of the enormous cornfields that I had imagined before, instead all we got to see were the traces the war had left behind. Abandoned army installations up and down the inclines, bombed-out houses, blown-up bridges, burnt-out Russian trucks tossed into ditches, and those damned booty trucks that I hated with a passion. Memories of Dünaburg that I had tried to block out threatened to come flooding back. Just don't think back now, I kept telling myself, you are the leader of a group, fifteen men are looking to you and see you as their model.

In Kischinew, we were greeted by the sound of cheering Romanian soldiers. On 7 July we had reached Tighina, and that was the end of our train journey. We unloaded and then continued, this time by vehicle. We crossed the Dnieper over the Marechal Antonescu bridge. After Tiraspol, with daytime temperatures reaching 40 degrees and enveloped by thick dust, we started that shit convoy drive all over again. The vast expanse was completely flat, there were no hills as far as the eye could see, nothing we could hold onto in order to orientate ourselves. Once in a while we would meet a group of labourers who were fixing the road. They were nearly all Russian women or girls, with remarkably large breasts. They were all toiling away in the sweltering heat.

We reached Odessa towards the evening and set ourselves up in the sports stadium, close to the city's port. For the hundredth time we got injected.[4] We continued our journey the following morning at 5 a.m., drove along the Black Sea coast and crossed the desolate steppes. The heat was relentless, and due to the dust, visibility was almost non-existent. When we reached Nikolajev at the Bug, we immediately stripped off and jumped naked into the water. Our good mood and high spirits returned, and we immediately set about organising a swimming race, which was won by the 4th Company. After this refreshing dip, we drove to the city, where we were assigned to our quarters, the Russian artillery barracks. But they were in such an incredibly miserable condition that we preferred to remain out in the open, in the city park. In the evening we strolled through the city. We found the Soldatenheim, but all that was on offer was hot green tea.[5] We soon left to go to some Russian theatre or cabaret, or something like that. Whatever it was where we ended up, the programme itself was pure kitsch. Some man hammered away on a piano which was totally out of tune, while a skeleton of a woman swerved her ungainly body along to the soulless melody. Featured as the main attraction of the evening was a 'floating female'. We preferred to return to our quarters and get some sleep.

The following day, after taking a brisk shower in the fountain of the park, we continued our drive and arrived in Bukojavlesnkoje, where we rested for a while in the shade of an orchard. Rumour had it that we would be stationed there for several weeks, which was a wonderful prospect for us, but things didn't quite pan out! For starters, and so we wouldn't get rusty and out of shape by lazing around underneath the fruit trees, we were ordered to do a practice march, organised right in the middle of the day when the temperatures were at their highest. That was meant to give us a taste of what it would be like to serve in the desert, joining up with Rommel and then operate in Iran, which was to be our next destination after our capture of the Caucasus. In full field uniform we marched beneath the boiling hot sun – the sweltering summer heat was unbearable. Our thoughts went out to those poor bastards in the infantry who had to go through this hell on a daily basis, and we thanked the good Lord that in our case it was just a matter of an occasional filler in our schedule. No surprise that this experience made us look upon our fabulous Opel Blitz with renewed respect and humble appreciation. Sweat poured down our bodies in rivulets, our feet were burning, our tongues were stuck to the roof of our mouths. After several hours of marching we arrived at a fountain. We literally raced up to it – finally, some water to quench our dreadful thirst! But who should stand at the fountain, blocking our way? Grabert, who forbade us to drink. We could only dunk our hands into the water, he said, or wash our faces, but whoever drank even so much as a drop of the water would be severely punished, he threatened. We filed passed the fountain in a single line, briefly dipped our arms into the water up to our elbows and wet our faces. Lieutenant Grabert stood by, observing us like a shark: would everyone obey his orders? At that moment, we truly despised the man. Nevertheless, thinking back, I know for sure that each and every one of us managed to sneak a handful of water into his mouth.

After this power march we just loafed around for two days, swam, and wrote letters home.

Out of the blue we received the order: '*Fertigmachen, Fertigmachen zum Abmarsch!* – Get ready to leave camp!' It turned out we had been assigned to the 17th Army. At 0400 we departed, direction Melitopol. Our journey, some 300 kilometres, took us over bumpy roads, with only the inhospitable steppes of Russia surrounding us; there was no bush in sight, no house and no hill, nothing but clouds of dust and dirt as our travel companions.

Once in a while we came across some Russian farmers travelling across the countryside with nothing but a few meagre belongings on their backs or stowed away in two-wheel carts they were wearily pushing in front of them. Where did they come from? Where were they heading? At lunchtime we had reached the Dnieper, which we crossed by ferry. In the middle of the steppes we set up our camp for the night.

We continued the following morning. Finally, the road was smoother, the countryside greener, and there was proper farmland everywhere. Enormous fields brimming with sunflowers bordered our road. We travelled through German communities. People greeted us and were friendly. The children had blond hair and sparkling light-blue eyes. We got to spend the night in Mariupol on the Sea of Azov.

The following afternoon we drove on to Stalino, the most significant centre for arms production in the Donetsk region, and one of the Soviet Union's most important industrial and economic centres. We looked for some place to spend the night in the city's ninth district, but all we found were some run-down mud huts; we stationed our trucks nearby and spent the night there. Most of the houses were empty as very few people had remained. My 'hostess' turned out to be an ancient woman who sat in a corner of the room the entire day, staring in front of her and constantly delousing herself. But the moment she realised that we were digging potatoes out of the garden soil, she perked up and started shouting at us, wretchedly blabbering some incomprehensible words. I decided to divert her by blocking her view to the outside, while my comrades committed the theft. Five days we stayed there, doing nothing. We played football, went for a spin, drove into the city, smoked. One day it rained from morning to night, turning the previously dust-covered roads into muddy, stodgy marshland. There would be plenty of opportunities for us to see how we would handle such conditions.

In the evening I joined Mania, a Russian girl, and her brother Josef. She wore a brown woollen dress and three-quarter-length boots. Underneath her kerchief her coal-black hair tumbled out. Mania made the tea and I brought some rusk bread, as well as some lard to spread on it. Josef, a young lad of slim stature, was an architecture student, but at the time we met he worked in a factory. Both of them spoke only broken German, but it was sufficient for us to have some kind of chat, seeing that my Russian wasn't much better either. We had heard nothing from the front; in fact, truth be told, we weren't all that curious – we would be informed soon enough. Each day we could spend in sweet idleness was a gift from heaven.

Our rest came to an end on Monday, 20 July. Early that morning the sergeant in charge shouted: 'At 0900, company to depart!' As always, these orders came as a shock, and thus were greeted with swearwords shouted everywhere and at everyone.

We had been assigned to the LVII Korps under General Kirchner, who was advancing to the Don and Rostov. At 1215 our convoy left Stalino, direction Artimovsk. We soon found ourselves wedged among vehicles that formed an apparently endless convoy. We inched forward with great difficulty, enveloped by a huge cloud of smoke and dust, driving past units marching alongside our cars, those poor devils who had no choice but to soldier on under the oppressive heat. On that day in July the sky was blue, there was no breeze, no relief. Full of envy, their red-rimmed eyes looked up at us sitting on our trucks, smoking and sheltered by the tarpaulins. Those were the inestimable advantages of being in a special unit, and for which one happily accepted all the risks and dangers. Mind you, there were no life insurance policies for the foot soldiers either. On the contrary, they would join the battle tired, exhausted and famished from the start, while our good selves were able to embark on an operation prepared, and properly rested.

Italian troops had also joined us. We smiled at them, feeling quite superior. We hardly made any progress, as the column was reduced practically to a walking pace. I sat next to the driver in the closed cab and read. It was a pocket edition of Goethe's *Faust* – one of my favourite pieces of literature.

On the evening of the following day we reached Nikolewka, near Taganrog. The spring of our truck had snapped, and the men of the 1st Staffel's repair section had spent hours trying to fix it. It was afternoon by the time we were able to continue our journey. We pretty much had to fight our way towards the front, and it was purely thanks to our cheeky overtaking manoeuvres that we were able to make some headway. Finally, we had caught up with our company, which had in the meantime set up for the night in some houses in Nikolewka. We had just enough time to write a letter home, as the field post was being collected a few moments later. Who knew when I would have another opportunity to write a letter, as word had it that the war would start the following day?

And the war did start. We were woken up at 0300, and by 0400 we were already advancing towards the vanguard. The 13th Tank Division and the SS Tank Grenadier Division 'Wiking' left Taganrog and advanced to Rostov. Our company was divided into two. The half company under Lieutenant Grabert was assigned to the Grisoldi marching unit, while the other half, headed by Lieutenant Renner, went to the Ulbricht marching unit.

At dawn, the men of Panzer Grenadier Regiment 93 threw the Russians from their position with a few swift manoeuvres and took the first three tank trenches. Our tanks followed. Rostov had been turned into a fortress protected by three rings of defence surrounding it. Three ravines had to be captured, all protected by numerous weapon installations, spiked with minefields and anti-tank devices, and it had fallen to us to ensure a successful outcome, which would then allow us access to Rostov.

It didn't take long for us to come across the first wounded soldiers with blood-smeared bandages. They sat at the side of the road, listlessly waiting for transport. For the time being this was the end of the war for them. Not far away lay the dead, their positions unchanged from the moment after they'd been hit. Landsers were busy digging graves.

The artillery fire had been pushed forwards. We watched explosions lighting up Russian field installations. All of a sudden, the air was filled with the roar of planes, and seconds later a Stuka raid sent everyone scurrying for cover, harrying enemy positions and bunkers while deafening us with the noise of their thunderous explosives. It seemed that the sky was black with the circling planes who dived down, then pulled up again, only to come roaring down once more. The earth trembled with the explosions of the countless bombs hailing down and detonating on the ground. Enormous clouds of smoke and dust darkened the sun. Just like fireworks, heavy aircraft cannons soaring with light tracers illuminated the sky as they hit their targets, then extinguished or ricocheted and spiralled upwards. The explosions engulfed us.

Open-mouthed and utterly transfixed, we simply stood next to our vehicles and observed the gruesome yet strangely beautiful spectacle. That was what was called the German Wehrmacht's concentrated fire – there it was at work again. We were once more filled with confidence and courage.

This map shows the city of Rostov, the Don river, the marshland south of the city and the dam with the railway on it and a single causeway and connecting Rostov with Bataisk.

Just as suddenly as the fire magic had begun, it ended. All that was left on the horizon was a thick cloud of smoke.

And then came the momentous occasion for us to observe our infantry and its methods of assault. First, they were tiny dots in the far distance, running, throwing themselves to the ground, picking themselves up again and racing forwards again until they finally disappeared over the horizon. The tanks came rolling in, and then it was our turn to depart. At 1400 we arrived at the dangerous second anti-tank ditch. The engineers had already managed to cut a track into its steep wall, sufficiently flattened and cleared of obstacles so that our cars could cross. Again, we came to a halt and had to wait. Up front, the battle was heating up. The closer we came to the city, the more resilient the enemy defence had become. The third anti-tank ditch seemed to be a particularly formidable challenge.

We waited. Two lorry drivers decided not to fritter away this excellent opportunity to have a game. Sitting in the shade of their truck, they shuffled their cards and played seventeen and four.[6] While one had already lost his pay for the subsequent ten years, the other one was gambling away everything he owned, including the shirt on his back. I just sat on the footboard of my vehicle and took off my shoes to switch to the more comfortable sandals, when, all of a sudden, I heard an awful crash to my left. A Russian artillery attack! We scattered in all directions and threw ourselves flat on the ground. All around us the shells came pounding down, but we were more worried about our cars than about ourselves. Fortunately, the attack was over before we knew it, and once again we were left to our own devices and reveries. But not for long.

'Group leader – the chief is calling!'[7] The shout travelled from one vehicle to the other, tearing us out of our lethargy. This order meant one thing and one thing only: it was our turn. Lieutenant Grabert was sitting in his open-topped car with an unfolded map spread across his knees. Second Lieutenant Hiller and Second Lieutenant Haut sat next to him and a heated discussion seemed to be taking place, which abruptly came to an end once they saw us approaching. Referring to the map, Grabert elaborated on the situation.

The scale of the grid map was 1:100,000. For the first time in this war we got to see the layout of Rostov, with its rows of closely built houses arranged on hills that sloped down towards the northern shore of the Don. Bordering the south of the city was the river, running in a ruler-straight line from one side to the other. Beyond it was marshland, criss-crossed by some wide and some narrow tributaries. Through the marshland and at the other end of a stretch measuring some six kilometres lay a dam. The railway ran across the dam, with a single causeway leading through the marshland to Bataisk. We were tasked with holding that railway bridge, the only bridge over the Don capable of bearing German heavy vehicles. The moment the third anti-tank ditch had been taken, we were ordered to cross the outskirts of the city on foot and in camouflage, reach the Don, then march up the riverbank towards the bridge, dismantle the Soviet demolition charges, and hold it. For how long? Well, for as long as the German troops needed to fight their way through the city.

The spectre of Dünaburg raised its ugly head. What had been envisioned was, to my mind, sheer folly. 'Even if we succeed in fooling the enemy with our Russian disguise and reach the bridge, we will surely never be able to hold it' – this was my own fear, which I kept to myself. We couldn't be certain that the German tanks would arrive in time to give us backup in the city, which, furthermore, was built like a fortress, and in which Russians had put up a heavy defensive line, fiercely defending each and every house.

Second Lieutenant Haut categorically refused to accept the plan, and only Second Lieutenant Hiller, utterly intent that this operation go ahead at all costs, supported it. What he really craved was the Iron Cross. Lieutenant Grabert hesitated, he was indecisive. Hiller was pressuring him – he felt that Dünaburg had been a success, and that all that was required this time round was for us to take the risk.

Let's face it, had he been at Dünaburg ? No. Not to mention the fact that Rostov was not Dünaburg. Circumstances were completely different. We had taken the bridges of Dünaburg on the sixth day of war, the operation took place as part of a swift advance and with the help of vehicles. Additionally, the element of surprise worked in our favour, and the speedy arrival of our tanks was yet another advantage. But in Rostov we had to deal with a fortified city with well dug-in defences. Tanks would have to fight every street one by one, with nobody having an inkling of how many barricades we would encounter, how many bunkers, how many sentries and fortifications we would have to crush in order to even come near to the bridge. In Dünaburg, the enemy had already been retreating, while here in Rostov the Soviet enemy was on full alert, in positions they were determined to defend to the bitter end. While Haut submitted all his arguments, passionately putting forth his objections, Grabert still hesitated, while Hiller insisted that his take on the situation was the correct one. There he was, anxiously pacing up and down, speaking non-stop, his voice cracking and his eyes flickering nervously behind his glasses.

At long last, it was Grabert who made the decision: the Hiller group would go ahead with the operation, but only once the third defensive ring had been taken and the German troops were within the city compounds. Everyone was to get ready!

'Steady on, Sepp,' I told myself, 'keep calm and don't lose it!' I still don't know whether it was my sixth sense or my experience, but somehow I didn't believe in this particular mission. In my opinion, it seemed too much based on rough estimates, and overall too emotive an issue for people at the top to decide, people who were motivated by too much ambition. Given all these drawbacks, the entire operation seemed doomed from the start. I, for one, thought the whole idea was downright crazy. But being able to make somewhat light of it myself put me in a sufficiently relaxed state to return to my group and calmly instruct them to get ready for the operation. Something inside me said that surely nothing would come of it.

We were set and ready by 1800. We drove to the front. We crossed the third anti-tank ditch where our engineers, together with Russian prisoners, were stripping down its steep walls. We didn't get far and had little success overcoming the fortified and heavily defended Russian positions. The fighting units of the 13th Panzer Division, Grenadier Regiment 93 and the SS Tank Division 'Wiking' under SS-Waffen General Steiner had a bitter fight on their hands.[8] They had to negotiate pole-mounted explosives, minefields and anti-tank blockades with which the outskirts of Rostov had been spiked.

Night had fallen. We stopped and drove our vehicles to one side of the road and left them there until the next day. With the help of two Russian prisoners, we dug out some foxholes and slit trenches. I spread out a Russian coat next to my vehicle, lay down and tried to sleep. The battle had not yet abated at the front. Over the city the night sky was ablaze. Every now and then a flare flickered like lightning and illuminated the city, followed by the sounds of it crashing down and exploding. This was the first time I heard the unsettling howling sound of the Stalinorgel, and first saw the distinctive smoke trail of its explosives.[9] Not knowing how to deal with my pent-up emotions, I simply withdrew into myself, tried to forget everything around me and hoped that I soon would fall asleep.

Thursday, 23 July. It was already light when aircraft artillery fire woke me up. A Russian plane cruised above us, probably on a reconnaissance mission. Behind him, tracer bullets generated by anti-aircraft guns caught up with him, and with a cloud of smoke trailing behind, the plane came swirling down, smashing to smithereens as it hit the ground.

I discarded the Russian coat which had been my temporary blanket for the night and got up. A cold wind was blowing and I was chilled through. I would have given a kingdom for a hot coffee, but sadly our field kitchen lay far behind us.

Our pilots were already busy at work. In relay formation, they zoomed towards the rising sun and dumped their lethal cargo over the city. As for us, our operation was yet to get off the ground. The targets of the previous day had not been reached and we were still at the outskirts of the city; the second lieutenant was busy somewhere, desperately looking for an opportunity to get this operation started. He seemed quite obsessed, but our lot didn't care all that much; we were used to waiting and had all the time in the world.

By the time we were ready to leave the outskirts and drive into Rostov it was already the afternoon. Barricades and tank barriers had been set up everywhere, and though we looked for a gap, driving every which way, back and forth and criss-cross, we didn't manage to make any progress. Tanks, mortars and assault guns, anti-aircraft artillery, armoured personnel carriers and armed formations all jostled for space in the narrow streets. Civilians peered out of their doorways, women wringing their hands screeched as they watched medics transport the wounded on stretchers. The bloated corpses of dead horses gave off an indescribable stench that seemed to seep into the furthest corners. Somewhere, in front of us and between the houses, the skirmishes continued, and though we couldn't actually see anything, we heard the rattle of machine guns and mortar fire.

Were we really expected to blag our way through this throng of people while disguised in Russian uniforms?

What total madness! Night fell once more. The liaison officer of the 13th Tank Division who accompanied us and was tasked to coordinate our operation with his division suggested that we leave the city, as he judged the situation too dangerous. In the city, fierce house-to-house fighting had erupted, with fanatical Russians piling through the streets, stubbornly and skilfully resisting us; Second Lieutenant Hiller, however, strictly vetoed our retreat.

'If we turn back now, we won't be able to advance tomorrow morning,' was his argument, and he wasn't completely incorrect, even though we ourselves certainly wouldn't have objected to that option. Meanwhile, he insisted that we take the bridge, though nobody actually had any updates on it at that point. Was it even still standing? Or had it been blasted? The messages we received were conflicting, some reporting that the bridge was still intact, others claiming it had been demolished. After a while, we assembled all the vehicles into one small spot and assumed a hedgehog position, but not without first ensuring that we had with us three 20mm anti-aircraft guns. Nobody could even think of sleep, which was a good thing, seeing as the shooting and detonations reverberated far and wide throughout the night. One of our men, Corporal Jakob was his name, was killed. Fetching some water from a nearby house, he was simply cut down by machine-gun fire.

Friday, 24 July. A new day; the sun had a hard time filtering through the huge cloud of smoke hanging over Rostov. With dawn breaking, the battle noise grew more intense.

A messenger, rushing from one group to the next, brought orders that we prepare for an urban battle. We weren't phased, nor did we object. We much preferred a normal infantry operation to a camouflaged one. We immediately armed ourselves with plenty of hand grenades, checked our MPis and loaded our pistols.

It was already midday when we departed. There were street bunkers, torn-up paving slabs and barbed wire halting our advance at every turning. With the utmost caution, we weaved through gaps torn in the Russian defensive lines and kept pressing ahead as far as we could, only stopping and dismounting when it was impossible to continue. Abandoning our vehicles, we attempted to infiltrate the city by approaching it via the outer districts, crossing gardens and climbing over fences. While one unit secured the area, the other one would move forwards, from one house to the next. At one point, we were fired at from the left, forcing all of us into full cover. But none of us could establish exactly which postion the shots had come from.

Meanwhile, the Wikings, who had turned up from God knew where, provided reinforcement throughout. Right from the word go, and without having to talk much, we got along famously. They provided us with covering fire while we moved forwards, and vice versa. Alternating our actions, we systematically tackled street by street, garden by garden, farm by farm. Then, as suddenly as they had appeared, the Wikings vanished and we were on our own once more. They had probably turned into a different street.

At long last we reached the Don. What lay before us was more of a stagnant and insipidly brown broth than a powerful river. Up the river, in the distance, we saw the bridge we were meant to have captured two days before. One of the bridge sections had been blown up and floated in the water below. Across the river, where the city reached the bank, not a single house had been left intact. All that still stood was a tall dam, across which ran a road and a railway track and which then led across marshland towards the south. Some men could be seen flinging themselves down the riverbank and into the water to get the sweat and dust off their faces. In spite of the scorching heat, I decided against doing the same; the idea of dunking my body into that murky sauce was simply too disgusting.

Eventually we came across a large barge, half full of water, and moored at the bank. Seeing it would have been big enough to transport an entire squad, we pulled it ashore, got rid of the water and fixed the leak as best we could. While we couldn't manage to get the barge completely watertight, we must have done a good enough job, as only a little water continued to seep through the cracks, which we stuffed with grass. If one of our men constantly baled out water with the help of an empty tin can, we figured that we would be able to cross the river. Second Lieutenant Rother and four men were assigned to attempt the first crossing. Would they succeed? Once at the other side, they were tasked with getting the lie of the land. Our SMGs were to provide them with protective fire.[10] Two hours later the Rother reconnaissance squad had returned and briefed us: the dam was occupied by armoured motorbikes; and so, our half-company had received sufficient intelligence to embark on the crossing. Squad by squad it was being ferried across to the other side, where we eventually gathered in the shelter of a barn.

With the city behind us, we were all alone. Over there in Rostov the fighting was still hotting up, while on our side, all was quiet. The peaceful atmosphere was only interrupted by the croaking of frogs, bustling around in the soggy wetland. This is a good place to mention that one of the most remarkable characteristics of a soldier serving at the front is his ability to seize every given opportunity to grab some sleep. No matter how uncomfortable the situation or the location, a soldier will always be able to sleep, even while marching or sometimes when standing, maybe it's because he can then forget everything around him: the filth, the heat, the cold. Thus, it was hardly surprising that we managed a nap until such time that everyone in our half-company had been accounted for.

The chief had gone to the dam to meet up with the motorcyclists. There weren't many of them, perhaps some thirty or so; they belonged to Motorcycle Battalion 43 under the command of Second Lieutenant Eberlein. They had crossed the Don to the east of the city and had attempted to seize the dam, a stretch of around eight kilometres, along with its three bridges. But they hadn't got far, only up to somewhere near the last bridge. There they got stuck and couldn't move an inch. The minute they lifted their heads from above the mud, a salvo of SMG fire and grenades would sweep across them.

At 1800 the chief returned, and that was the end of our rest. Our task was to drive forwards and capture the last of the three bridges. Some men were sent back to gather food rations, spades and ammunition. Additionally, they were ordered to bring *Haftladungen* as we needed to consider a likely offensive by enemy tanks.[11] Regardless of the leak they set off. Soon after, we too got ready for our advance.

The glistening dark red sphere of the sun was about to sink below the horizon, sending its last rays onto a city which was still in the heat of violence, death and a fierce urban battle. Black clouds of smoke, streaked with the smog from burning houses and countless explosions, were lingering above a ruined Rostov. Yet the fight to capture this gateway to the Caucasus continued relentlessly through the night.

Silently and in single file, we stomped through the marshland to the left of the dam. Dead Russians lay everywhere, covered by swarms of buzzing flies. A ravaged truck here, an upturned cart there, with dead horses, still harnessed, sprawled in front. Automatically, we held our breath, just so as not to have to inhale that ghastly smell of decay.

How would the young comrades cope in battle? For them, today was a trial by fire. Compared to these young lads, I suddenly felt terribly old. For me, who had been part of similar operations several times in the past, what was going on and what surrounded us was no longer new. But it was different for them. I stood still and let the young soldiers go past. Looking for support, their anxious eyes made contact with mine, some were smiling timidly while others didn't seem to take much in. I encouraged them, saying: 'Comrades, it won't be all that terrible, not every single bullet is a hit. Just don't lose your nerve. Remain calm and everything will be all right.' Truthfully, I myself could have done with somebody giving me a few kind words of encouragement. Or was this simply my way of cheering myself up?

We had caught up with the motorcyclists and they were visibly relieved to receive reinforcements at long last. In a few short moves we crossed the second bridge. Above our heads flew some SMG bullets, and down below grenades fell into the mud, causing loud thuds but little damage. By then it had become night. Under the cover of dark, we moved in on the last bridge. To the right of the road, our heavy weapons, which we had lowered into position and sunk into any shallow recesses we could find, returned enemy fire. The flare of fire drew tell-tale lines through the night sky, but one could hardly see the stars for all the thick clouds of smoke rising from Rostov. We tried to penetrate the dark but could barely see, grateful for the occasional shots fired across the bridge giving us occasional moments of illumination. One grenade hit the position where our weapons had been lined up, and in that same instant the painful wailing of a wounded soldier pierced the night. We suffered our first losses. Squeezed tight against the damp mud walls of the pits we had dug out with the grips of our MPis, we were cowering next to each other, anxious and terrified. It had turned cold and the damp seemed to reach our bones. I started shivering and my teeth chattered. I wondered whether it was due to the cold, the tension or just plain fear? Images of our earlier operations kept appearing in my mind: Greece, Lithuania, Latvia, but above all, Dünaburg.

Corporal Bohnhoff, who was crouching right next to me, seemed to have had the very same thoughts. 'Until now, we've never had to lie so close to a bridge for such a long time without being able to capture it,' he whispered into my ear. 'In the past we just got hold of a truck, zoomed across and right through the Ivans, and the next minute we'd captured the bridge. I kind of preferred that to just staying put, waiting until we get slapped in the face.'

Food was delivered. Only two men had managed to get through: they brought us a large metal container with cold soup, meant for the entire platoon. This was the first time that day that we received something to eat. It was just a few spoonfuls for each of us – and even then, there wasn't enough to go around.

Midnight had long gone, and we fully expected to report for duty any minute. It started to get light at 0300, and we would have to take the bridge at dawn, if this operation was to have any success at all.

'Gruppenführer to the chief, at once, conference!' Creeping out of my hole, I leaped across the road and crawled a few metres on all fours to get to the chief. The others followed one by one. Soon we were all gathered together.

'We are attacking at 0230,' Lieutenant Grabert began. 'Set your watches – gunners and the half-company to cross the bridge first under the command of Second Lieutenant Hiller, and then advance for another 100 metres. Listen up, chaps: you're to run for your life. You've got to get across before Ivan realises he has been attacked. When the first shot is fired, our covering fire starts. SMG and grenades to be launched until the pipes glow. Don't give a damn about the Ivans at the bridge, we'll take care of them – just push ahead. The minute we start attacking, the engineers are to arrive, storm across and take the enemy down. Then they'll take up position to ensure close security. Gunners of the second group to follow and to attack thick and fast and push forwards to the outskirts of Bataisk with the Hiller group. Heavy weapons platoons will provide fire protection and catch up with us later. Half the group of radio transmitters comes with me, the other half remains here. First aid underneath the bridge. Command post will be at the bridgehead on the other side. Any questions? If not, well then, good luck!'

As we were about to crawl back to our squads, we saw the sky flash and the bridge illuminated by a blaze of fire. What? Were the Russians actually going to blow up that bridge right under our noses? Soon we realised that the fire came from a truck that had exploded. Gradually it burnt out and it was pitch dark once again. I crawled back to my group and gave my orders.

The hands on my luminescent watch pointed to 0220. The order to prepare passed from one man to the other. Slowly, we crept out from our holes and onto the roadside. Once again, I turned to my men to ask whether they were ready to fight. The question was perfunctory. Every single one was prepared and ready for engagement, whether consciously or as an automatic response, I wasn't able to tell. Did we have a choice? Of course, we were all frightened, in fact to such a degree that our teeth didn't stop chattering and our hearts were in our mouths. So much so, in fact, that we were dripping with sweat despite it being a cold night. The more senior ones among us were frightened because we knew first-hand what fighting the Russians at close range implied. The young ones in our team feared the unknown, the moment of actually standing face-to-face with the enemy. They were scared because this was their first trial by fire, weapon in hand. Let nobody tell you that you can simply ignore such fear – it will never leave you and will forever remain part of you, gnawing at your nerves and your guts. What might change over the course of time is that one is somewhat more aware of what's going on in a battle, can judge more accurately what is happening from one minute to the next, can assess the circumstances surrounding an operation and thus be able to act accordingly. Experience helps ease the tension that can virtually paralyse one's limbs and senses; it is also vital for a clearer perspective in situations that can change in a split second. But, at the end of the day, everyone, be they an officer or a simple private, experienced or novice – we were all frightened.

A quick glance at my watch told me there were only two minutes to go before it was 0230. An eternity! Again and again my sweaty palms moved over the weapons. For the umpteenth time I checked whether my MPi was unlocked, if my cartridge sat properly, and if all the hand grenades were attached to my belt. Useless exercises all of them, as of course everything was in good order and where it should be. The hands on my watch clicked to 0230.

The first group jumped up. The silhouettes of their dark figures appeared but for a brief moment against the grey morning sky, then disappeared into the dark again, and all we could hear was the thumping of their heavy mountain boots on the concrete of the bridge. With hearts beating hard, we listened to the comrades who were the first to set off, running into the unknown. Nothing stirred. We figured that they must surely have reached the other side.

At that moment, the Russians realised they were being attacked. A Russian SMG glimmered – then another and another.

In that same instant Lieutenant Grabert shouted, 'Fire at will!'

Six German SMGs started firing all at once. Tracer bullets shot one line of fire after another into the sky. The barrels of our pistols were heating up. We had all leaped up and raced towards the chief. All tension had disappeared and the only thought in our minds was to cross the bridge as fast as we could and help our comrades! We stormed into the dark. We didn't shout 'Hurrah', as the infantry did. We Brandenburgers never did that sort of thing.

As was our practice, we stormed the enemy without uttering a sound. The panting of our comrades was drowned out by the firing around us. Barely an order was issued – each of us knew exactly what he was meant to do. We stumbled across dead bodies – were they Russians or comrades? There was no time to check.

Fast as lightning, we dashed across the bridge and reached the other end. Hand grenades were already dropping to either side of the road. Shooting from the hip and swinging a spade, we penetrated the Russian posts and wiped out their crews. Comrades followed us at short intervals, widening the bridgehead on both sides. By then both groups had reached the other side. It was crucial that we dug ourselves in before daybreak to be prepared for the Russian counter-attack which was sure to follow. We threw out the dead Soviets from their holes, jumped in and – with our spades and our bleeding hands, buried ourselves in the mud. Sweat was pouring from us, but nobody paid any attention.

Lieutenant Grabert landed right next to me, panting; he said, 'Look at this, Tschampetro, this is it for me, I've been hit, I can go home now!' He put the stump of his little finger of his left hand under my nose to show me. He really believed that nothing else could happen to him, he wasn't joking. Every Landser believed that if he so much as got zapped, he was done with the war.

It had become light by then, and the Russian defence had become heavier and more accurate when targeting us. We were lying at the bridge, protected by shrubbery about half a metre high. We could only move forwards if we crouched down low, but because daylight had broken, we didn't even dare do that. We were practically glued to the bridge. The village boundary was only 300 metres away from Bataisk. That's where the Russians were located, behind a long dense hedge, some two to three metres high, in well prepared positions and equipped with SMGs, grenades and anti-tank guns. The distance was only 300 metres, but for us an impossible stretch to overcome, seeing that the terrain was completely flat and marshy and offered us no protection whatsoever. The comrades out there stood no chance at all. The lucky ones were those who had found a hole in which they could lie flat. If anyone had raised his head, he would have become an inevitable target, and the Russian snipers were superb at their job.

The firing had died down. Both sides were gathering themselves for some rest, refitting and reorganisating. The wounded groaned or howled in pain. We pulled, dragged and pushed them below the bridge. That's where we thought they would be safest, and also it was the only spot that was somewhat shaded. There they were then, lying one next to the other, German next to Russian. Pataisky, the combat medic, who was a student straight from his first term in medical school, had his hands full. He bandaged the wounds as best he could.

'Medic!' Medic!' men were moaning, groaning and sobbing. The call of the wounded was urgent and demanded our immediate attention – these men were hurt but they were also angry. Finally, we had them all in one spot – that is, as many as we could manage to assemble into one spot. Our dead comrades were also here, stored away under the bridge and covered as best we could.

'Help! Help!' we heard all of a sudden. It had come from one of my men. He lay fifteen feet in front of the protecting wall behind which we had taken cover. Only fifteen feet, but there was no way for us to cross that small distance. The minute someone raised his head above the embankment, the bullets came whistling past his ears. One could just about get away with throwing a quick glance across while changing positions.

'Help! Help!' We simply had to do something, we couldn't abandon our comrade. We had to help him.

'I'll dash out and pull him inside. Who'll join me?' I asked.

'Me', 'Me', 'Me' came the response. Everyone volunteered to help our friend. Grabert joined us and listened to the plan. 'Fine,' he said, 'you go when I give the command. We'll give you covering fire, but be quick.'

Corporal Krüger and I put our weapons to the side and crouched down, ready to jump. We dug some starting blocks into the soil with our shoes and we tried to clutch onto some of the grass that was growing at the edge of our protective barrier wall, though failing, leaving only clumps of mud between our fingers.

'Ready?' asked Grabert.

'Ready,' I answered.

'Then let's go!' shouted Grabert.

Our legs pushed back against the toe holds. At the same time, we fired our machine guns. In a few short strides we were by our injured comrade's side. He didn't move and seemed to be unconscious, or was he dead already? We pulled him up.

That's when Krüger screamed and collapsed. 'I'm hit in the knee!' he shouted, and writhed on the ground. We were swept by gunfire, bullets ploughing into the mud around us.

I grabbed Krüger, pulled him up, slung one of his arms around my neck and dragged him back. It was only fifteen feet separating us from the ditch, but they seemed interminable. Head first, we flung ourselves into cover. Machine-gunner No. 1, Linhart, who had given us covering fire, got hit in the head and stumbled backwards. Meanwhile, a passing shot literally tore Grabert's cap into shreds. 'Help! Help!' we heard another comrade shouting. This long drawn-out cry filled with pain and sorrow went right through us. My heart tightened and I held my hands to my ears. I no longer wanted to hear the call. We aren't able to help you, my friend! We did what we could, the price was more dead and wounded. Why won't you stop shouting? Hearing these pleas for help, seeing all the anguish around me quite literally sickened me.

'Help! Help!' his cry had turned to a feeble moan, then a whisper, until it finally ceased altogether. Or at least it grew so quiet we couldn't hear it any more.

The Russians then attacked us from the right. We saw them approaching; it was as we remembered it from our training exercises. They would always take just five jumps, throw themselves to the ground, and disappear from sight, just like aphids who dig themselves into leaves. What we desperately needed was a curtain of artillery fire. Our grenade launchers threw their stuff across and truly outdid themselves in speed and energy; the attack broke down. To our right, far back, soldiers were still trudging through the mud. These were our comrades from the Waffen-SS Wikings. Our hope was that they would make it to the river and secure our bridgehead at least on one end. We watched them intently as they attempted to establish blocking positions.

But before we could breathe a sigh of relief, they were hit by enemy fire, forcing them to the ground. Their attack was aborted. They were unable to advance. Worse still, they seemed to be running to the rear. Grenadiers were attempting to reach us from the left. The Soviets intercepted that assault as well. These comrades then also rushed back, scampering like frightened rabbits. It was a rather depressing spectacle for us to witness.

Hours passed. At that point, we had lost all connection with the gunmen in front of us. Had any of them survived?

Casualties mounted on our side as well, and we mourned many dead and wounded engineers. At that point the Soviets still held the riverbank and were relentlessly battling on, but we held on, albeit tenuously, to the bridge of solid cement. Enemy anti-tank gunners accurately targeted the area underneath the bridge, releasing a deluge of fragments that hailed down straight on top of the wounded who had been assembled there. Realising we had exhausted our supply of bandages, we were forced to use torn strips of handkerchiefs and shirts as makeshift dressings. Ammunition was also running low.

'Only target clearly visible objects!' 'Keep calm and stand strong!' 'The Stukas are due any moment now!' 'Our artillery will soon move into assault position!'

Those were the words Grabert told his men while dashing back and forth, from one soldier to the other. The radio operators signalled incessantly for aerial and artillery reinforcement, ammunition and fresh dressings. Nothing arrived. Instead, we were hit by a Russian grenade, which put an end to the radioing.

Suddenly, on the other bank, we saw two men gliding down into the water, desperately attempting to swim across. The Russians had spotted the swimmers as well, and sprayed them with machine-gun fire. Unfazed by the bullets hailing down all around them, they continued. Watching them closely, we fervently wished them the best of luck. And indeed, they were blessed with it. Minutes later they scrambled ashore, and we welcomed them like messengers from the world beyond. It was staff physician Stabsarzt Dr Helmut Weber and Sergeant Fohrer. They were totally naked, but Dr Weber had a small pouch around his stomach containing a syringe and morphine, with which he was at least able to ease the pain of the wounded.

Sergeant Fohrer was then dispatched to swim back across the river to secure a radio that was still intact and with which he could message for urgent aerial and artillery reinforcements. We needed immediate support or we would be finished. With all our hopes pinned on him, he swam back and successfully reached the shore.

Again, Ivan was on the attack. Before I even saw him, I heard the screams of 'Urrah' that seemed to come out of every corner. This time, the assault was planned to target us from both sides simultaneously, thereby making it impossible for us to organise our defensive line. For just one brief moment I managed to lift my head above the undergrowth. I was horrified. There they were, jumping out from behind the hedges that had brilliantly concealed their positions near to Bataisk and charging forwards. Tight clusters of brown figures emerged, just as they had in Dünaburg; this time, they didn't just dash a few metres and then stop. No, this time they came straight at us. They shot with guns, pistols and machine guns. What came towards us felt like a heaving steamroller with sparks spraying in all directions.

There are no words adequate to describe these events. And, as often happened in such situations, suddenly all my fear disappeared. The once-paralysing terror simply dissipated into thin air, and in its place appeared the familiar shooting phantom of 'fire, load, aim, repeat'.

I lay on the embankment, a surefire target, but I didn't care. I emptied my entire MPi cartridge into that screaming mob storming towards me. Only then did I fall back, fumbled for a fresh cartridge on my belt and, while slipping it into the pistol, I looked sideways at my comrades. They too were shooting like mad. The guy at the far end at the pier of the bridgehead was busy switching his barrel – probably burnt out – for a new one. There was only a brief period of rest before we sent off a fresh volley of lethal bullets towards the Russians who were barrelling towards us. As if an invisible fist had come crushing down on them, the first ranks buckled. Those behind them tumbled over the lifeless but still twitching heap of corpses to then crumple too, pounded by our machine-gun fire.

Lieutenant Grabert lurched from one hole to the next, screaming orders, but it was of little use, as each of us was fully aware that we would lose the fight if Ivan succeeded in penetrating our hedgehog position. We would stand no chance at all if it came to close-combat fighting.

I had already replaced my used cartridge but couldn't stop my trembling. The sweat running into my eyes was burning hot, and drew lines onto the steamed-up lenses of my spectacles. Once again, I found myself lying on the embankment and shooting. I didn't care in the least whether or not I was a target. Why was that? Was it despair? Heroism? We'd often get called the elite, revered as this dare-devil lot who feared nothing, defied everything, the intrepid warriors. If there was an ounce of truth to this, then I certainly proved it at that very moment. We were indeed the diamond in the Wehrmacht's treasury.

Not a single Ivan came within range of a hand grenade. The 'Urrah' screams gradually faded away. What was left were heaps and heaps of dead bodies, a few of them still twitching. Some men were running away. Exhausted, I sank back into a ditch and my mind started working once again, becoming more conscious of what was happening.

That's when I noticed that Lieutenant Grabert was lying just three feet away from me. He groaned, pressing both hands onto his stomach.

'Lieutenant, sir, what's the matter?' I asked, and ran across to him.

'I … got … caught?' he strained to get the words out.

'Stabsarzt, quick, over here,' I shouted as loud as I could. 'Chief got hit!'

Dr Weber came in a flash. Nobody noticed that he was still naked. We dragged the chief very carefully underneath the bridge, where the doctor set to work. It was an abdominal wound! The doctor put a makeshift dressing on Grabert while we sat by his side, words failing us.

'Men … Back to your holes … and … pay attention,' said the chief softly.

We crawled back to our positions. It had become curiously still, apart from the odd shot that rang out here and there. It could just be a brief respite and they would soon come again; we simply didn't know what lay ahead of us.

It was lunchtime. The scorching July sun beat relentlessly down on us. The narrow strip of shade underneath the bridge was entirely taken up by the wounded and the dead. All that was left of our group was a handful of men, all of us exhausted. Shaking, Corporal Kiebacher handed me a cigarette. With trembling hands, I accepted. Silently, we puffed the smoke into the sky. The fact that our chief had got hit had shaken us to the core. We had always known that this operation was a pile of shit, but we never despaired as we believed in our chief. We were convinced that surely, *he* would get us out of it. But at that moment we were abandoned by our leader. Who would head up the operation? Who would issue the orders? Who had the seniority to succeed him? Dr Weber? He was a physician, not the leader of a troop.

Good Lord, it suddenly struck me. Why, of course, it looked as if I was the only sergeant still remaining. It was now down to me to think and also decide on behalf of our lot. I was feeling quite ill, but at the same time fearless. For the first time I felt like a real soldier. Never would I be able to look myself in the mirror without crumbling in embarrassment if I shirked this responsibility.

'Take cover!' Wasn't that the voice of the chief? At once we turned around and flung ourselves into the undergrowth with our eyes peeled to Bataisk. Nothing seemed to be moving over there. What was happening? Why this order?

Grabert, without anyone noticing, had crawled out from underneath the bridge and clambered up. Turning over onto his back and pulling up his knees, he then inched forwards, cautiously, slowly. We sat there, frozen, staring at each other in disbelief. What on earth was he up to? What the hell was he doing up on that bridge? The only explanation was that he was looking for trouble, looking for a suicide mission.

Ivan had also got sight of the slow-moving silhouette and targeted it. As the bullets collided with the ground around Grabert, concrete shrapnel sprayed into the air like water from a fountain. He lay there, flat on his back, stretched out and immobile. We did everything to hold down the enemy machine-gun fire, all the while preoccupied by our chief's motionless body up there on the bridge. Was he dead? No, painfully and ever so slowly, he was turning onto his stomach to then settle once again into a still position. A pool of blood formed beneath him. The firing ceased.

That's when he suddenly leaped up and darted across the bridge. Holding up his trousers and the bandages with both hands, his Iron Cross swinging wildly from right to left, and with his bloodstained head dressing slipping down his face, he ran. Yes, he literally ran.

Instantly, machine-gun fire came hammering down from across the bridge with bits of cement flying in every direction. He threw himself to the ground and stayed there, motionless. Finished. By this point he must surely have been killed. Some interminable minutes went by.

And then, would you believe it, he sprang to his feet, wanting to run on, but he could only stagger forwards a few metres. Where on earth did he get that energy from? Surely not even a drop of blood was left in his body. The bridge seemed to go on forever. Ivan shot repeatedly at him. Grabert teetered on. The now entirely blood-soaked bandage around his stomach had come completely loose and dragged behind him, with Grabert still clutching at it with both his hands.

Ivan took aim. Grabert lurched on.

We were frozen to the spot like statues. What a cruel sport target shooting is, we thought. Grabert fell to the ground again and stayed there. Was this the fatal bullet finally finishing its target? We had lost sight of him – done – it was over.

But no, we couldn't believe our eyes. There he rose again. Tumbled, attempted it again, swayed as if drunk and, with what seemed like a last burst of energy, he had reached the other end of the bridge. That's where he then collapsed and fell headlong down the embankment. We could still make out the few crew members from the heavy weapons platoon who leaped towards him and dragged him back to their positions. We were immensely relieved.

Suddenly we had once again become more optimistic. Chief was on the other side, and would surely give these tired staff gentlemen his piece of mind and put pressure on them to get moving finally. Surely the artillery and Stuka bombardment would set in shortly. Dear God, may this happen soon, we prayed, otherwise we'd all be lost.

Calm had once again settled in. I crawled up to the Stabsarzt underneath the bridge. Where on earth had he managed to procure himself a pair of trousers? His hands and upper body were smeared in blood. He was leaning over a wounded man.

'Unbelievable,' he mumbled, 'truly unbelievable.' The comrade he was treating was as white as chalk, his eyes wide open, staring into nothingness, his mouth agape with a thin river of blood spilling down and dripping to the floor. I inched forward to get close.

'What's unbelievable?' I asked.

'Well, that this guy is still moving, that he's even alive,' responded Weber. 'He was hit by a bullet straight into his open mouth, not a single tooth has been injured, entry point was his soft gum tissue, exit point, his neck, and he's still alive, a clean shot. Looks like he isn't even seriously wounded – unbelievable.'

Underneath the bridge there was total devastation. The scene of an infirmary at the front is probably absolutely the most horrendous sight one can imagine. Wounded everywhere, not a single one properly bandaged. Some whimpered, others groaned in terrible pain, while some seemed to be peacefully asleep. They might have been dead, or simply knocked out by the morphine. Pools of blood at every step, blood-soaked dressings, pale and exhausted faces covered in sweat, bloodshot eyes. You couldn't tell the living from the dead. An awful smell of decay hung over the whole area, and buzzing flies swarmed around.

'I am out of morphine – and out of bandages,' said the doctor, looking at me.

'And we are out of ammunition,' I responded. 'We only have one MG left and some eighty bullets in our belt. My MPi is on its last cartridge – and I have already half emptied it.' If the Russians resumed the attack, all we could have come up with was one last burst of fire. It wasn't hard to predict that.

'Sergeant, sir,' a wounded man broke our silence. 'What are we to do if Ivan attacks us?' Should we allow ourselves to be taken into captivity or should we shoot ourselves?'

What does one offer as a response? Those of us who at the time were still alive and not severely injured could well have saved our skins perhaps by swimming, but what of the wounded? What would happen to them?

'Just take it easy, comrade,' I said, trying to put on a confident smile. 'Nobody is going to get us down that quickly.'

'How many men do you still have ready to engage?' Dr Weber asked me.

'Seven, sir,' I responded.

'We'll clear out,' was his answer.

The only way out for us was to swim across the river. That would mean overcoming a stretch of some 200 metres, and it meant having to swim against the flow of the water. That option was out of the question, as when it came to swimming underneath or within the proximity of the bridge, firstly the enemy could easily spot us and secondly, if he got wind of us leaving the bridgehead, he would simply eat us alive. Apart from anything else, the Russians were excellent marksmen, having already cut down in the course of that day two men who, stuck to the bottom side of the bridge like flies to the ceiling, had attempted to claw their way across by clinging onto the girders.

But the wounded were our biggest problem. There were more than fifty of them. All we could do was to leave them to their fate. It was good that some of these poor devils weren't truly aware of the situation. They were either unconscious, or the morphine had blurred their minds. But those who were still conscious and who were still half able to move – it was them whom we worried about. We just couldn't leave them to some horrible ending, we had to do all we could to save them, even if we had to pay for it, probably with our own lives. We had to act swiftly. It couldn't be long until Ivan once again picked up his gun and started shooting.

We had to make good use of the few minutes granted to us. Those of us still capable of carrying a gun and still in possession of some ammunition were still in position. We were perhaps seven men, certainly no more than eight.

'Those who can crawl,' I shouted to the wounded, 'should crawl along the river some 200 metres, and that's where we'll cross.' I took off my heavy mountain boots and got rid of the uniform. We put one or two heavily wounded soldiers onto wooden planks and branches that had at some point been washed ashore and pushed them into the water. Others, who still had use of one of their arms or legs, did their best to cling to these makeshift rafts while pulling their living cargo across the river. Never before had I witnessed a more miserable retreat, and never would I forget the beseeching, the desperate and profoundly sad eyes of those left behind. Like me, they had enlisted into the Wehrmacht brimming with excitement, idealism and a thirst for adventure; they had imagined this war to be different. And there they were, helpless, a heap of misery, attended by a naked Stabsarzt who had neither bandages nor morphine, and to top it off, they had to watch how the few comrades still on their feet walked away, abandoning them. They remained there, alone, left to a fate which could not have been more cruel.

The first of our men were already drifting across the river, with only a piece of wood to hold on to, and pushed along by comrades who could barely keep themselves above water. Damn, hadn't I told them quite clearly that they were supposed to first crawl beside the river and only then cross? Why weren't they doing it? They probably just couldn't wait. Or perhaps the Russians had already positioned themselves at that other point on the river? Well, if that was the case, it was the end of it – for all of us.

I had no time to mull things over. It was total chaos, and the last act of the drama was about to begin.

'Here they come,' said someone suddenly.

I got up onto my knees to look out over the thicket, which reached to about my shoulders. I couldn't believe my eyes: there they were, coming forwards. Clusters of brown figures slowly heaved themselves towards us in a grotesque sort of dance. Who was to stop this fire-spitting bulldozer? Us? A dozen battered men who had barely eighty shots in their MG belt, and a half-empty cartridge in their gun?

'Go, into the water, now,' I shouted to MG gunner No. 1, who wasn't budging.

'I can't swim, Oberjäger,' he shouted back. Oh, dear God!

I crouched down, as if getting set for a race, because what I needed to do was negotiate twenty metres of flat shoreline and then reach the water in one move. All I was wearing was a pair of gym shorts. Into my back pocket I had stuck a egg hand grenade – one never knows. I dug my feet against my improvised starting block, shot up and darted across the pebbled stretch, where I took off with an expertly levelled jump, landing in the water. Well, at least that's what I thought had happened. But that brown sludge was only half a metre deep right at the riverbank, and with a huge thud, I ended up flat on my back on hard ground. Obviously, my body was scraped from head to toe, and it burnt like hell. Thrashing about like a trout, I quickly got my wits about me and crawled as fast as I could into deeper water before swimming upstream. I caught up with a comrade who was slumped over a treetrunk, barely holding on and only half conscious. I kept pushing him onwards while crawling hard behind. I could certainly measure up to any Olympic swimmer. I definitely must have set a new record in the 100-metre crawl – but what with a Russian on my heels, it was child's play.

And they literally were on my heels. Everywhere around me, right and left, behind and in front of me bullets smacked into the water, spurting little fountains into the air. These men, drained of blood, all doped-up and shredded to bits, their torn bandages drifting around their bodies, torturing themselves across the river – were an easy target for these Soviet marksmen.

A man from my squad was swimming next to me. All of a sudden, he flung his hands up, wailed at the top of his voice – a scream which went straight through my bones – and went under. He had been hit! I wanted to grab onto him, but he had already sunk into the thick brown muck. I swam on. Suddenly he bobbed up again, performed the same 'trick', screaming and throwing his arms into the air, and then disappeared once again into the stream. That wasn't stupid at all, I thought, and proceeded also to throw my hands up, ejecting a blood-curdling sound before sinking into the river. Pushing hard, I continued swimming under the murky water.

Finally, I had reached the other side. The riverbank was two metres high. Vertical wooden posts, constructed to protect the riverbank from erosion, loomed above the water. I clung onto them to get some rest. Pressed behind one of the posts, barely able to hold my head above water, I glanced back to the riverbank we had left behind. The first of the Russians had already landed and were taking aim, firing at the swimmers, while streams of brown-clad figures were spilling out of Bataisk.

Then, literally out of the blue, our Stukas appeared, roaring and dropping bombs right into the midst of the attacking Russian lines. It was one huge cacophony of screeching, crashing, bursting and howling. For me, however, it sounded like the most beautiful music on earth. Why hadn't they arrived half an hour earlier? On this side white flares were fired, but on the other side all that was left were the dead and the heavily wounded.

They had come late, these planes; very late, but not *too* late. They were able to crush Ivan, who had reached the bridge but for the last few metres, in one fell swoop. It was impressive work what these Stukas displayed to us, detailed and focused.

I was still hanging in the water. Gradually I pulled myself up and onto the riverbank which had been my saviour, but then I fell backwards. It was only at that moment that I felt the burning pain in my left leg. Goodness, I thought to myself, I must have been hit while swimming.

With the last bit of strength left in me, I raised myself onto the bank and hobbled as fast as I could across the marshland. Onwards I struggled and reached the dam, our starting position from what seemed ages ago, where I was received by the motorcyclists. I can only imagine that I must have reminded them of 'ecce homo'. I was stark naked but for the dog tag around my neck; I must have lost my gym shorts while swimming. Covered in wounds and bruises, bleeding and dazed, that's how I returned from hell. With no more strength left in me, I collapsed.

The motorcyclists didn't utter a word, and simply stood and stared at me. One of them poured me some coffee, but I couldn't swallow it, my throat seemed knotted together. I was shaking, and my teeth chattered incessantly. Second Lieutenant Eberlein, the leader of the motorcyclists, handed me a shirt and kept speaking to me. I couldn't comprehend. I came to only slowly and felt as if I had woken up from an awful nightmare. After what seemed like an eternity, I could once again recognise what I saw, and understand what I heard.

Second Lieutenant Eberlein gave me a motorbike, and that's how I drove back along the dam to Rostov, my shirt blowing in the wind and with an emergency dressing dangling from my left leg. In the meantime, the comrades had prepared a ferry, where I met up with my comrades who, just like me, had emerged from that hell on earth: Hundhammer, Sondermann, Kiebacher, Wieland, Dross and Raiss – all comrades of mine. This was the glorious remains of our half-company. One could easily make them out. They were all naked, like me, wearing only a pair of gym trousers or a shirt. Landsers from other squads just stood around and gawked at us.

An infirmary car took us sad lot to where we boarded a ferry which transported us across the Don, from where we were then taken through the city to our vehicles. Upon arrival we received a warm welcome from our comrades of the other half-company. It seemed that everyone had been informed of what had happened, at least sketchily, as they had received intermittent radio messages from the front.

While a medic looked after my injuries, Second Lieutenant Haut approached me. He was extremely cordial, and seemed quite concerned about my wellbeing. He wanted to hear my own account of what had happened and I told him, without exaggeration, as if detached from it all, as if I had been a mere spectator sitting in a theatre watching a gruesome scene unfold on stage – but who didn't play a part in it.

The grim and terrible slaughter which I had just lived through had churned up my insides more than I realised at the time. I had aged many years, and had matured beyond recognition. It felt as if a veil had been lifted from my eyes, making me suddenly see the world quite differently, much clearer, much more distinctly.

God only knows that our previous engagements with Grabert and Knaak hadn't all been cakes and ale, but, at least in retrospect, it seemed that I had been able to experience these as if in a trance. Somehow, I hadn't ever felt quite connected to what was actually happening, rather I had just gone through the motions – automatically, without thinking. 'At your command, Your Imperial Highness!' Perhaps this state of mind, this internal detachment, was a sort of protection that had enabled me to come out of it alive and without having gone mad. Granted, after Dünaburg when our rather ridiculous group of survivors had returned home and my nerves had reached rock-bottom, it had taken me weeks to regain control and feel that I was in charge of myself. But with Rostov, the situation was of a different order. I had lived through this last engagement entirely conscious of what it entailed, with eyes wide open. I saw it all, quite clearly, quite distinctly. All my senses had been attuned to every single detail, I was always fully conscious of each of my actions and what they would entail, and throughout the battles I never really lost sight of that. This fact alone might have been the most horrendous aspect of that war, namely that I had taken it all in, fully aware, and without hiding behind any defence mechanism.

How would it be next time round? How often would there be a next time? When might fate catch up with me as it had done with so many of my comrades? If only it could be quick: one, two, three, and then the end.

The Kuban Steppe: Kerch to Sussatski

It turned out that the battle to capture the bridge at Bataisk was a real tragedy for the 8th Company. The first half-company was completely wiped out. Only a few of the men from the heavily armoured platoon had survived; other than that, it was just the drivers who had stayed with their vehicles back in Rostov. We had suffered thirty losses, four were still missing, probably drowned in the brown waters of the Don. There were sixty-one injured, some of them seriously. How many of them died at the first-aid stations and in the field hospitals, I never knew. Lieutenant Grabert had died of his injuries shortly after having crossed the bridge while preparing to launch his grenade. Second Lieutenant Hiller was also killed, mowed down while taking cover in a mud pit some 100 metres before the bridge. Besides him lay the ambulance officer – he too was dead, a bullet straight to the head, his hand still holding a pouch containing dressings.

We had seized the last bridge before Bataisk and had held it. Yes, indeed, we had held it, even though we, as the last survivors, had swum back. The Stukas were eventually joined by the longed-for reinforcements. Bataisk was captured, while back in Rostov heavy street-to-street fighting to win the old city had continued on for several days and had caused heavy casualties.

On 27 July the tanks and the sniper squads of the 57th Tank Corps crossed the dam and our bridge and prepared to move south. The gateway to the Caucasus had been opened.

At the time, I had absolutely no inkling of the strategic significance of either the dam or its bridges, and quite honestly, I didn't much care one way or the other. We simple Landsers were too preoccupied with our own stuff to start deliberating about whether or not it made sense to engage in a particular operation; more importantly, we could never have condoned an operation which necessitated the deaths of our comrades. We did our duty and had committed to this operation as instructed. Both then and at other times we were always quite prepared to die, if this was what it had to be. But to send others to their death?

We were no heroes. Or were we? Perhaps this was best left for others to judge, those who hadn't been there. They never had any idea of how we were gripped by fear when we were preparing for an operation, and that even the most reckless and the bravest among us were terrified by an impending attack. They didn't know how our teeth chattered, how our hands sweated so much that we could hardly hold our weapons, and they'd never know how our bodies quivered while we lay in wait for the next assault. These people who only ever heard the stories afterwards would not have been able to comprehend how we would have loved to just curl up and hide somewhere safe and that, when it came to it, these so-called heroic acts just happened automatically, and that those who committed them were always surprised to be alive after it was all over. So, yes, for those on the outside we were heroes.

That battle to capture the bridge at Bataisk had a profound effect on me. It took me several days to regain control and think straight once more. I wandered around as if sleep-walking, or I would sit in my car feeling listless and apathetic. I had headaches and my whole body seemed to be on fire, still the effects of the chafing I had suffered during the operation.

Though incredibly tired, I was rarely able to fall asleep just like that, and if I did happen to drop off even briefly, I was plagued by terrible nightmares from which I awoke, bathed in a cold sweat. I felt completely alone. This was indeed the truth as I had lost my group and my own small crew. The crew of which I had been such an integral member no longer existed; everyone was dead, or lay in some field hospital seriously injured. Thus, my physical suffering was compounded by the emotional feelings of having been abandoned. Shortly thereafter I was assigned to the second half-company in the position of commando leader. While it was indeed a promotion, it didn't alleviate my loneliness.

At long last we departed, once and for all putting this dreadful city and what it represented behind us. Assigned some tanks, we drove north in the direction of Shachty. We stayed in Kerch for two days.[12] I was tasked to write up the combat report and include those soldiers' names whom I deemed worthy to be honoured with the Iron Cross.

I had arranged for myself a school bench from somewhere which I placed in my tent and that's where I would sit and write, using the opportunity also to write letters home and to my girl. Someone among us had brought a gramophone all the way out here, and he had actually managed to hold onto one and a half records which had survived all the turmoil we had been through. While it produced nothing but a scratchy and groaning sound, it was, at the end of the day, music, and it cheered us up to some small degree. Hour after hour we would have to listen to the same old melody, it went something like this: '*Mein Mädel ist nur eine Verkäuferin [In einem Schuhgeschäft mit 80 Franc Salär in der Woche ...]*'[13]

And in fact, nobody complained, quite to the contrary. The minute the record had come to an end, it wouldn't take long for someone to get up and crank up the old box again; the music continued. Indeed, we must have played it so many times that the cartridge with its blunted stylus was heaving across the dented record like a ship in rough waters. Each of us would dream about our girls back home.

Gradually, I returned to my old self. I had got over the trauma, was able to sleep without suffering from nightmares, and I ate as if there was no tomorrow. Once again, I was able to read and enjoy *Faust*.

As soon as the two days of rest had come to an end, it was back to the old grind. Yet again we found ourselves wedged in an endless columns of vehicles, all jostling for space to press onwards. As far as our lot was concerned, we were in no rush. None whatsoever. 'Please, by all means, why don't you drive ahead! Why don't you overtake us? As for us, we have all the time in the world,' we felt like saying. 'We have just come out of a real shit-hole, so now, gentlemen, it's your turn. Just you go ahead – we're more than happy to let you pass!'

We turned around and drove back to our resting spot, with the glowing red sun right in front of us, disappearing below the horizon. It meant that this was the first time ever since the start of the Russian campaign that we were heading westwards.

If only we could keep going in that direction, simply keep driving on, and in 2,000 kilometres as the crow flies we would be home again. Well, that would have been too good to be true. Already by the following day we were ordered to turn around and drive east, and further east and further. How long would that last? Would it ever end? What an earth were we doing there, did we even have any business being there?

We were chasing an enemy, and wherever we could catch him, we beat him and relentlessly stormed ahead, ever eastwards. Further and further away from Germany, deeper and deeper into Russia, a country which to me loomed ever larger, ever more desolate, gloomy and horrific. How would this war end? And how many of us would actually live to see the end? How often would we be assigned the role of painting on wooden planks the words: 'Fallen for Greater Germany!' and how many more times would we be ramming plain wooden crosses into foreign soil, into Russia's hostile and tortured ground? How many of these markers would tell the tale that over there, at the edges of Eastern Europe, at the far-flung borders of Russia, German blood had been spilled for the sake of... well, indeed, for the sake of what, for heaven's sake?

This was the first time I couldn't find any answers to my question; it was the first time something from within me surfaced and I was unable, or perhaps unwilling, to make sense of it. Petrified, I pushed aside these initial and tentative moves towards independent thinking, which would inevitably lead me to criticise and doubt the phrase that had been hammered into me: 'The Führer certainly knows what he is doing.'

But the spark had been ignited and was sufficient to keep a low flame of revelation glowing. It couldn't evolve, couldn't develop into a full-blown fire; there was no time for that as I was much too preoccupied with the war, just like everyone else, and it left no room for any of us to dwell on our doubts, let alone discuss them with friends. Then again, could any such defeatist deliberations add anything meaningful, given the decisive phase of the war we found ourselves in at the time, and with us continually dangling between life and death? We soldiers at the front couldn't afford to reflect upon the whys and ifs of the war – the likes of us were otherwise engaged, preoccupied with matters of survival.

In any event, we were travelling west at that moment, and enjoying it. I fully indulged in the illusion that this journey westwards would only then terminate once we were back in our homeland.

But the following morning our vehicles were headed towards the rising sun. We crossed the Don at Radorskaia, by crossing a pontoon bridge. It was oppressively hot with not a cloud in Russia's vast sky, but we actually couldn't see the sky as we were entirely covered in a dense coat of dust that covered our faces as much as an inch thick. The sweat dripping from our forehead drew deep lines into this brown skin patina, and we could barely see a thing.

We made a short break in Sussatsky, a small hamlet situated amid the seemingly endless sunflower fields. The village consisted of a few shabby houses around the centre, where the village's draw well was the only water source for the inhabitants. While parking our vehicles, we had spotted chickens and other poultry cavorting behind the garden fences of the cottages. Immediately a wild chase ensued, which had these poor birds clucking aimlessly between the shacks.

Mention the word 'food' to any of us Landsers and we instantly perk up. When it came to issues relating to our appetite, no order was ever necessary to get us going. That day was no different, and all of us happily went on the hunt. Certainly none of us felt that he had been forced into it. Even our good lieutenant dived straight into action and shamelessly chased a poor piglet, and even the laziest of our drivers got off his butt from behind the wheel and charged after a goose in flight. The race yielded but a modest taking, which was then instantly slaughtered, plucked and cleaned. Within moments we had a blazing campfire going and greedily inhaled the enticing aromas wafting across from the pans where those poor birds were sizzling in their own fat. War, hardship, dust and dirt, the heat and the distant homeland, death itself – it all seemed to have disappeared. And in its stead came joyfulness and laughter. Our excitement about the forthcoming opulent meal beckoning from the pan was great, with several among us constantly pouring more and more sunflower oil from out of the cans and watching gleefully as pig, chicken and goose practically drowned in it.

One of our comrades mused that *Palatschinken*[14] would be the ideal dessert following a meal of this kind, and no sooner had he spoken the words than his hope became reality. Someone must have found milk from somewhere, and it wasn't long before the batter was being whipped up in a bowl. The moment we swallowed the last bit of our delicious main course, the most marvellous *Palatschinken* magically appeared. Large, ripe tomatoes and onions were cut into thick slices, then salted and smothered in oil. We sat on the steps of our cars, or crouched on our steel helmets, or on anything really we could find to rest our tired bodies; we truly had the meal of our lives. It had been ages since we had been able to enjoy such culinary delicacies, so at that moment, having been offered the opportunity, we took full advantage of it. Grease was dripping from our chins down our elbows. Did that bother us? Not one bit. Why would we care about our liver or our gall bladder; we didn't worry for one minute about filling our stomachs as if there was no tomorrow. Eventually we just keeled over right where we were and fell into the deep slumber of the contented. We were full and for a brief moment we were also happy.

Fundamentally, the Landser is man of modest aspirations, and it doesn't take much to please him. A bit of booze, a bit of tobacco, a full belly, and he won't ask for more; this is all he requires to feel happy, to sing and to laugh. Indeed, short harmless breaks from the routine like the one on that charmed afternoon have always proven to be very important features in the life of a soldier, as they lift his morale and allow him to forget the misery that can surround him. Sometimes, however, such departures from the routine turn the Landser's head, and that's when he tends to fall down.

That's precisely what happened to one of our drivers. This unfortunate guy discovered a bee hive and, what with being a true glutton, he immediately turned desire into a plan, and a plan into action. The prospect of the sweet delicacy was too enticing for him to resist. Sadly, this poor fellow's craving for a treat backfired. The Russian bees were of course not much different to their German friends and, fiercely attacking the intruder, they sent him leaping up and yelling in agony. Unfortunately, this poor sod was only wearing his gym shorts, and it really couldn't have been much better as far as the bees were concerned. Much to our annoyance, this guy then came running towards us. Howling, screaming, cursing, and with his arms flailing and beating himself, he expected us – who had nothing to do with this entire escapade – to come running to his aid. The bees were clearly in their element, and there was nothing that could stop them. Next, the attacking swarm split up into several teams and descended on all of us in one fell swoop. Us lot who had been peacefully enjoying our lunch break had nowhere to escape. In the end, it was that stupid driver who was dealt the worst blow. His face was utterly disfigured and so swollen that he couldn't see out of his eyes. Worse still, he could no longer even sit down.

That same night, however, a far more tragic event took place. We were all fast asleep and only the guards were patrolling the camp, when we were suddenly woken by the sound of an explosion. One of our comrades had crept out during the night, thrown a grenade to the floor and lay himself on top of it. This man, who had gone through thick and thin with us, a soldier who had, like us, completed all the operations and who, on top of that, had survived Bataisk, had decided that life was no longer worth living. It was a crushing blow to all of us.

The following day at 1700 hours we had reached the Manytsch, crossing the river over the partially blown-up dam and, with that, left Europe for ... Asia. We learned that the Brandenburgers, under the guidance of Second Lieutenant Moevis, had played a decisive role in storming the crossing. We were told, that with the help of his reconnaissance troop dressed in Russian uniforms, the second lieutenant had first scouted the crossings over the Manytsch, which then enabled the surprise attack on Maitschstroij. This then allowed him to establish a bridgehead, preventing a total destruction of the dam.

We were in Asia! We were proud of what we had achieved, as never before had a European army penetrated so far eastwards. But alongside experiencing this deep sense of achievement and pride of being an integral part of such a historic development, I sensed fear smouldering deep inside me. To me, it somehow seemed that we were too far from our homeland, too deep in enemy territory. How would something like this end? Someday, surely, we would have to return, whether we wanted to or not. Surely our forces wouldn't be sufficiently strong or numerous to occupy this hostile and unwelcoming land? Wouldn't every single inhabitant hate us, we who had so defiled their home, and wouldn't they be justified and thus even more determined to fight us? Just by looking at us, small units who were constantly and everywhere surrounded by enemies, it wouldn't have taken long to realise just how awful our predicament was. And with our reinforcements having to face ever-longer roads – who would keep these accessible?

Dark thoughts like these were increasingly playing on my mind and plagued me. But I would quickly dismiss them as soon as they crept up. Why indeed would these be my problems, since it didn't really affect me personally? Surely the Führer knew what he was doing, and in him I trusted. That's how simple it was. What alternative did I have? Was I to desert? Was I to commit sabotage? Was I to consider treason or spying? For whom? For our enemies? It would have been utter nonsense.

Slowly, our truck rumbled through the desolate steppes. The only person whom we followed was our lead driver, as we were wedged in a column and covered in a thick sheet of dust which prevented us from seeing ahead. Progress had become incredibly depressing. No tree, no house, nothing in sight. I rolled up the window of the driver's cab and dozed off.

Once in a while dark silhouettes appeared briefly at the window: men with shaven heads and covered in rags. These were Russian prisoners. Looking at them made me feel both dreadful and anxious at the same time.[15] I delved deeper into the book I was reading.

Finally, our column came to a halt. Some mud huts stood next to the road. I grabbed my stuff, tucked it under my arm and went searching for the rest of my platoon. Frankly, that was the only place where I felt I was among friends, at home. Silently, we all sat on the ground, leaning our backs against the mud huts, smoking cigarettes. We could doodle on the walls with our fingers, the mud was so soft; I puzzled at how these miserable huts built from that stuff could withstand the winter storms without simply being swept away. We didn't even step into them, the mere thought of what would await us inside put us off, and we chose to sleep under the open sky. We lay close together as the night was going to be chilly, and we much preferred to feel the proximity of a friend, and even listen to him snore. I was still awake; two of my comrades on either side of me had already fallen asleep, breathing heavily and peacefully, while others were still whispering. I looked upwards at the sky strewn with stars and my thoughts inevitably drifted to my homeland. These were the same stars that shone down on German land, I mused, and though that idea ever so tenuously linked me to my distant home, it was a small consolation.

Once again, I reflected on what war meant, where lay its justification, its reason. Ever since crossing the Manytsch and reaching Asia, such thoughts tended to preoccupy me. What on earth were we doing here? While I had deliberated such and similar questions back in Greece, at the time they were just musings, fleeting moments which I hadn't taken too seriously, nor had I allowed myself to start grappling with them. But suddenly these questions persisted and demanded a response. What was Asia to us Germans, and more specifically, what were we South Tyroleans doing here in Kalmücken – in the Kuban steppe?

This was the first time I made a distinction between Germans and South Tyroleans. The thought had not quite crystalised, it was only vague at the time, still lodged in the subconscious. Indeed, it would have been senseless, even absurd to pursue it to its final conclusion. I pushed it away, but it kept resurfacing.

Were we actually defending our homeland? Which homeland? The one with our venerable cities and towns boasting picturesque alleyways, towering church steeples and historic buildings where bay windows looked onto trees lining the streets below? Or was it the land boasting traditional farms, cultivated in the most remote villages for centuries, or of the mountains reaching up to dizzying heights? Or was our homeland the place where the most delicious fruit and wine ripens in the luscious orchards and vineyards of our fertile valleys? Or perhaps it was the homeland of proud mountains and glaciers majestically stretching into the blue sky? Was it any of these lands that revealed the undying persistence of our Tyrolean farmers?

No, it was not those lands we were defending, I concluded. We had voluntarily given these up. We no longer had any homeland; in fact, we had pawned it off. Sure, it looked as if we were allowed to keep it for the duration of the war, and indeed we were obviously permitted to fight in order to win. But then, at the time of victory, would it ironically turn out that as a reward we would have to give up this homeland of ours forever?

I realised that the hoped-for outcome of this war in fact entailed some absurd repercussions for us South Tyroleans: along with our victory, we would stand to lose our homeland. So, bizarrely, we were fighting a war which would end in the sacrifice of our homeland. My conclusion was that we were fighting the wrong war.[16]

Had we acted wisely when we had left our homeland to become part of the Grossdeutsche Volk, which in fact gradually turned out to be the Grossdeutsche Heer?[17] Had we not, instead, betrayed our homeland, our very own South Tyrol? Who would deliver judgment on that choice?

Yet there we were, stranded on the steppes of the Kamücken, and our brethren were out far away at the Arctic Front, and in Africa and on the high seas. Where we should really have stood was at the foot of the Ortler, in Salurn or the Dolomites. That's where we really belonged, weapons in hand, ready to fight anyone who dared touch our homeland.

These thoughts were awful, horrendous really. What was I thinking? Had I gone mad?

Looking up at the stars in the sky, they appeared different. Gone was the familiar glow which had brightened my dreams when I was young. It had vanished. Instead, it seemed to me that smirking faces peered down at me from the night sky, their twinkling eyes mocking my existence.

At the Caucasus[18]

Before us lay the sheer endless Kuban steppe, lying there as flat as a pancake. Not a tree in sight, nor hedge nor burrow; in fact there wasn't even the slightest dip in the ground which could have helped signpost the area or orientate us. All we could see was that hard grass so particular to the steppes, burnt by the relentless sun to a brownish colour and reaching hip height. The few villages we drove past lay far apart from each other, often by as much as 100 kilometres, and were connected only by a pathetically narrow and bumpy field path. I wondered how long it would take a traveller by horse carriage to ride from one isolated village to another. Two days, even three days, perhaps? How terrible it must have been in winter, with its icy winds and snow storms blowing across the land. I tried picture to myself what life was like for these poor folks to live in these miserable huts, squeezed tightly together. Surely their spirits would become dulled and their way of relating to each other would become ruthless and tinged with cruelty. Gradually I came to comprehend why their folk melodies had such a sorrowful and melancholic air to them.

Once again, we were assigned to the 13th Tank Division. The lead tank, not taking notice of anybody, stubbornly followed the compass like a captain at sea. The tanks in his column followed his track, and after five or six tanks it was us, the Brandenburgers, the first unarmoured vehicle in this convoy.

We are, as our name zbV indicates, assigned for special purpose and ready for orders. We can be found at the front, mostly right at the front.

The tanks stopped. Hold on, what was the matter? We looked at each other, not knowing what was going on. We were ordered to send out a reconnaissance troop. What that meant in plain language was that someone had to check out the area for as long as it took for them to encounter some enemy fire. Two reconnaissance vehicles were dispatched to move to the front, and we followed in our three Opel Blitz cars. That was our expedition into no man's land.

All of a sudden, we came across some planes parked in the fields. We couldn't believe our eyes. But indeed, there they were: three, four, no, six Russian planes were actually lined up close to some barracks. Was it an actual airfield? Cautiously, we inched forwards. Everything remained still, not a soul in sight. We were convinced that they were lying hidden in their trenches, waiting to reach for their guns as soon as we were within range. Wanting to play it safe, we moved at a snail's pace, remaining seated and ready to jump at a moment's notice. Our vehicles fanned out. Then, suddenly, we saw that these weren't real planes. What the Russians had done was position wooden dummies to mislead the air reconnaissance. We approached, shaking with laughter, and could only marvel at what we had assumed to be the Russian air force: it consisted of nothing but card and paper! It was a Potemkin village in every sense of the word.[19] Shortly afterwards, some Russian soldiers – with their hands raised above their heads – emerged from the trenches, fear and terror written large on their faces. We carried on driving, criss-crossing the rugged area before finally catching up once again with our column.

On 5 August, at lunchtime, we had crossed the Kuban steppe. From afar we could already make out the mountains of the Caucasus. At long last, we saw some mountains again. What that meant for us was forests, shade and above all fresh water to wash off the disgusting dust and dirt that had seeped into all our pores. Our fervent hope was that this mad race with our tanks storming ahead would surely soon come to an end, which would mean that finally, we, the Gebirgsjäger, would get a piece of the action. But for now we were still pushing forwards rapidly and not making a single stop until it was pitch dark. We then spread out, parked our vehicles for the night and put our heads down.

At dawn the drive continued. We had been assigned to the Scholz combat unit. With the scorching sun relentlessly burning down on us, it was unbearably hot. Not the slightest breeze offered relief and not the tiniest bit of shade could be found; our throats were parched and we had nothing to quench our thirst. Once in a while, however, we came across some large red water melons, and years later, the image of the watermelons still loomed large in my memories of our march towards the Caucasus. Without them, I am certain that we wouldn't ever have got out of those barren, vast and treeless steppes. With the first slice we washed off the grime from our faces, ready to then shove the second slice squarely into our mouths. Oh, what pleasure, what blissful joy to feel the cool wetness drip down your chin and onto your chest.

We advanced further. We must have put some 100 kilometres behind us each day. The dreary grasslands of the barren steppes had finally given way to vast sunflower fields that reached far beyond the horizon. We drove while navigating exclusively with the help of a compass. We had hardly any contact, let alone direct encounters, with the enemy, with the exception of the occasional shell flying by us, but they never caused any serious damage. The relative calm of these days did me a lot of good. Gradually the awful days of Bataisk receded into the background, and slowly my old drive to be involved returned. When it came to the Prochaska's operation, I actually didn't mind not having a major role in it.[20] The guys who had been assigned to this particular platoon were basically those who couldn't be put to use in any of the other operations, or men whom nobody wanted. Ever since it had been created, it was rather looked upon with disdain, and derisively called the idler pulley.[21] Prochaska himself was a calm and modest man, who neither placed himself into the background nor pushed himself into the limelight. He was quite the opposite of the sharp and ambitious go-getters that all the other officers of the Brandenburg Division were. He performed his duties conscientiously, of course, but didn't go above and beyond. He always gave the impression of being worn out and deep in thought; his appearance was relaxed, laid back, and even his uniform wasn't as sharp as it could have been, what with his belt not being buckled tight enough and his heavy pistol – he always carried with him a .08 Parabellum in a holster – pulling it down to one side. This in turn caused his uniform shirt to bulk up and no longer sit perfectly tucked in. His stirrup trousers were much too long and usually dropped down, bunching up over the puttees that he (probably the only one in our entire company) insisted on wearing at all times.

Even his mountain cap, which tended to sit straight on his head, seemed much too large for him. Additionally, the poor man had zero projection, nothing in the vein of the commanding voices we were used to, and this in turn made his orders sound more like polite requests. All of this, of course, led to him not being taken very seriously, either by his colleagues – the other officers – or by his crew. But, against all the odds, it turned out to be precisely Second Lieutenant Prochaska with his idler pulley who achieved the singular most amazing operation of the entire Caucasus campaign. It truly represented a model of what a Brandenburger operation consisted of, and which was quite deservedly entered as a glorious chapter into the annals of the division's history. It was they who, on 9 August 1942, drove through the city of Maikop in camouflage, were hemmed in by Russian columns, and then proceeded to capture a bridge on the road to Tuapse. Because of these Brandenburgers the city of Maikop fell into German hands and Second Lieutenant Prochaska received the Knight's Cross – and posthumously the Iron Cross – for his hero's death on that very bridge.[22]

Two days prior to this operation I had been appointed substitute leader of operations and transferred to Commander Grube. I struggled with this order. Why wasn't I permitted to remain with Second Lieutenant Prochaska and his so-called idler pulley instead of once again joining a mission whose leader had a 'sore throat' and whose only aim was to be decorated one day with the Knight's Cross? I rather enjoyed being part of a calm platoon that served more often than not merely as reserves, and of whom no big achievements were expected. Being part of them, one just kind of floated along without making big waves, and Second Lieutenant Prochaska never pushed himself to the front, always giving way to his more ambitious colleagues.

I approached Prochaska and tried to convince him that he simply mustn't stand for such nonsense, that he shouldn't allow his men to be ordered to leave his squad willy-nilly. If he were to insist that he wasn't prepared to let me go, seeing as I was his deputy, then surely I would be given permission to stay on. Could he please insist on the configuration of his crew and not just silently swallow anything that came from above? But Prochaska wasn't that sort of man, and thus nothing changed and my transfer proceeded as planned. In fact, on that same day, Second Lieutenant Grube arrived personally to pick me up. I had no other choice but to accept my lot. As had become my habit, and one which had stood me in good stead in the past, I kept repeating to myself: 'Who knows what good might come of it'.

And, by God, good certainly came of it. In fact, it turned out to be for the best! Thanks to this transfer I was able to avoid the Maikop operation. But what this mission actually involved, and what its implications were, only transpired once we had collected all our dead comrades on the bridge of Maikop. It must have been an extraordinary, albeit gruesome, show of fire, with powerful explosions detonating all around, typical of the Brandenburgers, as there were piles and piles of dead bodies lying around. We actually had to spend quite some time with our bare hands groping around to find our dead comrades, as they were still wearing Russian uniforms. When we found them, we lined them up next to each other: seven dead comrades of the idler pulley, now covered by a tarpaulin, brave men every single one, who had carried out their mission with unmatched courage, thereby disproving all the ridicule and scorn that they so often had to endure. Ultimately it was these guys who had confirmed to us all what it meant to be a Brandenburger, even if he was a member of the idler pulley.

We had captured Maikop and actually managed to push through and arrive at the Caucasus. The town had remained intact: not one house had been destroyed, and not a single street had been turned to rubble – even the electric lights were still working. We set up our night quarters in the house of a Russian doctor, obviously a cultured gentleman, who owned a

Bechstein grand piano. One of its legs was broken and the piano had been cleverly propped up with some crates that made the instrument look quite lopsided; and though terribly out of tune, it obviously took pride of place in the owner's home.

At long last we had some time to ourselves and the opportunity to wash properly and get our kit cleaned and sorted out. But the biggest pleasure by far was finally to be able to sleep in a soft bed and have a roof over our heads.

The dream was short-lived. By the afternoon of the second day, Second Lieutenant Haut came running and sounded the alarm: 'Operation Grube, get ready at once with camouflage and captured vehicles!'

We didn't even have time to swear. No sooner had Second Lieutenant Haut given his command than all of us – dressed in the filthy and stinking Russian clobber – were seated on those miserable trucks. Our staff medic, Weber, desperately wanted to come along. He too was wearing camouflage, and on his back a satchel with a red cross painted on it. The rest of us deeply appreciated his gesture as he could easily have chosen to stay back in Maikop and send a paramedic in his place.

We had been given no information, no situation report. The only detail we were briefed on was that the tanks en route to Tuapse had got stuck. So that's when we Brandenburgers were called to the rescue! Apparently, we were to seize a tunnel, or something like that – nobody knew the specifics.

The route through dense forests along a valley took many twists and turns. Tanks and other vehicles were crowding the roads, making it near impossible for us to advance. Sitting on the trucks and wearing that Russian kit, we were quite a sight to behold, and we got many puzzled looks. My vehicle was an honest-to-god booty vehicle, with no doors, no windscreen, and no hood. On top of it the brakes didn't work. But we only found this out once we had landed smack in the ditch. With everyone's help we finally managed to get that heap of scrap onto the road and continued driving. But it didn't take long for the whole piece of crap to come to a complete standstill.

Once you have spent enough time doing service at the front, you'll have certainly found yourself in the shit many times or, as it is said so euphemistically, you'll have 'accumulated quite a bit of experience'. You just develop a sixth sense. Somehow, you tend to sense danger before it hits you, and you then go into automatic, doing things which are inexplicable at the time but which turn out to have been exactly right in hindsight. You just learn to listen to your inner voice, and in time it turns out that this voice doesn't deceive you and you simply need to obey. It's precisely that sense of impending danger and its corresponding appropriate reaction that make up the soldier's experience in war, and which distinguishes the old hand from the rookie. All it really takes to develop this sixth sense is to remain alive long enough.

Well, at the time I had the distinct sense that absolutely nothing would come of this operation. While I didn't know exactly why I had that feeling, I was quite certain that I would be proven right. So, I wasn't at all surprised when eventually it was already night-time and the whole operation was called off and we were ordered to travel back. We spent the night in a forest clearing not far from the road. Both sides kept up their random artillery fire, but it didn't disturb us one bit. We remained camped out in the same clearing the following day as well, simply waiting for the order to engage. Once again, the day turned out to be really hot, but at least we had the forest and shade of the enormous trees to cool us down. The only disadvantage of that rest was the penetrating and pungent odour that hung in the air. A slew of dead horses lay around, with burst stomachs and millions of flies swarming about them. We had to tie our handkerchiefs over our mouths in order to breathe through this stench of decay.

At lunchtime we received our mail. After a long wait, finally some post arrived from back home. In one go I received a dozen letters, from my parents and from my girl. There was even a small field-post parcel included. My mother had sent me a marble *Gugelhupf*.[24] But it sadly hadn't borne up quite as expected to the long journey from my home to the Caucasus. It had been reduced to a heap of crumbs, so that I had to eat it with a spoon. Nevertheless, it tasted fantastically delicious, and for a brief moment I forgot the war, the putrid stench and the blistering heat. All of us were deeply immersed in reading our letters, with only one interruption tearing us from our reveries. A Russian spy had been captured. He had been caught hanging around our tanks and wearing a German uniform. When he was stripped down, they found a pistol which he had clenched in between his buttocks. A large plaster had kept it in place. He was hung from a tree. The Russians would certainly have made equally short shrift had they got hold of any one of us wearing Russian uniform![25]

What had started off as a fast and furious advance had come to an abrupt halt in the mountains of the Caucasus. The tanks could get no further and the plan was that they were to be replaced by the Gebirgsjäger who had been summoned to arrive as fast as they could. They were ordered to cross the mountains and proceed down to the port city of Tuapse at the Black Sea, about

100 kilometres away. We certainly expected them to manage that. Having done our bit, it was now up to the others to give it their all. As for us, we were relieved to get a few days' rest and recuperate.

We were certainly gobsmacked when only two days had passed since our capture of Maikop and there they were already: the first Gebirgsjäger had arrived. That really was one hell of an achievement. While we of course had also struggled through the desolate, barren and windswept steppes, we at least had the privilege of being able to drive through it, while they had had to march on foot. It really didn't bear imagining! In a scorching heat of 55 degrees Celsius, coated with dust, with dry throats and lips, these poor sods had had to drag themselves through the treeless Kuban steppe, sixty kilometres every day, wearing their cumbersome hobnailed boots and carrying their whole combat pack with them: their gun belt and gun, their munition pouch filled with heavy bullets, their gas mask and steel helmet, and then on their shoulder their rifle and the MG or flamethrower. In their flasks was some tepid tea. How very fortunate we were in comparison to them, and how obviously lazy. No 100 kilometres on foot for the likes of us! And yet I wasn't sure whether even one Gebirgsjäger could be found who would have voluntarily taken our place.

We enjoyed the days in Maikop to the fullest. The inhabitants seemed to be far from hostile towards us. They heaped upon us tons of eggs, tomatoes, onions, fruit and cheeses, with pork and chicken featuring daily in our menu. We took our meals at properly set tables and with actual crockery. When the heat became unbearable, we would drive down to the Prochaska bridge and bathe in the river.[26] Come evening, we would sit together and get drunk on vodka. Meanwhile our 5th Company had also arrived. This get-together with old friends was, of course, dowsed with even more alcohol.

A few days later we found ourselves once more in the midst of the desolate steppe and engulfed by a thick cloud of suffocating dust. We had been allocated to the motorised infantry division, the 'Windhund' division. At the start we were all in high spirits as we were heading north.[27] We crossed the Kuban at Armavir and then turned east, with the 5th Company driving ahead of us.

In Kurgannaia, a tiny hovel situated on the Lewa, we rested for two hours and bathed in the river. After that, the advance continued. Our vehicles were battered, shabby and badly worn out. My car, for example, had lost its windscreen several days earlier. Given the state of disrepair our cars were in, we were both an embarrassment and a hindrance to the rest of the column.

Just so that we could breathe, we were forced to keep a certain distance from those in front of us, which in turn tore the entire column apart, and this again landed us in the shit, with the commander constantly having to give us a dressing-down. To top it off, the spring on our car had snapped and we had to pull to the side. So, there we were, in the middle of the vastness of the steppe, while the entire division, the entire advance troop in fact, passed by us. God only knew where our I-Staffel had got stuck, but then it finally arrived, albeit without a spare spring.[28] Very fortunately, about 100 metres on, a burnt-out Russian truck lay in the ditch and, though to this very day I would never know how they did it, they managed to dig out the spring from the wreck and insert it into our vehicle. Although the car was lop-sided, we were still able to drive it, and so we returned to the road once again, trying to catch up with the others. Who knew how far they'd got, but one thing was for certain, we had to meet up with them. We drove like mad, without any consideration whatsoever for the others, just so we could to push forwards and get closer to the front. We overtook wherever we could, using all kinds of tricks and manoeuvres in order to beat the column.

At long last we arrived at a paved road which went up a hill, winding its way in a wide serpentine up to Voroshilovsk, after which it was a straightforward drive taking us into the city. We were searching for our comrades when I spotted Sergeant Burrer, who was standing in the middle of the road and gesticulating at us to stop.

Burrer turned to me, saying: 'Tschampetro, get out and take all your stuff. Here are your orders: you're off to Baden near Vienna. Looks like the two of us have been drafted to join the war school.' I was beside myself, not believing what he was saying, and I just stood there, stunned. But he urged me to hurry up and get going, and said that he would give me the full details later on. He didn't want me to waste any more of the company's time; they had been ordered to take the lead in the front line. I gathered myself instantly, jumping from the car as my comrades tossed my rucksack down to me. There was a quick exchange of handshakes, good wishes, and then the truck disappeared.

I could no longer understand the world. With my mouth still agape, I was unable to grasp the fact that I had obviously got extremely lucky, and so I kept reading and re-reading the order that Burrer had handed to me. There was no doubt about it – it was there in black and white: 'Destination: Baden near Vienna'! Reason: 'Drafted to attend the war school'. Gradually it dawned on me what precisely this little piece of paper actually meant, and how significant it was. I hugged Brunner as if he himself was the cause of this incredible stroke of good fortune, and together we performed a joyous twirl, right in the middle of the road and in front of all the other Landsers.

It was difficult to fathom what had just happened. There I was, in the middle of an advance, surrounded by the vastness of the desolate steppe and at a point in time when nobody knew if they would even live to see the next day – I, a simple Landser, was told that as far as I was concerned, the war was over and I was to return home.

With that, the two of us, rucksacks on our backs, were standing at the roadside in Voroshilovsk, wondering how this would all pan out. While our papers were all in good order, we had no vehicle. Well, surely this problem would be solved. At first, we of course required a place to spend the night. So, we just went into the building closest to us, which turned out to be a college, either for veterinary or agricultural studies, we couldn't quite figure it out. We settled down on the wooden benches in the main auditorium and fell into a deep and peaceful sleep.

At dawn, we took our rucksacks and went to the city entrance. We stood at the roadside, hoping that a passing vehicle would let us on and take us in the direction of our home. But not a single car was headed that way. Looking out from Voroshilovsk, which is situated slightly higher, we could actually see north. The endless columns, huffing and puffing, wound their way towards us, but nobody was returning home. We sat there for three whole days. Nothing. In the evenings, we returned to our university lodgings.

On the morning of the third day, just when we were on our way to take up our seats in our 'waiting area', we saw a BMW Cabriolet with our insignia on it. Who should be sitting in it but Sergeant Barth from the 5th Company. He too had been drafted to attend the war school. Finally, our big opportunity had arrived to leave it all behind. But it wasn't quite as easy as we hoped. The driver had been ordered to drive his superior's car to the repair shop in Voroshilovsk, as there was something minor wrong with it. We thought long and hard, but finally decided to take the risk. It was eighty kilometres to Armavir and, after dropping us off, the driver would be back in Voroshilovsk that same day, so it was unlikely that anybody would notice his detour. We stowed our luggage before anyone thought twice about it and off we went. All went smoothly on the paved roads, but when we hit the steppe we got bogged down. We were going against the tide since everything and everybody was advancing in the opposite direction, and it was only us in our vehicle who were driving back. Inch by inch, we had to fight the columns heaving with all sorts of vehicles, marching troops, horse carriages, Flak, heavy artillery and even labour service units, children really, whose faces were haggard from the enormous hardships that had befallen them. When the going really got tough, and in order to press through, we simply used a small trick: one of us would stand upright in the car, grip onto the windscreen and shout: 'Courier service, courier, army post!' That was the only way to get through.

We reached Armavir. Spotting the airfield from afar, we watched the heavy Ju 52, loaded to the hilt with war supplies, landing and taking off again. Our aim was, of course, to try and hitch a ride with one of the planes. When we reached the airfield, a Ju 52 had just touched down. We dashed towards it, hoping to make it before it took off again. The aircraft came to a stop, all the doors flew open and within seconds the unloading process had been completed, oil containers and munition boxes all stacked up at the side. The pilots also came out, just to stretch their legs briefly. Not wanting to miss our one and only chance, we explained to them who we were, that we had been drafted to the war school, and that we needed to get there – somehow. One of the pilots, the captain, looked us up and down, eyeing us sharply: 'Well, get yourselves in there, but quick, the minute the bird is fully unloaded I'm off.'

We quickly took all our stuff from the car and said goodbye to the driver, who left immediately. He wanted to grab the opportunity to fill up his tank at the airport and then return at once to Voroshilovsk.

I climbed up the ladder to reach the inside of the plane when I noticed, to my horror, that I had left my waist belt, together with my card pocket, behind in the car! My heart stopped. I had tucked the document ordering me to attend the war school into that card pocket! Damn and damn again! I turned around just long enough to see the car disappear behind the barracks at the far end of the airfield. I jumped off the ladder and ran – well actually I raced towards the car. Never had I run faster than at that time. Panting and totally out of breath, I reached the barracks, and at the back, thank God, stood our vehicle. The driver was trying to make a deal with the quartermaster to purchase some fuel. I dived into the car, grabbed hold of my waist belt with the card pocket and yelled at the driver to immediately drive me back to the plane, as it would otherwise take off without me.

The driver didn't hesitate. He pushed the quartermaster to the side, jumped behind the wheel and sped diagonally across the airfield back to our plane. Once inside, I practically collapsed on the floor and just thanked my lucky stars. The consequences had I not found my marching orders would have been unimaginable. Well, unimaginable is not quite the correct term. In fact, it wasn't that hard to imagine what my lot would have been had I not found them. I would have ended up being ordered back to the front line within a matter of a day.

Our flight to Artemovsk took two hours. From there we took a lorry and drove eighty-five kilometres to Stalino, where our commander, Colonel von Lanzenauer was based, together with his staff.[29]

That's how it was with the Brandenburgers. While the men were in the thick of things, the headquarters – believe it or not – were positioned no less than some 1,000 kilometres behind the front line! This was surely a necessary measure, we assumed, and perhaps we were actually better off not having anything to do with them. The following day, after having reported for duty to the colonel, we were put on a train specially assigned for those on leave and were taken from the front to Dnjepropetrowsk, Kirowograd, and then onto Lemberg, where we arrived after three days. After going through the obligatory delousing station, we were bathed, shaved and combed, and only then were we allowed to travel onwards to Vienna.

— TWELVE —

The End of the War,
Early 1943 to Spring 1944[1]

Ohrdruf and Greece to Munich

After a well-deserved leave and time spent at home, I joined the military school in Ohrdruf in Thuringia. It was there where we were trained in strategy and tactics and practised – in sandboxes – how to head up companies, battalions and regiments in different terrains. We were taught every secret and theory pertaining to conventional warfare, but learned nothing which even so much as vaguely touched on what a Brandenburger operation would typically involve. Who would there have been to teach us? No template for such missions existed, no regulations, no norms. What counted for someone like a Brandenburger was flexibility, adapting to the situation at hand and improvisation.

While we were there, we followed closely the deadly fight of the 6th Army at Stalingrad. We were utterly devastated. Even if life at the military school seemed abhorrent to us, filthy and strenuous, we were relieved not to have to share the fate of our comrades, whom we knew to be stuck deep in the Caucasus; as for us, we could lie in clean beds at night, relax in heated lounges during the day, and eat at set tables in the casino.

The time spent at the school passed swiftly, and I was eventually promoted to second lieutenant. I took great pride in my epaulettes, my new silver cord attached to my cap, and my belt buckle. Spending some time in Berlin, I strutted up and down Unter den Linden boulevard like a peacock. With an air of dismissive nonchalance, I acknowledged soldiers who greeted me with a sharp salute; eagle-eyed, I made sure that not a single sergeant or corporal dared ignore me. One day, taking a walk and turning in and out of lanes, I finally reached the Reichskanzlei, which I wanted to see with my own eyes, having been curious for such a long time as to where the Supreme War Leader resided. The guards performed their present arms to perfection, outdoing each other by striking and gripping their rifle butts with a loud cracking slam. It actually startled me, and I didn't know for whom they were snapping to attention, but when I realised that they had recognised my epaulettes, I simply smiled at them rather awkwardly, secretly pleased at such honour being bestowed on me. When I reached the next street corner I rested for a bit and then gathered myself and turned back on my heels. That time round I greeted the soldiers with due poise; they just stood there stiff as boards.

That officer's uniform filled me with pride and heightened my self-confidence even though I was continually plagued by doubts about whether I really was up to the job which would be coming my way in the very near future. The soldiers who would then be placed into my trust would surely view me critically and would most likely observe closely how I behaved, not only during regular duty but above all during a mission. I had to be their role model. I was fully aware that my platoon would reflect how I performed both in everyday and in difficult circumstances. They would turn out to be either a courageous unit or a miserable bunch of losers.

How was I to instil the fighting spirit in my men, the desire to be brave and crave for action? How was I to be a model to them if I myself couldn't justify that fight?

The glimmer of doubt which had been ignited in the steppes of Russia was still alight. What had once just been a spark had become brighter and stronger, despite me desperately attempting to extinguish, or at least dampen, it. I couldn't deny its growing presence. While I was preoccupied with work during the day, my nights were disrupted by awful dreams, by sinister and alarming plans and visions, from which I woke up drenched in sweat.

Whom could I speak to, in whom could I confide or consult with? Did my comrades think about the sense or nonsense of this war? Where would I find a friend with whom I could speak openly? Was it even right or appropriate for me to raise in others the doubts that I was experiencing? Would it not be considered subversion of the forces, sabotage, a betrayal of us all? If we, who were the elite of the German Wehrmacht, were starting to doubt the guidance of our Supreme Leader, didn't that amount to the most abominable and devious treason imaginable, and wouldn't it have come close to some kind of collective suicide? Was it really possible for us to jump off the train and abandon our people at a time when the outcome of the war was on a knife edge? Not only would we lose our lives but – and this was actually of far greater importance to us – we would lose our honour. Our comrades of the Wehrmacht, next to whom we had bravely fought through the years in so many of the war's battlegrounds, would certainly curse us. The German people, for the sake of whom we had gone to war, flags waving, would condemn us, while the enemy would surely feel nothing but contempt for us.

I desperately tried to push all these terrible thoughts away. Gradually I calmed down, or was it that I had simply resigned myself to my lot? I was determined to continue fighting in this war until the bitter end, and fulfil my mission as an upright and conscientious soldier. We had been burdened with this war, and it was our responsibility to deal with it. What mattered was only to win the war, and surely everything else would fall into place. While my faith in the Führer and in Greater Germany had been shaken to the core, I had nothing to put in its place, no convincing alternative I could have invested myself in. And while I myself deeply despised carrying out missions at all costs, without a care as to what they entailed, many of my comrades in our division didn't have such qualms. They were known to forge ahead blindly, commit and engage without any consideration whatsoever to the losses that might ensue.[2] Hell-bent on being awarded an honour, they doggedly pursued the Knight's Cross.

No, I refused to ask any of my men to commit to something to which I wouldn't willingly commit myself. I shuddered at the thought of giving anyone in my platoon the order to kill or to die, if I myself wasn't prepared to give up my life. That was my motto and I clung to it, and in the end doing so restored my emotional equilibrium.

In the meantime, our battalion had been called to report to Füssen in the Allgäu. I joined them as a brand-new second lieutenant. We were transferred to the northern part of Greece. Once I was back with my comrades at the front, I felt safe and at home again, and all the recent defeatist thoughts disappeared, or at least had been pushed to the far reaches of my mind. Here, at the front, the invigorating and rough spirit of the troops who had been toughened up by battle was still alive and well.

While the devastating retreat from the Caucasus had taken its toll on our battalion, and many an old comrade was missing, the spirit of the Brandenburgers had remained as strong as ever. It was unaffected by the badly battered esprit de corps which – inevitably extremely contagious – had otherwise poisoned units both away and at the front.

In fact, we had no time to either dwell on such morbid thoughts or engage in any deep discussions. War, with all its worries and challenges, preoccupied us all, without exception and to the utmost. Yet I felt quite sure that never again would I be as wholeheartedly committed to the cause as I had been. The feeling that we were fighting for the wrong idea, for something utterly utopian, became more concrete by the day, and it increasingly consumed and paralysed me. Rather than actively engaging and being proactive, I drifted along. The doubts that had arisen in the steppe at Kalmücken, fledgling at the time, had become bitter certainty. The war bore no justification. I suddenly realised this truth, and all its implications, and I was filled with profound sadness. Nobody noticed my inner despair. I continued my service to perfection and led my group successfully during the war against the Partisans. I was in good spirits dealing with my comrades, but deep down my heart was not in it.

I had been promoted to adjutant of the battalion. We were sent from Greece to Montenegro, where, in December 1943, fighting alongside my commander in a large-scale operation in which the entire regiment participated, I was seriouly wounded.[3] I was transported to a field hospital and then made my way to Munich, where I started my studies in medicine. I had evolved from a soldier at the front to a student at university. To others it might have appeared as if the war had abruptly come to an end for me and that peace had set in. But it wasn't like that. I was about to live through the bombings of the German cities, which were just as terrible as fighting the war.

At the beginning of my studies I still had to receive outpatient care at the hospital, but since I had recovered well enough not to be an inpatient, I didn't take up one of the private hospital rooms that were so badly required for the seriously wounded who were brought in. Instead I decided to rent private lodgings. My left arm was still in plaster – it had been fractured by a bullet – and I wasn't able to walk unaided, thus I hobbled along, supporting myself with a stick.

This didn't prevent me from immersing myself straightaway and with utmost zeal into my studies. I didn't want to hear anything about the war, nor see anything; I wanted to forget, rid myself of it all; I wanted to pretend it hadn't happened. I sought refuge in books and lecture notes, I didn't read a single newspaper and didn't listen to the radio. The intensive studies had become my drug, lifting me out from the tragic reality of everyday life and putting me into an unreal state of illusion and fantasy.

Where else should I have turned to find some support or footing? All my ideals had been shattered, all my hopes and dreams of a Greater Germany as a home for all Germans, and consequently of all us South Tyroleans as well, had been crushed. What was left was disappointment and resignation.

Though the fact that the war was lost had certainly occurred to me by that time, I still hadn't fully acknowledged it, and was still hoping for a miracle. This was in spite of incredibly heavy and almost daily bombardments which pounded the German Reich, turning it into rubble and ashes. The nights were alive with explosions and fires which signposted the way for the incoming flying fortresses.

How was one to focus on studies under such circumstances? While Munich was being hit by bombs day and night, the only means of remaining sane and studying was some kind of what I called auto-suggestion which I prescribed for myself: I refused to believe in reality and conjured up the fantasy of peace. I believed that if I stubbornly focused on something completely different, something abstract and something that was diametrically opposed to what was happening around me, then I could survive. I transported myself to an impermeable realm of autohypnosis, against which all external influences simply bounced off.

— THIRTEEN —

The Return

In February 1945 I was declared GVH and was dismissed from the hospital and ordered to report to our divisional headquarters in Brandenburg an der Havel.[1] There, since the Russians were preparing for their last assault on Berlin and were already on the banks of the Oder, I was assigned to join the instruction team that had been put together for the Volkssturm.[2] But I couldn't stand this place, and so, though not actually fit for war purposes, I volunteered to serve at the front in Italy where one of the Brandenburger units was operating.

With my marching orders in my pocket, I left Brandenburg the day after I had arrived and travelled to Bozen. I reported to General Feuerstein, who sent me off to Meran, where I was commanded to await further orders.[3] Well, no such orders ever arrived; instead, the Americans did.

A wide-meshed, oversized barbed-wire fence with another wreath of barbed wire on top encircled us. Only a single bolted gate led out to freedom. An armed guard stood in front of it. Looking straight ahead with his bored red eyes protruding from his black face, he kept rotating his lower jaw. Once in a while a white balloon popped out between his lips, grew larger and larger until it burst. If the guy didn't quite manage to blow the bubble, his lip would stick out at the corner of his mouth and in one swift movement the chewing-gum ball would disappear inside.

The fenced area, about the size of half a football pitch, was crammed with prisoners representing every branch and rank of the military. Some, like us Brandenburgers, were dressed in scruffy old clothes. There was no tree that could offer us any shade, no tent or any structure with some kind of roof under which one could have crawled for protection. Some men were crouching on the ground, leaning with their back against each other, searching in vain in their knapsack for something to eat. Others drew pointless shapes in the sand. Others put their heads between their pulled-up knees, dozing, and a few tried to pace up and down, like wild animals in their cage.

The true misery of our situation hit me hard. It had taken me a while to allow the reality to sink in and for me to grasp fully that we had lost the war

225

and were in the hands of the victors. Who knew how that would turn out for us – better or worse? To them we were nothing but numbers and objects, sheep whom they had gathered into a corral, and whose fortune depended on luck and on their new masters' benevolence.

During the years of the Blitzkrieg, I had often come across prison camps, and the hopelessness of the inmates, their fear and indeed terror in their eyes had always bothered me. At the time, I couldn't understand why they were so frightened, I felt that they had no reason – for them the war was over. They had survived it, nothing else could happen to them; all they needed was patience and to wait for their return home! Returning home – the thought struck me like a bolt of lightning. With it also came the idea of escaping.

I had been but one short hour behind this barbed wire and there I was, already thinking of escape. I had to get out of there, I wouldn't be able to survive this imprisonment. Just looking at the fence made me feel a physical pain. A good few in that camp had already been in captivity a fair amount of time and had clearly been affected by apathy, but I was determined not to allow this to happen to me. I felt the urge to do something, to act and get myself out of that situation. I had to get away from there, hide somewhere, go back to the mountains.

How could I have been so stupid and voluntarily given myself up to the Amis?[3] Whatever had made me believe the rumours that the South Tyroleans would immediately be liberated and that imprisonment would be nothing but a formality? The two days spent in captivity back in Meran had not been so terrible actually, thinking back – in fact they'd been quite tolerable. We had been put up in the officers' casino in the Alpini army barracks, our beds had been freshly made up, we ate at tables with tablecloths, played football and were in good spirits.

Then they had taken us to Bozen, allegedly to give us the release documents, but what had happened instead was that we were chucked into a camp and kept behind barbed wire, with nothing to do but watch prisoner transports depart and head off deep into the furthest parts of Italy. There we were, prisoners of war with no rights and no idea how long it would last.

And yet, I had to be grateful not to have to share the cruel fate of those many prisoners of war who wound up in Russian camps. After all, we were still in South Tyrol, our home. To disappear and go into hiding until things calmed down would surely be easy, I figured. But once we were down in Italy, escape would be much more difficult, perhaps even impossible. If we wanted to run away, this was the time to attempt it. We had to act swiftly. On that day no transport was due to leave, there was only one planned for the following day, or at least that's what we had picked up in passing. Thus, with only a few hours left, we had to make a move that same afternoon.

I discussed the situation with my friends and tried to convince them to join me.

'We have to get out of here,' I urged them. 'Who knows what's in store for us here and how long they will keep us? We can go underground in Meran or hide out on some Alp.'

'How would you manage that, Sepp?' they countered. 'It's impossible to get out of here! There might be a better opportunity, why not wait a while. They might let us go as soon as tomorrow and might not want to transport us down to Italy, that's what they promised us back in Meran.'

I was of a completely different opinion. Only one desire was on my mind: to get out of there as fast as possible and regain my freedom.

'If you don't want to, then I'll try it on my own,' I finally said, but they questioned me further. 'Do you have any idea of what you want to do? Do you have a plan?'

'I'm not quite sure,' I responded. 'I have to give it more thought. I'll definitely think of something.'

'Don't be foolish,' they advised. 'Don't put your life at risk, the war is over. You won't be able to hide forever, surely, you'll need your discharge papers as without those they'll catch you sooner than you think. Right now, we're in deep shit, and we'll stay in deep shit unless we get ourselves some appropriate documents.'

I was determined to leave, determined to be free at all costs, and none of their arguments convinced me otherwise. I started looking around much more carefully. Slowly I circled the barbed wire, inconspicuously but nonetheless meticulously searching for a weak spot. But the entire fence had been erected only recently, it had been embedded deeply into the ground and there didn't seem any possibility at all of slipping through. It would have taken several nights and an inordinate amount of effort to somehow cut a hole without anyone noticing. And even if one could have managed to squeeze through the fence, freedom was still a long way off. This huge prison cage had been constructed right in the middle of the courtyard of the army barracks. Once you'd managed to get past the fence, you still had to find your way out by passing through the gates of the barracks where two Amis were standing guard.

Not only that, but the place was literally swarming with armed American soldiers. At night, the entire area was lit by searchlights, the gate would be locked and additional guards would do the rounds circling the cage. I knew all of this only too well, as that was how we would have done it. It would have been sheer folly to attempt an escape under such circumstances, and it was bound to fail.

The only way it could happen was by resorting to some ploy. Wasn't that what we Brandenburgers were good at? Wasn't it precisely our art of deceiving the enemy, our talent for cunningly pulling off covert operations that had tricked and misled the enemy in the past? Hadn't we been taught to carry out brave and adventurous missions? How many times had we put our lives at risk to get through absolutely insane operations! Hadn't these toughened us up to such a degree that we were now good and ready to go ahead with this one last assignment? Weren't we trained to react within a few seconds – ready at all times to adapt swiftly to the situation? Didn't experience prove to us that relying on luck paid off in the long run, rather than on deliberating whether or not we were superior? If my escape was to be successful, it could only happen if I was bold and audacious to the extreme. I had made up my mind. I was going to risk it, and I wasn't going to wait for another moment. I hadn't a clue how or what had to be done, but I knew that something needed to happen.

As I slowly and nonchalantly approached the narrow and only door of the wire cage, the guard, still chewing his gum, unlocked the door to let in some prisoners who had just been offloaded from a truck.

The door was open – I could leave! I was dressed in civilian clothes, though old and dirty. Leaning on the stick which I still required due to the bullet wound in my left leg which hadn't quite healed, and hoping fervently that the bad English that I could just about remember would hold me in good stead, I quickened my pace and pushed against the incoming new prisoners. Roughly shoving one or two of them sideways, I squeezed through the door. 'I have to speak to the captain,' I shouted to the gum-chewing guard and, without waiting for an answer, I hobbled not to the gates of the barracks – that would have been too obvious – but towards the barracks that were just twenty metres away and on which hung a large sign with the word 'Headquarters' on it.

Before the baffled Ami could cotton on to what was happening – or perhaps the chewing gum had glued his jaw together, preventing him from calling out – I had reached the barracks and disappeared inside.

But instead of reaching freedom, I ended up in a hornet's nest. Amis were busily swarming in the long narrow crossway of the barracks, going in and out of offices. I didn't have time to think things over, no possibility of hiding somewhere. However, I also didn't want to draw any attention to myself. I had to pretend that I belonged, that I knew my way around there. Without hesitating, I turned into the left hallway, desperately hoping to find somewhere to hide and take a minute to catch my breath, perhaps consider my next move. My heart was pounding so loudly that I feared the Amis passing by might hear it. My knees were buckling underneath me and I had to lean on my stick. At long last I had reached the end of the corridor. But what then? Was I to just turn around? Surely that would be suspicious.

At the end of the corridor, I noticed a staircase on my right which led up to the next floor. I didn't pause or waver, just climbed up the steps. A scene similar to downstairs presented itself on the next floor: a long hallway flanked to the right and left by doors on which hung small signs. I couldn't linger and read them, as here too the Amis flitted from one office to the other. I decided to do likewise, took on a very officious air, hurried to the end of the hallway, hoping to find a toilet where I could remain for a short while to cool off. And indeed, it turned out that the last door in the corridor didn't have a label on it and, firmly pushing down the handle, I entered. But, oh dear, this wasn't a toilet but an office. Behind a large table standing near the window sat an American officer speaking on the phone, the American flag propped up in a corner. I couldn't see much more. I bowed, mumbled the English word 'sorry' and quickly shut the door again. As fast as I could without raising undue suspicion, I hastened down the hallway and descended the staircase. Luckily nobody accosted me and I reached the outside.

In the meantime, the door of our cage had been bolted shut once again and a different Ami stood in front of it, also chewing gum. Without even glancing in his direction and without so much as a fleeting look at my imprisoned comrades, who just stared at me in disbelief, I hobbled towards the exit gates. I smiled, mumbled 'hello' to the guards in English, tapped my forehead with my stick in a sign of greeting and was outside, on the street, free.

Walking slowly at first and then quickening my step in the direction of the city, I reflected upon my current situation. I was under no illusion that the freedom I had been able to gain so quickly hung by a thread. I was pretty helpless and indeed poor without the friends I had left behind. It didn't feel right to me to continue and make use of the help that their parents had so touchingly offered me before. Though they would surely have taken me in, I simply couldn't reasonably expect them to allow me to stay while their own sons were being held prisoner. I probably would also have endangered them if it had become public knowledge that they had sheltered a German soldier who had escaped imprisonment. I owned nothing except for the filthy clothing I was wearing, and I feared that the little money I still owned wouldn't go far. My parents at the time lived in Bad Ischl and I was certain that they were extremely worried about me. For several weeks I hadn't had an opportunity to even let them know that I was alive. I didn't have a choice, I simply had to find a way to Bad Ischl.

What I needed above all were some proper papers, an identity card or something similar. Without any sort of document, my freedom would certainly be short-lived. The first military or police patrol crossing my path would most definitely put a quick end to my journey. A pass issued by an American agency would have been ideal, but the issue was how I was going to avail myself of something like that.

Somewhere at some point I had been told that the only man who had any authority to deal with these matters in Bozen was a Captain Brown from the CIC. So, having found out where he was based, that's where I was heading. A long queue had formed in front of his office, with everyone having the same request as me.

Just as I was about to join the queue, mulling over how I could convince Captain Brown to issue me with an identity card, the man himself appeared in the hallway, pointed his finger to the clock which hung on the wall and said in a loud voice and broken German: '*Nix Ausweis, schon 5 Uhr, morgen wieder, 9 Uhr.*'[4]

The group of people, disappointed and grumbling, just meekly walked away, but I hobbled over to the Captain and told him in my faulty English: 'I need absolutely an Ausweis, I must go home.'

'Where are you from?' he asked me.

'From Sterzing, Captain Brown,' I answered, putting on my most innocent smile.

He told me, still in poor German, that I should go to Sterzing, seeing as there was nothing I could accomplish right here. As soon as he had fobbed me off, he disappeared. Well, although I hadn't actually succeeded, I had made some progress. If a police patrol stopped me on my way to Sterzing, I would be able to tell them, without lying, that Captain Brown from the CIC in Bozen had sent me to Sterzing without an identity card.

That got me going. My next goal was to reach Sterzing.

I found shelter for the night in a small inn, had a cheap supper, and wasn't pressed by anybody to divulge anything about myself. Early the following day I went to the station, enquiring whether there was any chance of getting on a train going to Sterzing. And indeed I managed to catch a train that would take me without any further incident not exactly as far as Sterzing, but at least as far as Franzenfeste. That was the final stop. Further north, the railway bridges had been destroyed by the bombings, so I had no choice but to continue on foot.

To avoid falling into the hands of the patrols of the US military police who were known to have put up checkpoints at city entries, at bridges or road crossings, I did my very best to avoid the main roads, and chose the field paths which ran along the Eisack. I marched for hours, and my belief that I would reach Sterzing safe and sound grew with every step. The reason was, of course, that I was once again on home soil and knew the area like the back of my hand. All roads were familiar to me; I recognised every turn and every corner, and I had no problem choosing the route which would avoid those spots where I suspected there would be US posts. There was absolutely no danger that I would inadvertently fall into the hands of the enemy, as I was well aware of all the potential tricky places. Towards evening I reached Sterzing, without encountering any difficulties whatsoever.[6]

I had returned to my hometown. It was astounding how much had happened since I had left exactly five years before. Then, my heart was filled with enthusiasm and excitement at leaving. I was so proud to have been given permission to enlist in the German Wehrmacht, to be allowed to fight with it for the goal of creating the Greater German Reich for a unified German people! Back then, I was embarrassed to walk in civilian clothes while others put on the uniform – the nation's dress of honour!

Five years had passed and I was returning home in tattered rags, an old floppy hat pressed over my forehead, which was intended to cover my face. Even though I knew practically every single person in this town, and every one of them would surely gladly have helped me, I preferred to remain unrecognised. Nobody should realise that this filthy and worn-down *Heimkehrer* was once the young, vigorous and proud officer so filled with self-confidence.[7] There is nothing more depressing in a man's life than to return home beaten and humiliated, realising that all the ideals for which he had fought and for which he had risked his life had crumbled into smithereens.

Avoiding the main road, I hurried down the narrow back lanes until I reached the Weisses Rössel inn,where the son of the innkeeper had been one of my best friends, and a Brandenburger like me.

Perhaps he had already returned from the war, I thought. Sadly, the news his mother gave me was that he had been reported missing in Yugoslavia. I knew, of course, what that meant. I stayed for a while, trying to give as much comfort and hope to the poor woman as I could. She invited me to stay with her until her son returned. He never did.

The following morning, I decided to tackle what I feared would be a really tricky visit to the town hall, but I simply had to try and get an identity card. I didn't get my hopes up, quite the opposite – perhaps my errand would even end up in me having to return to imprisonment – but I carried on.

After entering the impressive building, I mounted the steep staircase to get to the offices and felt quite a bit of trepidation. At the top, I leaned against the balustrade, trying to catch the sound of voices coming out of the room in front of me in order to determine whether English was spoken, but I couldn't hear anything. I entered with as much determination in my step as I could muster.

At first, all I could see were cupboards full of files, tables covered in documents and papers, and chairs on which more piles of files were stacked. Finally, my eyes fell upon a frail little old woman sitting behind a table and engrossed in the documents in front of her – there was something about her that was awfully familiar to me. She was in fact the factotum of our community, the honourable Fräulein Toni Stark. She had been, at least in my mind, connected with each and every one of our community member's fortune, as well as with the town's welfare, since time immemorial. Life without her was unimaginable, everyone was dependent on her support, plain and simple. Even the fascist masters had to resort to her help. She knew us all, and helped wherever she could. Without even knowing it, she was truly the *éminence grise* of the town hall.

Looking me up and down with her eyes peering over her glasses, she eventually seemed to recognise me in spite of my squalid appearance and changed looks, so different from how I'd once been. With outstretched arms and a friendly smile spreading across her wrinkled face, she approached me and launched into a warm welcome: 'Well, look who's here, if it isn't Peppele boy![8] How are you? What are you up to? Where have you just come from? How are Mum and Dad? Well, indeed, what is it that you're needing?' I loved hearing the familiar dialect.

'Ha, indeed, what I need is an identity card,' I didn't want to withhold my real purpose, and wanted to get it out of the way as soon as possible.

'No worries,' she replied in the same happy Tyrolean dialect. 'That won't take me long.' She was a decent woman.

Two hours later, I held a valid brand-new Italian identity card in my hands.

Everything was now completed and no further obstacles to my continued stay in Sterzing stood in my way. Thus, finding somewhere to stay, and even finding some work which would allow me to remain undercover until the Americans had lost interest in former German soldiers would no longer be a problem for me. I had every reason to believe that I was all settled and could start putting my life together again. I had safely weathered the stormy years of the war and had been able to avoid the humiliating fate of being a prisoner of war. Though physically diminished and morally destroyed, I was now in possession of an identity card and had reached my hometown safely; it was as if I had never left it, nor ever opted for Germany. I had achieved what millions of soldiers the world over, whether victorious or defeated, had dreamed of, and in truth, I should have been the happiest man alive. And yet the only thought I had and which kept me going was to leave town and embark on the long journey to Bad Ischl and join my parents. That's where my new home was, and the beloved hometown I knew no longer existed for me.

A feeling of guilt about my hometown had started creeping up inside me, which at first I wasn't conscious of. It seemed as if I could no longer face Sterzing with a clean heart and soul; after all, hadn't I abandoned it?

It was not an entirely defined and rational thought; it was vague and subconscious, suppressed by the sheer desire to find the ways and means to survive. Only much later would I truly realise its full implications, and why I was embarrassed to so much as look at the houses and roads, the arcades, the hills and the trees. All that should have been holy and precious to me I had voluntarily left behind, all for an idea.

I shouldered my rucksack and left town as soon as I could. Walking over the creaking wooden bridge that crosses the Eisack, I stepped over the train tracks along which I intended to march in the direction of the Brenner. One last time I ascended the steep path leading to my beloved seat under the cherry tree. That was the spot where I had decided to leave the homeland that had been so very dear to me. For one last time I wanted to drink in the image of the old town in which I had spent the happiest years of my life, and imprint it on my memory. Those old stones I myself had buried into the earth – it seemed an eternity ago – had shifted a little bit, and some of them had tumbled down the slope. I gathered them up and, placing them back where they belonged, fixed my seat. When I had sat there last, I had been a child. The cherry tree growing along the border of this field harboured all my dreams and knew all my desires; it was familiar with all the worries and all the troubles, all the joy and all the sadness I had confided in it. This was where I had sought refuge when I was downcast and when I was happy. This was where I had dreamed about love and heroic deeds.

The storm that had shocked the entire globe to its core appeared to have passed over this tiny piece of land. The wheels of extermination and fire had rolled over all of Europe and reduced it to dirt and rubble but here, in Sterzing, it hadn't left even the faintest trace. Everything, even the most remote corner of the town, had remained exactly as it had been before, as if nothing had happened, as if the world wasn't lying in ruins.

And yet, these past five years *had* left their mark, and this oasis of peace hadn't quite emerged unscathed. A stream of blood and tears had flown through it. Where are you now, oh friends of my youth? You have fallen. You are lying dead in the mountains of Norway, in the tundra of Finland and in the steppes of Russia; in the Caucasus, in the valleys of the Balkans and in the deserts of Africa. You are resting on foreign soil, nobody knows your grave, there is no cross, no stone marks the place where you have died. You will only live on in the memory of those of us who were fortunate to have escaped the hell of what turned out to be an insane war. All of us, young and old, had merely been blinded by the shining light of an ideal, and we hadn't been able to recognise that this very ideal, had it become reality, would have meant both the downfall of our homeland and also of our people.

We had fought for a freedom that we could never have even obtained. We had been prepared to sacrifice everything we possessed for Germany, including making the biggest sacrifice of all: our land and soil. Having renounced it, we were left with nothing.

What would become of South Tyrol? What would become of us? Would South Tyrol go to Italy permanently and would we once again have to become Italians? Had the German dream come to an end, and had we made all these sacrifices in return for nothing? Those were the questions that deeply troubled me.

I got up with a heavy heart, slung my rucksack over my shoulders and took leave from my hometown for a second time. Dressed in rags and with my spirit broken, I slunk quietly away.

The present required my full attention; I could not spend more time either lingering or reminiscing. My journey towards the Salzkammergut involved a tricky stretch and I had to figure out how I would manage it. What I needed to do was pass unnoticed across the border between Italy and the recently re-established Austria.

I wanted to get this behind me as soon as possible, since at that time the borders were still being occupied by American troops rather than by Italian custom officers who, of course, knew the area very well. The Americans were only positioned in those areas that could be reached by jeep. That was rather fortunate, as field and wood paths or steep mountain ways that couldn't be traversed by vehicle didn't worry me. Despite possessing valid travel documents, I didn't want to run the risk: that's why I only travelled along very secluded paths, but ones I knew from my youth like the inside of my trouser pocket. Unchallenged, I reached the Beim Wolf inn only a few kilometres away from the border. I was confident that the innkeeper would remember me, and it was from him that I wanted to receive more intelligence as to what the situation was near the border.

Before leaving the protection of the forest and approaching the house from behind, I rested for a while, carefully scanning my surroundings. I fully realised that already I was in the so-called *Sperrgebiet* that covered an area stretching up to five kilometres in the respective countries on either side of the frontier.[9] No civilian who didn't live in that area was allowed to enter. If I had fallen into the hands of the Amis, my escape would have ended right then and there.

But there was no sign of any American sentry or guard. Even when I checked the roads as best I could, I wasn't able to detect anything untoward: they were empty, nobody in sight, and no engine to be heard. I thus decided to go up the open path leading up to the inn. Swiftly but carefully, I approached.

Just as I was about to turn the corner of the house and head towards the entrance door, I spotted a jeep standing there. I instantly moved back, ducked and pressed myself behind a stack of tree logs. In the nick of time, as no sooner had I hidden myself than the door opened and out came American soldiers. I knew they were American because I heard them speak to each other in English. If they had found me behind the wood pile, I would have been done for. I wasn't able to run back into the forest, and I couldn't find a better hiding place right then and there, so all I could do was bluff my way through this tight spot. I quickly tossed my rucksack behind the stack of wood, grabbed the axe which was lying there and started splitting one of the logs with some powerful blows. When the jeep carrying four Amis with the white letters 'MP' written on their helmets slowly rolled past me, I briefly raised my hand to wave at them, then immediately bent back down and carried on with my work.

As soon as they had gone, I entered the house.

'Well, well, well, what on earth are you doing here?' the innkeeper asked, and then carried on in the familiar regional dialect: 'The cops have just come by, did they catch you?'

'I wouldn't be here if they had,' I responded in the same dialect, 'but in the meantime I chopped some wood for you!'

Sitting with a glass of red wine and some hard black bread, I learned from the innkeeper all I needed to know in order to continue on with my journey.

'You're of course familiar with the smuggling routes over the border,' he said. 'Well, don't take the lower one as they can look down onto it from the pass up above. Take the middle one and make your way to Kerschbaumer, my friend lives just behind the frontier line and he will definitely help you out.'

After resting for a bit, I carried on. It didn't take long for me to reach the woods, which provided me with some shelter, and I ascended the slope that took me halfway up the mountain, where a narrow, barely visible pathway ran in a straight line across the border. It wasn't an actual path, but rather a well-concealed trodden trail favoured by game. That was the route the smugglers took, and I cautiously moved along it. Far below me lay the Brenner Pass. Some lonely wagons and locomotives stood ranged on the rail tracks, not in use, as travel by train hadn't yet picked up since the bombs had destroyed the tracks on both sides of the pass. Instead, the roads were full of American trucks – long columns of them. If I came across paths that could have been spotted from down below, I simply either avoided them and took detours, or ducked and crawled along the ground.

Finally, the pass lay behind me, and I had thankfully reached Kerschbaumer, whose farm happened to be the first one on Austrian soil. As his house lay in a small valley away from the top of the pass and one could only get to it by taking a very badly paved road, there was no real danger I'd encounter an MP patrol. On top of that, the farm lay at the edge of the forest, allowing me to remain under cover until I reached the front door. I only stayed as long as it took for the farmer to provide me with as much information as I needed to continue onwards. I was running out of time. It was 7 o'clock in the evening already, and the entire area was a strictly closed-off no-entry zone for civilians. Everyone had to return to the valley and was only allowed to come up again the next morning to work the fields.

'Under no circumstances should you walk down the road,' the farmer warned me. 'The road leading down to Steinach am Brenner is extremely well policed, with constant patrols going back and forth. Best if you walk alongside the train tracks. The Amis can't get there on their jeeps so it's highly unlikely that you would bump into any of them.'

To provide me with some sort of cover, the farmer handed me a hay rake, and with that I was on my way, shouldering my rucksack and the rake, heading down to the train tracks, crossing some open fields, and filled with confidence and even joy that I had successfully managed to cross the border. The worst, at least in my mind, was over.

Perhaps it was precisely this euphoric state of mind which sort of lured me into letting my guard down, as I stupidly stumbled into an American army patrol. I had nearly reached the train tracks, blindly turned the last corner, when suddenly there in front of me stood two Amis. I was so shocked that I just stopped dead in my tracks. That was, of course, my first error, as nobody behaved this way unless they have a guilty conscience. There was no way of turning back. I had no choice but to heed their request and approach. Only then did I notice that they had caught two other guys as well. I immediately recognised them as fellow sufferers. Despite their civilian clothing, they were unmistakably German soldiers.

'Come on,' they yelled, 'you're an SS.'

'No,' I answered, 'I am a farmer.' I replied in the best English I could remember and waved my rake about, trying to convince them that I was just returning from the fields.

'Do you have an identity card?' one of them asked me.

'Sure.' I had luckily recalled that expression, and I drew from my pocket the identity card which I had received in Sterzing just that morning.

He glanced at it only briefly, handed it back to me and told me it wasn't the right card, claiming it was an old German card.

Well, I was actually relieved that he hadn't noticed that it was in fact an Italian card. I took it and pointed with my finger to the date, which was of course of that same day, but he refused to listen. They ordered us three poor sods to follow them down the road. The entire way I just loudly swore both in German and English, and decried the fate of us poor farmers who weren't even allowed to do their work.

Once we had reached the road, they ordered us to sit down and wait.

They mounted a jeep and drove in the direction of Steinach, while one soldier was tasked with watching us. I immediately started a conversation with him, hoping I would have more success with this fellow.

'What are you doing here?' I asked him, trying to intimate that this was a waste of his time.

'Sit down and wait for the captain,' he responded lazily.

I was certain that the Italian captain wouldn't be taken in by an Italian identity card and would very quickly see through these shenanigans. I could already picture myself back with my friends in the prisoner of war camp in Rimini.

I told him that I didn't have time to stay, since I was a farmer who was working on his land, and I pointed to the fields in the direction of the Kerschbaum farm, whose roof you could see from afar. Once again, I pulled out my identity card and tried to explain to him that as far as I was concerned, everything was in good order.

Nothing seemed to interest him, neither my card nor my chattering, but what did catch his attention was my wristwatch. It was a German Wehrmacht watch.

He thought it was an American watch and tried to grab it from my arm. I insisted it was a German watch and this fight went on for quite some time, with him insisting he was right and me insisting the opposite. He finally won, and simply removed and pocketed my watch.

I begged him to return it to me, telling him as if in confidence that it was memorabilia of my brother who had fallen in Africa. He didn't pay any attention at all, and with a wide grin fastened the watch on his wrist. He thought the case was over and done with, but he certainly hadn't reckoned with me.

Again, I beseeched him to return the watch to me and promised that I would bring him a much nicer one the next day, a better one, if only he returned this one to me. I gave him my word that I would return at precisely 7 o'clock in the morning, seeing as I didn't work far away and swore to him that I would keep my promise and bring him another watch, a Swiss one this time.

He finally agreed, said the familiar 'Okay', spat out his gum and made me promise that I would indeed return the next day with a Swiss watch and he would then give me back my watch. All the while he was giving me this large grin, baring his teeth.

In the same entrepreneurial spirit, I okayed the agreement as well, and for good measure made him promise that he would keep his word and be there the next morning. Not waiting for his response, I took my rake and rapidly marched away without giving him so much as a further look.

The minute I was out of his sight, I hit the shrubland and reached the train track after just a few minutes. I had lost my watch, but regained my freedom.

For the first part the train track leading from the Brenner to Innsbruck ran at a height of about fifty metres above the road, and could not actually be overlooked by it, except for in a few areas. A narrow footpath continuing along the embankment was patrolled by lineworkers but I didn't care, and followed the tracks at a fast pace. Time was of the essence, as I needed to reach Steinach before 2100 and leave the dangerous *Sperrgebiet* behind me. I had just passed a signalman's hut when I heard a sharp whistling sound. Turning around I saw an Ami, who sternly waved at me to come towards him. I had no choice but to obey. He had probably spotted me from his hidden position in the small cabin. In the meantime, he had been joined by a second Ami, as well as an elderly fellow who was obviously the lineworker as he was wearing one of those official blue caps.

The Ami asked me whether I spoke English, to which I responded that I did, a little bit. 'Okay,' he said, 'explain to your friend here that he should go home immediately and that he is only allowed to return tomorrow morning. As of 2100 hours we shoot any civilian in sight and without warning.'

Well, being able to fulfil his request without a problem, I did so happily. Explaining to the linesman what he had to do, I then waved a friendly 'bye' to the two Amis and continued on my way along the embankment until I could finally see, way down in the valley, the top of the church steeple of Steinach am Brenner.

I climbed up the embankment, thankful that until then the bushes had protected me well, then scanned the area and tried to figure out how to get down to the village. Although it had started getting dark, I no longer felt I was in danger. Walking just a few metres down the track I suddenly heard a bullet whizzing past and sending bits of gravel flying through the air, right in front of me. At that same moment the cruel and blinding headlights of a jeep standing far down on the road shone straight into my eyes and once again I heard the now familiar and dreaded word: 'Come on.'

What was I to do but accept this invitation, which, judging by the warning shot, was not to be declined. Had I jumped behind the embankment, my escape would only have raised the alarm and made my situation worse. So I stopped and waved my rake in the direction of the Amis, in what I thought was a friendly hello. Turned out that my gesture was misinterpreted, as no sooner had I stretched out my arm than a second bullet came whizzing past over my head with that familiar hissing sound that I hadn't heard for a long time. It was patently clear that the Amis had no interest whatsoever in negotiating with me at a distance.

Shouting to them that I was coming, and more sliding than running, I got down the steep slope.

Four Amis stood ready to welcome me. Immediately they started frisking me from head to toe, looking for weapons and, without any further ado, paying absolutely no attention to my blabbering, they shoved me into the jeep and sped off towards Steinach. En route, they searched my small rucksack but couldn't find anything apart from an old shirt, a pair of socks, some dry sausages, a bit of chocolate and a few packs of cigarettes.

Immediately upon arrival in Steinach, I was reported to the local commander. He was a small and chubby man who sat behind his desk with his shirtsleeves rolled up, chewing on a fat cigar.

Fortunately, it quickly became apparent that he spoke a perfect German, tainted even with a Viennese accent. He was obviously a Jew who had emigrated at the time. These circumstances were extremely fortuitous in my case, as it allowed me to come up with my excuses in German. In such a tricky situation my English simply wouldn't have sufficed, and I wouldn't have been able to lie in any convincing way. Surely, I thought, my Tyrolean dialect would also be an advantage, as insisting on my innocence in High German would likely have sounded much less credible.[10]

Without a word, he examined me for quite some time, searching my eyes with a curious look. All the while I stood demurely in the middle of the room – lit dimly by a bulb hanging from the ceiling – and leaned heavily with my right hand on the rake, clutching with my left the small rucksack. My pulse was racing like mad, but I did my best to keep my face looking as innocent as possible, mustering all the humility I could.

Finally, he asked me what I had been doing up there in the woods.

'I wasn't in the woods, I was on the embankment.'

'What were you up to on the embankment?'

'I wanted to return home.'

He wanted to know why I had chosen to go home via the embankment and hadn't used the road.

I then launched into a lengthy explanation, in heavy accented Tyrolean dialect, that I owned a tiny patch of land right near the small signalman's hut, which I had wanted to rake down to clear for next day's planting of lettuce and carrots. I then explained further, my accent exaggerated even more, that the wiring leading up to the railway tracks were blown, so I started fixing them so that if the train came by, all would be fine. I wasn't quite finished yet, I added, and would certainly need another two or three days to complete the job.

'Where is your home?' he wanted to know. Pointing my finger in a random direction, I told him where it was. But he wouldn't let it go, and continued questioning me as to why I hadn't used the road but chose the embankment instead.

I decided to offer him information that I knew would reflect the virtuous behaviour of a slightly obtuse but law-abiding farmer: how I had been late for work, didn't own a watch but was aware of the curfew, how the train tracks didn't have as many curves as the road so it was the shorter route to take in order to avoid being out at the forbidden time, and that I certainly didn't want to cause anybody any inconvenience.

It seemed to make sense to him as he then leaned towards me and, speaking very strictly, he said I could leave, but that he would give me a piece of advice for the future: 'If you find yourself running late once again, take the road and not the embankment. One could easily take you for a German who is on the run. There are many of them out and about, and many more in the mountains.'

Not dropping my charade, I feigned consternation and exclaimed: 'Oh dear me, Herr Offizier, let this not happen to me. I will never again be late and will forever more take the road.' I decided that it would be wise not to be too presumptuous and simply leave, so timidly I asked: 'Might I now be permitted to go home, sir, I mean, seeing as it's already so dark outside, or do I have to spend the night here?'

He obviously didn't want that and gave me permission to leave, but told me to hurry and to take the direct route home.

Winking at the soldier who stood guard at the door, he mumbled something incomprehensible. I took my rucksack, bowed politely and got myself outside as fast as it seemed appropriate.

Oh, the blissful fresh air of freedom! I breathed in deeply and quietly cherished the moment, though my knees were still trembling. I didn't actually know where to go, but the only thing that mattered just then was to move away quickly, disappear and find somewhere to hide.

The streets were dark and empty with only an occassional ray of light penetrating through closed curtains. I had to be quick in finding somewhere to spend the night, as I had to avoid at all costs being picked up by a patrol for the second time. I passed a house where I could hear children's voices through a door that stood ajar. I stopped, not quite knowing how to proceed. Should I risk going inside and ask to stay the night? Despite the darkness, I could make out what was written on the plaque: 'Primary School'. I was in luck: the school had been turned into a home for children who had been evacuated here from Berlin.[11]

The head of the home, a woman, seemed extremely sympathetic and, fully understanding my situation, permitted me to stay the night. She even handed me a bag of hay and two blankets. Dead tired, I crawled into a corner and fell asleep instantly.

I rose with the sun and was on my way. Leaving the still-sleeping village behind me, I went up the mountain. I had to climb fast and gain height so that I could escape the radius in which the jeeps were cruising. I knocked on the door of a farmer, begging for some milk and bread, but above all I wanted to get information about which routes I should take to avoid any likely checkpoints.

He told me that there were military positions at every entry and exit point of every village along the main road leading down to the valley, and that every pedestrian was being checked thoroughly. Without a specific document, nobody could either enter or leave a village. Thus it was advisable to remain up here in the mountains and avoid the villages in the valley. I was also told that the train line from Steinach to Innsbruck was already operational, and every day a team of labourers was brought up from Innsbruck tasked with fixing the tracks up to the Brenner. That particular train returned with its labourers to Innsbruck at 4 p.m.

Marching towards Steinach over fields and meadows with my rake over my shoulder, my thoughts continually drifted to that train filled with labourers. Wouldn't it be wonderful to be able to board that train and drive to Innsbruck, I thought? It would be so much more comfortable and above all, so much quicker. It was no doubt much safer to be on foot. My farmer disguise had worked well until this point, why give it up now and become a labourer? How would I get onto the train? And even if I got on board, how would I be able to leave the station in Innsbruck? Surely there would be checkpoints there that I would have to manage and pass through?

I mulled everything over, considered both the advantages and disadvantages before finally deciding that it would be worth at least giving it a try. The idea of no longer having to walk was simply too tempting. Having made this decision, I had plenty of time. The train was only due to leave at 4 p.m. I meandered along and started chatting with just about every farmer I came across, man or woman, and asked them whether they knew of any Americans being nearby. Everyone was only too happy to help me out. Without having to ask, they immediately recognised me for the *Heimkehrer* I was. They were all friendly and readily offered support. I was invited for meals and offered accommodation. At practically every farmyard, families were expecting the return of a son, brother or husband, and I somehow came to represent for them the fate of their own loved ones.

It was already 3 p.m. when I approached Steinach am Brenner, and having had no problem avoiding the American checkpoint at the entry to the village, I reached the train station. I quickly got rid of my rake, settled down in the shade of a railway wagon and waited for the labourers to return. When they did, I slipped in among the throng and boarded the train. The few wagons were quickly fully occupied. Sitting tightly crammed together, I was nevertheless extremely relieved that everything had gone so smoothly, without even a single American soldier in sight; in fact, there wasn't even a ticket inspector to be seen. So, my decision to try the train had obviously proved the right one. Once in Innsbruck I would, or so I assumed, blend in with the labourers and leave the station together with them. I chatted with them, impatiently waiting for the train to depart, but mindful not to let anything on.

Suddenly the door of the compartment was pushed open and an American soldier appeared. The white letters MP gleamed on his steel helmet, with the chinstraps hanging down each side of his face. Open-mouthed, I just stared at him. He glanced around, finally resting his eyes on me. I quickly found out why of all of us it was me he focused on. The minute the Ami had appeared, all the labourers had pulled out of their pocket a red card, which they lifted high up in front of them. It was only me who just sat there with hands folded across my rucksack. His eyes rested heavily on me. I pulled my mouth into the smile of an imbecile and, trying to look sheepish, simply shrugged my shoulders.

'Come out and wait,' he snarled at me, and when I intensified my grin he yelled at me again. I winced, grabbed my rucksack, pushed past the labourers and got myself out of the compartment and off the train. In the meantime, he checked the next compartment. The minute I was outside, I knew that there was no way I was going to just obey and wait there, but instead, I was intent on getting away as fast and as far as possible. It took me no time to run the few steps towards the station building. Without looking back once, I disappeared out of sight and started climbing the slope. From a safe distance, though now thoroughly disappointed, I watched the puffing and steaming train slowly leaving the station.

I walked north. I had some good friends who lived in Matrei. A family from Sterzing had moved there after exercising their right to opt for Germany. I was hoping to be able to spend the night with them.

It was already late in the afternoon when I reached Matrei, which had suffered badly under the bomb attacks that had targeted the Brenner railway. Death and destruction had left deep marks on the city, and also on the Sterzing family whom I had wanted to look up. After a lot of searching, I finally found the youngest son, Karl. It turned out that his family had been found under the ruins of the house – they were all dead.

We had lots to talk about, but the only really enjoyable part of our chat related to our childhood memories. When I got to tell him about the situation I was in, and about what had happened to me with the labourers and the train, he had an idea.

'Maybe you can still catch the train,' he suggested, and told me about a bakery that received its daily bread supply from Innsbruck, as the entire city had practically been bombed to pieces. The bakery seemed to have permission to travel, and could thus pass the roadblocks undisturbed. Karl knew the driver and believed that he would most certainly take me. Together we set off to see whether I could still catch this ride.

Not much later, there I was sitting in the back of an open delivery van, waving goodbye to my friend. I sat among the empty boxes, metal containers and car tyres, and tried to curl up as much as possible, with only my head above the side planks.

Driving towards the town entrance, we approached the American checkpoints and the driver had to stop. It was only going to be a short stop. The guard knew the vehicle and waved it on. As we passed him, he spotted me.

'Stop!' he shouted. He wanted to see my permission slip that would say I was allowed to leave the village. He then enquired why I didn't have one. I answered that the captain didn't have time to issue one. I then explained to the Ami that the captain knew me well, and since he was well aware that I belonged to the bakery he also knew that I would return the following morning, and that therefore I didn't really require a permission slip.

The driver of the truck joined in, and, tapping on his wristwatch, he pressured everyone to hurry up and get a move on. The officer was unconvinced, but because he felt that the decision to let me go without that damned piece of paper went beyond his remit, he walked over to the guardhouse on the other side of the road to make a phone call to the captain. I was standing there, right next to him, on tenterhooks, watching him rotate the hand crank of the field telephone.

He was working continually to get the generator going, but finally gave up, swearing and hitting the machine with his fist. He had obviously not managed to get a connection. I certainly blessed the American technology, wondering to myself how they had won the war if they couldn't even get a simple field telephone to work.

Speaking in English, I offered to run to the captain, get my permission slip and return very shortly. The lorry would wait in the meantime. Before the angry Ami could react, I ran back to the village and returned to my friend, totally out of breath.

The following day was Fronleichnam, the Feast of Corpus Christi, and waking on that Friday morning, I marvelled at the first rays of sun reflecting off the snow of the mountain peaks. My friend Karl, whose place I had spent the night in, wanted to accompany me halfway, as he owned a permission slip that allowed him a degree of freedom to move around. This, however, was limited to a radius of one and a half kilometres. Had he wanted to move beyond that circle, he would have required a special document.

We thought that the left side of the valley, where the road ran, was too risky. So we decided to head to the right-hand side and try our luck there. We crossed the torrential river Sill and ascended the hill, while the bottom of the valley still lay in shadows. Before the sun appeared from behind the mountains, shining down onto the valley, we had reached a good height, allowing us to continue our march north without having to worry ourselves too much. We heard the majestic and sonorous tolling of the big church bell rising up from the valley, and eventually more bells, both large and small, chimed in. The sound was so calming and so festive that it eased my mind and allowed me to forget the deafening noise of battle. Under different circumstances this march of ours would have been a delightful spring excursion, but at the time, we hardly paid any attention to the beautiful nature which had just awoken to new life. The closer we got to Innsbruck, the more cautious our footsteps became. We had learned in the meantime that Igls was just crawling with Americans. No surprise there, as Igls was the most beautiful area of Innsbruck, full of gorgeous villas. The occupying French troops had also arrived there, and they were known to have enforced very strict checkpoints. Yet if I wanted to get to Innsbruck, there was no way of avoiding Igls.

When Igls was within sight, we abandoned the footpath and mounted a small hill from which we could more easily see the lie of the land. Only a few hundred metres lay between us and the first houses, but the control checkpoint was right there, and we could tell that it was guarded by the French. Could we just risk it, go down there, and if the soldiers held us up we would simply think of some excuse and hope we'd be believed? Or should we look for an alternative route, one which would be less dangerous? Weighing up these options, we realised that an alternative route would necessitate considerable detours, and other entries to the town were surely being guarded as well. Also, it wouldn't have been advisable, we thought, to wander around in an open terrain as it could well be that the French weren't quite as laid back as the Americans and didn't mind making their patrols on foot. That certainly would only increase the potential danger, we concluded.

The bells of Igls were ringing persistently and my friend had to return home. He wouldn't have been able to help me much further anyway, and would only have put himself at risk for nothing. I had to continue by myself and in any event, being on my own made me feel somehow more secure and wouldn't draw so much attention to myself. Then, suddenly, I was wondering whether it was absolutely necessary for me to walk through Igls – why couldn't I remain up on the mountains and circumvent the city?

At that moment Karl interrupted my thoughts, pointing to the Fronleichnam procession. At first, all we could see was a large cross hovering above the fields, as if floating in the air all on its own; when the plateau which had initially concealed the procession became flatter, the altar boys who were carrying the crucifix became visible. Their gleaming white gowns with red collars stood out, and behind them traipsed a throng of schoolchildren. Eventually I could see the whole procession in its full glory, complete with flags and images of saints and virgins. They even carried with them a canopy under which the priest, dressed in his full regalia, was carrying the Eucharist. They, in turn, were followed by a band we had already heard from afar and after them, eventually, came the women and men, their hands folded in prayer. The procession went up a hill and on the summit they formed a semi-circle around the canopy. The priest stepped into the middle and, holding the Eucharist, recited the prayers in a loud voice. The soft murmuring of the praying congregation grew louder, joined by a mixed choir singing in solemn voices. They then all knelt, with the priest blessing the land around him with his monstrance. The band started playing again and the procession reformed to return to the church.

My moment had arrived. I pressed Karl's hand, said goodbye and raced towards the procession, where I mixed in with the congregants, tucking my hat under my arm and folding my hands over my chest in prayer. I was careful to stay right in the middle of the men, who were now no longer walking in an orderly fashion but rather in loose formation. I felt quite certain that I was the only one who really offered up his prayers, speaking clearly, loudly and with fervour. That's how I got past the French checkpoint and finally arrived in Igls. The minute the procession had reached the church and dispersed, I was well on my way to Innsbruck.

I found myself within the restricted zone of the city and was no longer in any danger of being picked up. Without a care in the world, I got onto the Mittelgebirgsbahn leading from Igls to Innsbruck and since I have always preferred to drive rather than walk, I continued by tram, travelling all the way in the direction of Hall.

It was midday by then, the sun was hot and there were only a few people out and about. I was relieved that everything had gone so smoothly, and truly enjoyed my tram ride through the city. I very much hoped that the occupying troops were taking that day as a holiday as well and, if luck was on my side, had reduced their patrols. I simply had to make full use of the day and intended to put a fair distance behind me. By the same token, I didn't want to test my good fortune, and thus eventually I got off the tram and searched for the more remote footpaths. Leaving Innsbruck was not a problem, and shortly thereafter I found myself on a hiking trail through the forest – thereby also able to circumvent Hall – and I had no further difficulties.

I was getting tired but carried on regardless. Every step was bringing me closer to my destination, and there was still a long way ahead of me before I was going to reach Bad Ischl.

Darkness started setting in when I reached Vomp, a village situated on a slightly elevated plateau in Tyrol. I knocked at the first farm and asked to stay the night. They couldn't have been friendlier, and all they wanted in return was for me to tell them my story, which I did that evening over hot potatoes, cold milk and hard bread. They wanted to know everything, where I came from, where I was headed, where had I fought during the war, and which unit I had belonged to. As for them, they were waiting for their son to return, not having heard from him for months. At the end, the master of the house offered me farm work in return for remaining there. He would, he assured me, get me the necessary residency documents and work permit from the mayor, and I wouldn't have to worry about anything. He continued planning, assuring me that I could review things come autumn. I was much too tired to decide on the spot, and all I wanted to do was sleep. I assured him I would give him a response the next morning.

After sleeping well, I contemplated the farmer's proposal. Of course, I wouldn't cut short my return home right there and then, but an idea popped into my head which I immediately turned to action. It was incredibly attractive to get a residency permit, as once I was in possession of such a document, many of my problems would instantly be solved. I would have an identity card in my hands that would allow me a certain amount of freedom to move around. It just didn't seem quite fair to me to deceive the farmer, and I thus decided to approach the mayor myself.

I was the first to be admitted to his office.

'I am a student from Innsbruck,' I explained to him, 'and farmer X – ' I don't recall his name – 'has given me work in the fields. I will stay here till autumn, until university resumes, then I will return to my studies. The farmer has sent me here to apply for a work permit, so I can start work immediately.'

It only took a few minutes, and then I owned a valid permit. It allowed me freedom of movement within a radius of one and a half kilometres. Not much could happen to me any more, I calculated, as this distance allowed me to continue on the way home. I quickly returned to my host the farmer, packed my rucksack, borrowed an old rake from him and set off.

Although I had full confidence in my silly permit, I only really wanted to make use of it in the direst of circumstances. I hesitated to put its usefulness to the test and decided instead to remain extremely careful for the time being.

There was still a major problem I had to overcome. To reach Bad Ischl, I had to cross the Inn. But rumour had it that all the bridges were being occupied, and every passer-by was thoroughly checked by the French. To get to the right side of the river I therefore didn't dare use the bridge near Schwaz, but decided to walk along the left riverbank. I was hoping to find a spot further along which was less risky. Maybe, I hoped, there were some Amis down there and they knew less than the French and, being ignorant of where Vomp actually lay, weren't so fussy about the documents handed to them.

I merrily marched alongside and down the river. I certainly wasn't the only hiker in those troubled times. It was quite busy, in fact. It wasn't difficult for me to spot among the men, mostly dressed in rags, returning soldiers who were all heading south. Our encounters were mostly restricted to a simple greeting. With some, a brief conversation would ensue, and experiences and advice were exchanged. Quite often I would get some valuable tips regarding certain guard posts or patrols that were best avoided. One of these men informed me that a bridge across the Inn was under construction further down the river. Nothing but the pillars were standing, held together by a rickety scaffolding. It should, I gathered, be quite possible to climb it with a bit of skill and luck and then swing over onto the other side. Before parting from my comrade, I asked what use he intended for the hammer and long nails which he was carrying.

'When I hear a jeep approaching,' he explained to me, smiling slyly, 'I just busy myself next to a tree or fence and hammer a nail in. It has always worked wonders. Cheerio, and good luck!' We parted ways.

It didn't take long to reach the construction site of the bridge. Concrete piles were rising high into the sky and the bridge piers were connected to each other by nothing but a flimsy scaffolding made up of a few planks and bars. Leaving the road, I climbed down the embankment, hid in some bushes and studied the construction in front of me. If the cross-struts held, I figured, and if the nails securing them weren't rusted, and if the planks connecting the piers were sufficiently well fastened and could take my weight, I should be able to climb up and crawl across. I knew that it had to happen quickly, as once up there, I would be clearly visible and had nowhere to hide. What kind of excuse was I to come up with if I was discovered? I certainly couldn't make anyone believe that I was up there picking mushrooms or sunbathing. It was definitely a risk, but one I had to take.

I picked up my rucksack, listened out to hear whether anything was coming down the road, and then began to scale the first pillar. The cross-struts did hold and I had soon reached the top. Flat on my stomach, I very carefully crawled forwards on the wobbly planks. Way beneath me the Inn flowed, but I didn't dare look down. The further along I crawled, the more the plank bent dangerously. Sweat was pouring down my forehead and completely misted up my glasses. I barely dared move, and yet I had to get across; there was no going back. I didn't lift my head. My arms started aching and my hands were full of splinters. Just don't look down, I told myself, hoping that the board wouldn't break.

Bridges seemed to be my destiny. For five years they had literally been my life. How many bridges had we captured during that long war, how many had we destroyed? There had been wooden bridges, rail bridges, concrete bridges, long and short bridges, nothing but damned bridges. And there, on that day in June, I crawled over my last bridge, which wasn't even a proper bridge, and only consisted of a narrow, wobbly plank of wood. Suddenly I had gone back in time, and memories of the battlegrounds came whooshing into my head, with all its cacophony of noises ringing in my ear: the rattling of the MGs and MPis, the explosions of hand grenades, the yelling of the commanders and the cries for help from the wounded. Just don't think about it, I said to myself. Keep going! I had to get this bridge behind me, I wouldn't allow myself to give up now, facing the last bridge. Only once I was on the other side would my path home be free, only then would the war be over for me, and all these damned bridges could go to hell. At long last I arrived at the other side and quickly slid down the pillar, throwing myself, exhausted, into the grass.

After resting a short while, I marched downwards along the right-hand side of the river and reached Wörgel without any incident. I set up for the night in a shack near the railway station. It was already quite dark when another *Heimkehrer* sat down beside me. It transpired during our chat that he was headed in the same direction as myself, and we decided to join forces for the rest of our journey.

We were fast asleep when suddenly we were woken up by the sound of a train. We leaped up immediately to see what this unexpected rattling could signify, and much to our surprise saw an electric locomotive engine moving some wagons to a different track and leaving them standing there. The train driver then left his cab and headed towards the station building.

Curious as to what this was all about, we asked the driver where he came from and where he was scheduled to go to. He told us that he had brought the carriages which he had just left on the tracks from Bischofshofen and was headed straight back there.

'Goodness, Bischofshofen! That's precisely the direction we want to go!' we exclaimed and, without wasting another second, asked him if he would allow us two *Heimkehrers* to get on the train.

'You are out of your minds,' he replied. 'I am returning on my own, without any carriages, and I am not permitted to allow you into the locomotive cab, nor would I have room for you. It is forbidden for any passengers to travel in the cab.'

Nothing helped change his mind, neither our arguments, nor our pleading with him or cursing his stubbornness. But we didn't give up. The prospect of being able to put behind us such a long stretch during the night and by train, even if it was in the cab, was simply too wonderful to give up on so quickly. We thus tried to bribe him. We offered him a bar of chocolate, a tin of pork, cigarettes and, would you believe it, we actually got somewhere with him.

'I've never set eyes on you, and I haven't seen anything,' he finally said, before adding: 'I'm leaving in five minutes.'

That's all we needed to hear. Off we ran, back to our shed to fetch our rucksacks. We handed the promised delicacies over to the train driver and climbed up onto the locomotive. But we weren't allowed to get into the driver's compartment, we had to remain outside, in the open air. We lay down flat on our stomachs behind the cabin, fastened our belts as best we could around the many protruding pins around us, and before long the train departed into the darkness.

Our hearts leaped with joy at every kilometre we put behind us and never for one moment did we care about our discomfort; pressing our heads against the cabin to have some minimal protection from the blasts of wind, we were practically glued to the outisde of the driver's cab, but it was certainly preferable to walking. Without stopping, we rattled through the night. We passed one railway station sign after another, with each of the towns behind them still fast asleep and covered in darkness. Hour after hour ticked by and, what with the airstream being so cold, we started to freeze terribly in our positions. On top of that it started to rain, so we just huddled together, trying to protect each other against both wind and rain. But we were happy, happy to be travelling home.

At long last the engine slowed down. Far away we could see the very well-lit railway station of Bischofshofen. The locomotive gradually slowed down even more and stopped completely before it was within the range of the station lights. We jumped off quickly and took cover behind the carriages that stood in long lines on the tracks. Rid of its passengers, the locomotive continued into the station building. Protected by the height of the carriages, we crept forwards. Nobody was to find us out, least of all the military police standing on the platform, closely observing the incoming locomotive. We had to leave the railway station while it was still dark, otherwise our journey homewards would end in a prison camp. Crouching low, we scampered from one carriage to the next until we were finally out of danger, away from the lights. Sitting down on a carriage step, we discussed our next move.

Suddenly, we saw a train leaving the station and coming towards us. It had three carriages, heading in the exact direction we wanted to go in.

'Gosh, we must catch that train!' I shouted to my companion and ran as fast as I could, over tracks and between carriages, towards the moving train. I stumbled, fell, picked myself up, lost my rucksack – what did I care, I ran as perhaps I'd never run before. My comrade followed hot on my heels; the train started accelerating, I only had a few more metres to go, a last sprint and I would make it. I managed to get hold of the handle on the last carriage, I grasped it and heaved myself up with the last bit of energy I had left.

'Quick, give me your hand!' I shouted to my companion, stretching my arm out to him. But the train drove ever faster, the distance between us increasing.

My fellow escapee was left standing there, waving to me until I lost sight of him in the darkness.

Totally exhausted, I collapsed on the footboard. I had to catch my breath. Sweat was pouring from my forehead and my heart was beating like mad. The station lay far behind and the train continued to pick up speed. As soon as I had recovered just a bit, I pulled myself up and tried to open the carriage door to get inside.

There I was, inside a carriage, it was hard to believe! It was dark, not a single compartment was lit, and only one bulb hung from the ceiling, giving a weak and shaky light. I opened the door to the first compartment and saw that it was occupied. On both benches were outstretched silhouettes. Closing the door, I went to the next compartment. Here as well, two sleeping guys. Well, it sure didn't look like the train was fully occupied, seeing as all of these guys found space to lie – perhaps I could at least find a place for myself to sit and rest my weary bones. I was just about to open the door of the third compartment when the ticket inspector appeared and stared at me, shocked, as if he had seen a ghost.

'How on earth did you get onto the train?' he whispered to me, once he had recovered from his fright. 'If the Amis catch you, you'll be done for! The train is only meant for American officers, no civilians are permitted.'

It was my turn to freeze in terror. I realised that those sleeping characters in the compartments were American officers on their way to Salzburg! And what had I done? I had run for my life, just to end up in the hands of the Amis!

'Sit yourself down on the footboard outside and just as soon as the train slows down, jump.' That was the ticket inspector's advice.

I did as I was told. How low I had sunk. What had become of the German officer, where had his pride gone, his honour? He had turned into a wretched tramp, a fare dodger who was huddled on the footboard of a train's last carriage, hoping that nobody would catch him. A miserable vagabond who clutched with his frozen and stiff fingers to the planks of the step. And those who had won the war? They were comfortably spread out, sleeping in their warm compartments. *Sic transit gloria mundi!* I was nearly sick just thinking about it. Suddenly, my whole situation just seemed so demeaning. Wouldn't it have been more honourable for me to have given myself up after the war, capitulate like the rest of them, to submit myself, for better or for worse, to the mercy of the victors? Had my friends, who had remained in captivity, not acted with more honour than me, who instead fled? At least they had been able to retain their military honour in spite of suffering deprivation and humiliation.

Yes, I would give myself up to the Amis, report as a German officer, beaten, defeated, but with a clear conscience and with his honour intact. I would surrender and hand myself in. Whatever came my way, I would accept and endure it. But my honour would remain unblemished, they would never ever be able to tarnish it, not if I kept it pure.

The train rumbled through the night. Gradually the day was dawning. I had a decision to make. Should I really give up now, so close to my goal? Hadn't luck been on my side until now, wasn't it true that my good fortune had brought me almost to the doorstep of my home? Would it actually abandon me at this moment? Wasn't it my duty to carry on to the end of my path, no matter what it looked like? My parents were anxiously waiting for me at home, and wasn't I meant to do everything I could to get home and embrace them? So what if some honourable feelings of mine were stung. Wasn't it too late, what with everything having been destroyed and the world lying in ruins? All the ideals for which we had fought and for which we had suffered and on which we had built all our hopes, all of that had been annihilated. I had always held freedom to be the highest form of human experience, and firmly believed that it was worthy of all imaginable effort to both avail oneself of it and receive it. Should I be expected to give it up voluntarily?

The train had slowed down. We were approaching a bridge that had been destroyed by the bombing and had only been fixed temporarily. There were barracks around us, and I noticed some construction workers who had obviously just woken up and were still rubbing the sleep out of their eyes. The train very slowly crossed the bridge. The workers stared at me with open-mouthed surprise. The minute the train had fully crossed the bridge, I jumped off and hid in the bushes.

I didn't have far to walk to get home. If I followed the Admont valley, I figured, I would be able to mount the Postalm at some point, where I would surely find a good path. Then, on the other side of the mountain range, I would find the Wolfgangsee and Bad Ischl. I was incredibly tired and hungry. My sparse rations were lost in my discarded rucksack. But being so close to my destination filled me with energy.

I entered the valley and asked for some refreshments from a farmer on the way. I was immediately recognised as a *Heimkehrer*, and properly hosted. A glass of milk and a piece of bread always seemed to become available for me. When I explained my plan to the farmer, that I wanted to cross the Postalm and then reach Ischl, he thoughtfully shook his head, saying: 'You have to watch yourself like hell. They are still fighting back there in the valley. There are still some SS units scattered there and the Amis want to smoke them out. They're still shooting.'

That was all I needed to know. I ate my bread and drank my milk, then the farmer allowed me to rest a while in his haystack. I fell asleep immediately. Towards lunchtime I woke up. The farmer's wife brought me some fried eggs and the farmer explained how I could find my way to the Postalm.

He told me how to find a path in the middle of the valley that would take me over a wooden bridge, after which I was supposed to take another path up through the forest. It was apparently a very steep path and no jeep could manage it. If I got that far I was out of danger and could reach Postalm without further worry.

I thanked him for his hospitality and set off. It was a lovely early summer's day, the sky had turned blue again, and after the rain of the previous night, the air smelled fragrant and had a crisp freshness to it. The birds were cheerfully tweeting away, the sun was warm, I had had a good rest, my stomach was full, and the world looked much more beautiful. I made good progress.

In my mind I had already reached home and was imagining what my mother would say once she saw me standing in front of her. Would she recognise me? What with my tattered rags, the old crumpled hat on my head and my haggard and bearded face, I looked so different from when I had last seen her, dressed in my handsome uniform, with the medal on my breast and the portepee hanging down at my side. I could already envision how she would embrace me with tears rolling down her cheeks. I would be home the next day, I figured, and on that day the war would have come to an end for me. I made plans for my future, thought about how life would continue, how it would shape up to live in peace, without war, without fear, without orders or the damned obligations that had made up my life up to that day. Would I find my bearings quickly?

I was deep in thought as I marched to the valley. And there they were again. A military police jeep stopped right alongside me. Behind it stood several vehicles with Amis, complete with full war paint on their faces. I hadn't heard them approaching and was furious with myself. Why hadn't I been more careful, I thought, surely I could have noticed them earlier and could have hidden? But it was obviously too late and the only option I had, I concluded, was to rely on my nerve. The interrogation started.

'Who are you, where do you live, what are you doing here, do you have an identity card?' the officer sitting in the first jeep asked me.

Looking completely innocent, I fumbled in the pockets of my trousers and jacket and eventually pulled out the piece of paper the mayor of Vomp had issued.

Again, I played the imbecile: 'Here it is.' I smiled stupidly, handing him the piece of paper.

He just glanced at it and asked where Vomp actually was.

'Over there,' I answered and pointed to a church steeple peeking above a hill far away. 'And that's where I'm headed to, to work the field over there. Over there – don't you see the farmland over there behind the trees?' I feigned stupidity.

He threw me another quizzical look, returned the card to me and waved me away with an okay.

The convoy set off and disappeared in a cloud of dust. I breathed deeply a few times, then I also continued onwards.

Soon I had reached the bridge the farmer had described. I found the steep path leading up the woods and avoided the road, as I was aware how easily accessible it was to jeeps. I ascended the mountain, and only once I had reached the summit and was able to look down onto the other side of the valley, recognising the blue Wolfgangsee, only then did I sit down on the grass.

The world lay peacefully before me. Not a sound, no noise of engines penetrated up to where I rested. How beautiful the world was, how marvellous it felt to be free! Soon my journey would come to an end, I mused, soon I would embrace my loved ones and finally be able to embark on a new life in peace, and at long last I would be allowed to sleep, to sleep …

The sun had already set and it got dark quite quickly. I crawled up to a haystack and was soon asleep.

The following day, at lunchtime, I was home.

Afterword

Thinking back to my youth and reflecting on the emotions, the dangers, worries and the deaths of so many of my friends and comrades, we are inevitably confronted with questions that need to be answered. Was what we had done in those years right, were the orders we had followed correct, when we needed to opt for either Germany or Italy? Were the blood sacrifices offered by the South Tyrolean people justified? Or should we have gone down a different path, decided differently, acted differently?

When I look back on how history evolved, I would say this: what we did at the time was right. While before 1938 Italy had pushed for our total denationalisation and assimilation, the fact remains that after 1943 the possibilities for our people to be recognised *as* a people could finally at least be considered; to some degree this possibility presented itself after 1945 as well; in fact, developments after 1945 might indeed have resulted from what we had achieved in 1943.

Let's cast our minds back to the years that preceded the decision. After the First World War, Tyrol was split apart, and those who had won the war allocated the southern most parts of this ancient Austrian land to Italy. It was meant as a recognition of and reward to Italy for having broken the Tripartite Agreement with Austria and Germany and for then having sided with the Central Powers. Italy hadn't conquered South Tyrol through a military invasion; South Tyrol was merely occupied by Italy after the ceasefire. In the three and a half years of war at the southern front, not a single Italian soldier had set foot on South Tyrolean land, not a single drop of Italian blood had soaked our fields, while on the other hand, streams of South Tyrolean blood had been shed in order to defend our land. Italy only took final possession of South Tyrol when all hostilities had ceased. How prescient was Cesare Battisti, Italy's national martyr, when he warned his people not to annex the German land of South Tyrol lying north of Salurn.

After that war, swept by frenzied nationalism, Italy set about the Italianisation of South Tyrol. With whatever there was at their disposal, Italians strove to turn the ancient German land and people into an Italian one. Brutally, systematically and without any consideration, the fascist regime imposed Italianisation on the area. All villages, towns, rivers, mountains, valleys, meadows and farms were renamed and received Italian names. Everything that brought to mind German culture – be it costumes, songs, even Christmas trees or German gravestones – was forbidden, extinguished, banned. The South Tyrolean people were to become Italians, even if this necessitated the use of violence.

But just as all political coercion boomerangs, so too repercussions were not long in coming here. While the South Tyroleans succumbed to the dominant power, what smouldered underneath in response to the humiliations was opposition to the fascist dictatorship.

Then comes along this man in Germany who wanted to set right the injustice and the mistakes made in the Treaty of St Germain, and who intended to bring back the groups of people who had been severed from Germany, a man who planned to unite the entire German people into one single Reich. It was only natural, and thus nobody can fault the desperate South Tyrolean folk, that they would then place all their hope in that man. What they expected from him was to be saved from certain ruin and survive as one nation, one people, trusting that he would reunite the South Tyrol that had been so cruelly torn apart, fervently hoping that they be reunified into the German Reich.

But, instead, and against all expectations, Hitler proceeded to personally guarantee to Mussolini that the boundary of the Brenner would forever remain untouchable. And to top it off, both dictators, cynically and authoritatively, entered into mutual agreements which went over the heads of the people living in the land. That's how the 'option' came about. The choice put before each South Tyrolean demanded that they make a decision and, as it turned out, this went on to have an unbelievably tragic and long-lasting impact, and in so many cases led to utterly unsolvable moral conflicts.

When it came to the 'option', the people only had the choice of opting for German citizenship, with its obligation to emigrate to Germany, or of remaining in South Tyrol, but declare themselves prepared to retain Italian citizenship, which in turn would amount to them no longer being entitled to consider their nationhood as protected.[1] There was a third alternative, which was to not submit any declaration at all, remain passive so to speak, and those who went down that route remained Italian citizens.

As it happened, the majority (87 per cent) declared themselves German, choosing freedom; only a very small part opted for Italy.[2] I am not certain what reasons those South Tyroleans had when they committed themselves to Italy and not to Germany, but they would surely have weighed up the pros and cons of their decisions and these must be respected. But it was only a small portion of the population, mostly from within cities, and hardly any from the rural communities. Often the explanation for why some chose to remain is that these people realised that Hitler would embroil the world in a war. But this is a cheap argument, as this could surely only have dawned on these people *during* the war at the earliest, and certainly long after the South Tyrol Option Agreement had been not only been entered into, but also warmly welcomed and accepted.[3]

Perhaps there were indeed some very foresighted men who had an inkling of what the future would hold, and who might have thus preferred to remain in a fascist Italy than in a national-socialist Germany.

Often it was suggested that choices were based on financial and economic reasons. However, many people opted to hold on to their Italian citizenship in spite of having nothing to lose, either in terms of their career or in terms of their economic position. Their only reason to remain was that under no circumstances did they want to leave the homeland with which their families had been connected for centuries.

Those who remained founded the Südtiroler Volkspartei in 1945, surely much to the surprise of the Italians. In its mission statement they demanded their return to Austria.[4] After the war, the Allies viewed those *Dableiber* as the only trustworthy representatives of South Tyrol. They did in fact contribute to the eventual narrowing of the rift between those who had opted to leave and those who chose to remain, and have thus helped to unify the people once again. The vast majority of those who had left eventually returned to their homeland. I want to stress that the great majority of the South Tyroleans who at the time decided to take on German citizenship and thereby emigrate, loved their homeland just as much as those who declared that they wished to remain in South Tyrol. The world has many examples of people, groups and nations who much preferred to give up their original home and go out in the world than to stay put and sacrifice their nationhood, their character and their belief, and thus be oppressed. And nobody would dare declare those people traitors.

It seems a stroke of fate that today all South Tyroleans, both those who had declared themselves as Germans and those who decided to become Italian now live together as South Tyroleans in their old, original homeland, one which they all share. This way at least the injustice inflicted on them by history has partially been rectified.

The youth of South Tyrol did not fight and bleed for Hitler's Germany, nor for Austria, which of course didn't exist at the time, but only ever for their freedom, which they thought they had finally obtained, and which they simply could not bear to lose again. We were never National Socialists, we were only Germans who wanted to remain Germans. And because we couldn't live as Germans in our homeland, we were prepared to leave it behind.

How bitter the eventual disappointments were that we young soldiers had to endure in the course of the war can only be fathomed by those who had experienced them. The bright enthusiasm with which we had gone out to war turned into the bitter realisation that we fought a battle that had been forced upon us. Yet the truth is that we went through the war to its bitter end as upright, honest and conscientious soldiers, despite it all. None of us would ever have thought to switch to the other side; no South Tyrolean would ever have shot at a German.

The fact that in South Tyrol there exists a strong German people is entirely thanks to the efforts of all South Tyroleans, both those who opted for German citizenship and those who decided to remain in their homeland. One group proved that the South Tyroleans are German, the others have laid the building blocks for the creation of a new South Tyrol by founding the Südtiroler Volkspartei. Soon after its creation, all South Tyroleans were ready and able to acknowledge the Südtiroler Volkspartei as their only legal representative.

If Hitler, and with him Mussolini, had won the war, there would be no South Tyrol today, only an Alto Adige; no South Tyrolean could have changed that. But even the Italians had to recognise that in a democratic state, brute force cannot suppress or annihilate a cohesive group of people; only a dictatorship can do that. That's why a compromise was reached in the peace negotiations in Paris between the Allies and the Italians: while South Tyrol would remain part of Italy, the rights of its German minority would be fully recognised, and they had the legal right (within the framework of the state of Italy) to retain and indeed cultivate their language, culture and German traditions, in whichever way and manner they wished to do so.[5]

Our fallen comrades had sacrificed everything for the sake of retaining the ethnically German group of South Tyrol. It was they who died a hero's death, and thus gave testimony to how profound the fight for freedom of our German people was. I truly hope that today's younger generation, for whom freedom is natural and obvious, think about the fact that their fathers fought hard for this freedom and paid for it dearly with blood, sweat and tears.

All those involved, Germans and Italians, must draw lessons from our tragic past, one caused by confusion, fanatic nationalism and their disastrous developments. It must not be that violence, hate and terror inform our lives. Instead it is a duty for us all to ensure that our shared homeland is grounded in civil and human rights, and this can only come about if we are committed to mutual tolerance, mutual respect and a willingness to strive for it.[5]

Translator's Notes

All notes are by the translator.

Foreword

1 Landser is a colloquial German term for a German army soldier, a private, perhaps best equated with 'squaddie'.

1 Sterzing, 1938

1 The 1919 Treaty of Saint-Germain was signed by representatives of Austria on one side and the Allied Powers on the other. It declared that the Austro-Hungarian Empire was to be dissolved, and specified that South Tyrol be ceded to Italy.

2 Baiuvarii or Bavarians, a people who populated the majority of Old Bavaria, Austria and South Tyrol from the sixth century.

3 Andreas Hofer (1767– 1810), leader of the Tyrolean rebellion against the Napoleonic invasion during the War of the Fifth Coalition. He was captured and executed but is still seen as a folk hero and Austrian patriot.

4 The Kaiserjäger were regiments officially designated by the Imperial and Royal (k.u.k.) military administration as the Tiroler Jäger-Regimenter (Tyrolean Rifle Regiments). Despite the name, the regiments' members were not just recruited from other regions as well as the crown land of Tyrol. The regiments were disbanded in 1918 with the end of the k.u.k. monarchy.

5 A *Gstanzl* (Viennese German for 'stanza') is a mocking song that is especially known in the Austrian-Bavarian regions. *Gstanzln* are about simple folk, usually rural people, and are generally humorous, making fun of the authorities and the peculiarities of other people.

6 *Volksgemeinschaft* – people's community, an expression popularised during the First World War that appealed to the idea of breaking down elitism and uniting people across class divides to achieve a national purpose.

7 Here Sepp is referring to the two competing socio-political pressures he and his compatriots were under: Mussolini's political goals versus the goals of the German-speaking ethnic Germans who made up 90 per cent of the population.

8   Sepp writes '*klassisches Lyzeum*' which was a humanities-oriented upper secondary school usually teaching Latin and Greek, philosophy and theology and generally attended by the upper middle classes. The Matura is the equivalent of A-levels or the Baccalaureat allowing entry to university. In Switzerland this exam is called *Matura*, in Germany *Abitur*.

9   The Opera Nazionale Balilla (ONB) was an Italian Fascist youth organisation between 1926 and 1937, when it was absorbed into the Gioventù Italiana del Littorio (GIL), a youth section of the National Fascist Party.

10 *Schuhplattler* – traditional style of folk dance popular in the Alpine regions of Bavaria and Tyrol in which the performers stomp, clap and strike the soles of their shoes (*Schuhe*), thighs and knees with their hands held flat (*platt*). For the *Schuhplattler*, lederhosen and dirndls are a must.

11 Verein für das Deutschtum im Ausland (Association for German Cultural Relations Abroad), now the Goethe Institut, was a German cultural organisation engaged in espionage, using German minorities living in other countries. Its other goals included the preservation of German culture among 'racial Germans'. Hans Steinacher (1892– 1971) was chairman of the VDA from 1933 to 1937. He introduced the racial principle in the VDA, according to which only 'Germans of German descent' could be members. The agreement between Hitler and Mussolini of September 1937 brought about Steinacher's downfall. Mussolini granted Hitler a completely free hand in Austria and Czechoslovakia; in return, he demanded a free hand for the Italianisation of South Tyrol. Steinacher opposed Mussolini but also Hitler in his aim of having the German South Tyroleans repatriated into Germany. This offered his opponents a welcome opportunity to 'release him from office'.

2 The Big Disappointment

1   Adolf Hitler and Italian Duce Benito Mussolini met at the Brenner Pass to celebrate their Pact of Steel on 18 March 1940.

2   *Roaner*, dialect form of *Rain* – slope.

3   'W' stood for *Willkommen* – Welcome.

4   Hitler's special train, the *Führersonderzug* was named Führersonderzug 'Amerika' in 1940, and later Führersonderzug 'Brandenburg'. It was used as a headquarters until the Balkans campaign. Afterwards, Hitler continued to travel on it throughout the war between Berlin, Berchtesgaden, Munich and other headquarters.

5   *Blut und Boden* – Blood and Soil – was a maxim expressing the nineteenth-century German idealisation of a racially defined national body (blood) united with a settlement area (soil). The concept of *Lebensraum*, the belief

that the German people needed to reclaim historically German areas of Eastern Europe into which they could expand, is tied to it. Sepp in fact changes this, probably deliberately, to '*Feld und Blut*' – Field and Soil – perhaps in an attempt to distance himself from the Nazi slogan.

6   During French control of the region, it was officially called Haut Adige, or Alto Adige in Italian, in order to avoid any reference to the historical county of Tyrol.

7   Ortler – or König Ortler, as it is commonly called in German – is the highest moutain of the Ortler Range of the eastern Alps.

3 *Deutschland, Deutschland über Alles*: Berlin

1   In fact, it is not the Berlin dialect which is considered a sign of education, but rather the German spoken in Munich or Frankfurt.

2   The Hegelhaus at this address was at that time the home of the German Institute for Foreigners at Humboldt University.

3   Twenty Reichsmark equates to not quite £2.

4   Johann Wolfgang von Goethe's *Götz von Berlichingen* has the famous line known as the 'Swabian salute': '*er kann mich im Arsche lecken!*' – 'he can lick me in the arse!'

5   The German occupation of Norway and invasion of Denmark began on 9 April 1940.

6   'Der Grosse Kurfürst' – 'the Great Elector' – was Frederick William, Elector of Brandenburg and Duke of Prussia (1620–88). 'Der Alter Fritz' – 'the Old Fritz' – was Frederick II or Frederick the Great, King of Prussia and Elector of Brandenburg (1712–89). Gottfried von Berlichingen (1480– 1562), also known as Götz of the Iron Hand, was a mercenary knight and poet, the title character of Goethe's *Götz von Berlichingen*.

4 The Beginning Was so Innocuous: The Pfeifermühle, Allgäu

1   Siegfried Grabert was a highly decorated major of the Reserves in the Wehrmacht during the Second World War. He also received the Knight's Cross of the Iron Cross with Oak Leaves. He was killed on 25 July 1942 during a commando operation to destroy a dam between Rostov and Bataisk. In the text Grabert is referred to as second lieutenant, lieutenant and captain (which is the rank given on his gravestone).

2   Sepp refers to him as Hiller throughout, although other sources have his name as Hüller.

3 *Spiess* is the colloquial name for the mustering and administrative non-commissioned officer of a company.

5 *Zur Besonderen Verwendung*: Bad Vöslau

1 *Zur besonderen Verwendung* (zbV) translates as 'for special purposes'. In the army it implied that a military official had special duties assigned to him.

2 A pioneer is a soldier used in engineering and construction tasks. During the Second World War, pioneer units were used extensively by all major forces, both on the front line and in supporting roles. In this text, the terms pioneer and engineer will be used interchangeably.

3 The 'Bozner Bergsteigerlied' – Bozen mountaineer song – was one of the two unofficial hymns of the South Tyroleans (the other being the Andreas-Hofer-Lied). It was sung to the tune of an old Tyrolean craftsmen's song. Sepp quotes the first line here: 'How the world is so big and wide'.

4 Eduard Dietl (1890–1944) was commander of the 20th Mountain Army. Wilhelm Franz Canaris (1887–1945) was an admiral and chief of the Abwehr, the German military intelligence service, from 1935 to 1944. The Abwehr was divided into sections I, II and III – espionage, sabotage and counter-intelligence, respectively. He was among the military officers involved in the clandestine opposition to Nazi Germany and executed in the Flossenbürg concentration camp.

5 Here, it needs to be noted that 'adopting civilian dress or enemy uniform' did not contravene international law as long as the soldiers involved did not engage in combat dressed in foreign uniform. While the Brandenburgers were taught to always disguise themselves, they all did wear uniforms under their disguises. This made sure that they would be treated as uniformed enemy combatants and receive their due rights, rather than be executed as spies in the event of capture.

6 Sepp is referring to Peter Mayr (1767–1810), a Tyrolean innkeeper and freedom fighter against Napoleonic France and its allies.

7 Sepp's surname is spelled Giampietro. However, throughout the book, when he relates how he was addressed by his German colleagues or superiors, Sepp spells his name Tschampetro. This might be to convey how the Germans pronounced it, but perhaps also to Germanise his name, as the Italian spelling of his name must have rather pointed towards the Italianisation of the South Tyrol, which he, as a German South Tyrolean Landser, so opposed.

8 It might not be unreasonable to assume that Grabert, who was Sepp's role model, and who had wanted to become a doctor, influenced Sepp's later decision to study medicine – which he started during the war and then

resumed afterwards. Grabert continually calls Sepp by his Italian first name, which is indicative of how Grabert might have viewed him.

6 The Balkan Campaign

1   Kraft durch Freude (KdF) was a political organisation designed to supervise and synchronise the leisure time of the German population under the Third Reich. Among other things, it was a tour operator.

2   Kübelwagen is an abbreviation of Kübelsitzwagen, meaning 'bucket-seat car'; all German light military vehicles that had no doors were fitted with bucket seats to prevent passengers from falling out.

3   Pak – Panzerabwehrkanone, anti-tank gun.

4   General der Panzertruppe Rudolf Veiel (1883–1956) was a veteran of the First World War. In the Second World War, Veiel commanded the division during the Invasion of Poland in 1939, the Battle of France in 1940, Operation Marita, invasion of Yugoslavia and Greece, and Operation Barbarossa in 1941. On 3 June 1940, he was awarded the Knight's Cross of the Iron Cross. He was relieved of command because of complicity in the 20 July conspiracy to assassinate Hitler. Veiel spent two years in American captivity after the end of the war.

5   Wine with bread and salt is a welcome greeting ceremony in Slavic, some European and Middle Eastern societies.

6   The Model 39 Eihandgranate (or Eierhandgranate, 'egg hand grenade') was introduced in 1939 and produced until the end of the war.

7   *Geballte Ladung*, a concentrated charge or bundle charge was several stick grenades tied together with wire. Even though a concentrated charge might not be effective against armour, the concussions of an explosion on top of the turret or engine deck might break a track or penetrate upto 60mm of armour.

7 The Vale of Tempe, Early Spring 1941

1   Troops often sought protection in shell holes. Apart from the obvious shelter the craters offered, the soldiers believed that grenades or shells would never land in the same place twice.

2   Sepp writes that Litochoro was a fortress, but he is probably referring to the sixteenth-century fortified monastery, later destroyed by the Germans in 1943.

3   *Gepanzerte Mannschaftstransportwagen* or MTW, armoured personnel carrier.

4 OKW – Oberkommando der Wehrmacht, the High Command of the Wehrmacht.

5 *Sanka* is an acronym for *Sanitätskraftfahrzeug*, a term for German field ambulances.

6 The Panzerbüchse 39, or PzB 39, was a German anti-tank rifle.

8 Athens, Spring 1941

1 *Schmarren* is a German or Austrian sweet dish made of eggs, flour and milk, often served with compot, sugar and cinnamon.

2 HDV – Heeresdienstvorschrifft, the army service and conduct guidelines.

3 '*Thálatta! Thálatta!*' (also Thalassa, Thalassa) – 'The sea! The sea!' A quote from *Anabasis* by Xenophon.

4 BdM – Bund Deutscher Mädel, was the girls' wing of the Hitler Youth. There are no reports of BdM girls actually being in Greece, but film footage shows blonde girls waving and throwing flowers at the German soldiers entering Athens on 27 April 1941.

5 The army's Streifendienst was in charge of discipline and soldiers' conduct.

9 The Invasion of Russia, Summer 1941

1 Soldiers captured wearing foreign uniforms were not protected under the Geneva Convention 1929.

2 Hans-Wolfram Knaak (1914–41). In 1937 he was promoted to second lieutenant, and joined the Brandenburgers. As early as 1938, he was involved in the conspiracy by generals von Witzleben and Oster to assassinate Hitler. During the war he was awarded both classes of the Iron Cross and served as a company commander of 8th Company Lehr Regiment zbV 800 (the Brandenburg commandos). He received a posthumous promotion to Rittmeister.

3 These one-man holes were nicknamed *Russenloch* – Russian hole – and were used when necessary, but the two-man (*Wolfgrabhuegel* – wolf's den) was preferred as it offered soldiers moral support and allowed one to rest with the other on watch. Also, if a one-man position was knocked out, a wide gap was created in the defensive line, whereas with a two-man hole, if one man was lost, the other could still conduct the defence.

4 OKH – Oberkommando des Heeres, the Army High Command and Army General Staff from 1936 to 1945.

5 V-Leute – Vertrauensleute, a liaison person who worked as a permanent informant.

6 BK — Bordkanone, heavy-calibre (usually over 30mm) cannon on aircraft.

7 An orange signal meant: 'we are here'; a red one meant: 'enemy attacks'.

8 Sepp uses the word *Feuerzauber*, which indeed was the German Wehrmacht codename in 1942 for an enterprise to capture Leningrad. In this context he probably wanted to describe a barrage of firing and explosions.

9 Sepp refers to a *Seitengewehr*, a close-quarters combat weapon, first incorporated into the German army as a bayonet for the M1898 Mauser rifle, with a blade 50cm (19.7 inches) in length.

10 Dünaburg – modern-day Daugavpils, in Latvia – is a city in southeastern Latvia, an industrial centre that was one of the most important centres of Jewish culture in eastern Europe.

11 It is unclear why Sepp would write that the Brandenburgers 'were left in the dark', since they did know what their mission was. Perhaps he was distancing himself from the subsequent murder of the 16,000 Jews of the city, which he only found out about much later.

12 While in English 'masquerade' might equate to camouflage and a deceptive act, in German the word generally connotes carnivals and fancy-dress. Hence, the laughter.

13 I wonder whether Sepp is mistaken here as I cannot find a reference to Russian soldiers wearing the MG pistols on their shoulders.

14 During the German invasion of the Soviet Union, and with the loss of thousands of Russian men, there was a mass mobilisation of women too, called 'shotgun women' by the Gemans.

15 Erich von Manstein (1887–1973), a German commander who attained the rank of field marshal.

10 Bad Vözlau and Oberjoch im Allgäu, Early 1942

1 A few months have passed since the start of Operation Barbarossa and Sepp's arrival in Bad Vöslau in summer 1941. From this point the chapter covers the first winter months of 1942. The Oberjoch is some three hours away from his hometown of Sterzing.

2 RAD – Reichsarbeitsdients, the Reich Labour Service, was an agency created to help mitigate the effects of unemployment on the economy and to militarise the workforce.

3 Franz Hofer (1902–75) was the Nazi Gauleiter of the Tyrol and Vorarlberg and hence the most powerful figure in the region.

4 In Germany a war school was a military technical school that served to train officers.

5 A cheap *Volksempfänger* – People's Receiver – was put on the market primarily for propaganda reasons. The *Wunschkonzert für die Wehrmacht* – Request Concert for the Wehrmacht – claimed to broadcast music requested by men in the armed forces.

6 Sepp uses the term *Kameradschaftsabend*, loosely translated here as 'social evening'. The German term contains the component of 'camaraderie', connoting unity, cohesion, close friendship and loyalty – all elements so important to Nazi ideology.

11 Russia, Summer 1942

1 Wilhelm List (1880–1971), who had commanded the 14th Army in the invasion of Poland. From 1939 to 1941 he commanded the 12th Army in France and Greece, and was Commander-in-Chief South-East. In July 1942, he was Commander-in-Chief of Heeresgruppe A (Army Group A), on the Eastern Front.

2 'Muss i denn' is a Swabian German folk song. The melody and some verses of the song became widely known through Elvis Presley's 1960 adaptation of it as 'Wooden Heart'.

3 The Hungarian Puszta is part of the Pannonian Steppe.

4 Sepp does not specify what those injections were.

5 Soldatenheim – 'soldiers' home', a wartime institution designed to offer the German troops entertainment, good food, clean beds and regular friendly (but not solitary) interactions with the German Red Cross aides who worked there.

6 Seventeen and four is another name for the card game twenty-one, or blackjack.

7 The Gruppenführer, group leader, in this instance was Sepp.

8 Felix Martin Julius Steiner (1896–1966), commander of the 'Wiking' Division, which was mostly made up of non-German volunteers.

9 Stalinorgel – 'Stalin organ', the Germans' nickname for the Soviet Katyusha multiple rocket launcher because of its resemblance to a pipe organ, and the distinctive howling sound of its motors.

10 SMG – submachine gun.

11 *Hafthohlladung*, or *Panzerknacker* (Tank breaker) was a magnetic anti-tank grenade or mine. Sepp uses an abbreviated form: *Haftladung*.

12 Kerch is a city on the Kerch Peninsula in the east of the Crimea

13 'My girl is only a shop assistant in a shoe shop wiht a salary of 80 francs a week'. These lines are from a song with lyrics by Josef Benatzky from one of his very successful musicals, *Meine Schwester und ich*.

14 *Palatschinke* or *palacsinta* is a thin crêpe-like kind of pancake common throughout Central and Eastern Europe.

15 'Hitler wanted to denude the area of its existing inhabitants, up to 45 million through starvation and disease. He started by the deliberate extermination of prisoners from the Red Army, who were simply penned into barbed-wire enclosures in the open, denied food and medication, and left to rot. Altogether 3.3 million of them died in the course of the war, nearly 60 percent of the total Red Army prisoners taken; 300,000 were dead already by the end of 1941, before the German armed forces and war economy administrators began to use them for forced labour in Germany'. (Richard Evans, *The Third Reich at War*, London, Penguin, 2009)

16 This particular question resonates with the German title Sepp had given his book: *Das Falsche Opfer?* (*The Wrong Sacrifice?*). In Sepp's mind, the war was wrong, the decision for the South Tyroleans to join the war was wrong, and in that light the sacrifice – i.e. South Tyrol – could not be justified.

17 i.e. The Greater German army rather than the Greater German people.

18 On 29 July 1942 the Germans cut the last direct railway link between central Russia and the Caucasus, causing panic among the High Command of the Russian armed forces , which led to the passing of Order No. 227 'Not a step back!'

19 A Potemkin village is any construction (real or figurative) built solely to deceive others into thinking that a situation is better than it really is.

20 Ernst Prochaska (1917–1942) was the new company commander who took over after the death of Grabert.

21 In German Sepp's sentence alludes to a clever play on words. The German word *Zug*, platoon, comes from the word 'to pull'. *Flaschenzug* is a pulley, one part which is called an 'idler pulley' a piece of the equipment which, while not exactly a waste of space, only serves to guide or take up the slack as opposed to the driver pulley, which applies force.

22 In the literature it is Freiherr Adrian von Fölkersam (1914–1945) who seems to get more credit for the Brandenburger operation. He was a German Brandenburger and Waffen-SS officer who headed a different unit which launched a simultaneous attack on Maikop.

23 The literature often points out that risky operations carried out to obtain honours and awards cost many soldiers their lives. An officer who wanted to decorate his naked neck with a Knight's Cross at the expense of his men's lives suffered, in military jargon, from *Halsschmerzen*, a sore throat.

24 *Gugelhupf* is a traditional yeast-based cake, usually made in a distinctive round mould.

25 Sepp uses the German *kurzen Prozess*, which translates as 'short trial' but in this instance, of course, there was no trial whatsoever.

26 After the operation a sign with the inscription 'Ernst Prochaska bridge' was attached at the Belajabrücke as homage to him.

27 The 16th Infantry Division was nicknamed Windhund (Greyhound), as their divisional motto was: 'Quick as a greyhound, tough as leather, hard as Krupp steel, Greyhounds in front'.

28 I-Staffel – infantry squadron.

29 Paul Alois Octavian Hubertus Maria Haehling von Lanzenauer (1896–1943).

12 The End of the War, Early 1943 to Spring 1944

1 Sepp skims over many months of his own war engagement, offering little information on the operations to which he or the Brandenburgers were assigned. The war with the Partisans to which he refers included some excessive and brutal incidents that were condoned and encouraged. Perhaps this might explain Sepp's lengthy moral considerations in this part of the book.

2 Lawrence Paterson writes in *Hitler's Brandenburgers* (London: Greenhill, 2018) that the tenor of the partisan fights was 'ruthless destruction' as per Hitler's directive (18 October 1942): 'no one should be held to account for conducting themselves with excessive harshness.'

3 Sepp is probably referring to the codenamed 'Kugelblitz' mission. Carlo Gentile writes in *Wehrmacht und Waffen-SS im Partisanenkrieg: Italien 1943–1945* (Paderborn: Ferdinand Schöningh, 2012) that excessive and brutal incidents against civilians committed at the time by the German units relate to 'the radicalisation of the then pervasive climate and dictated from above' which condoned the 'panorama of terror'.

13 The Return

1 GVH – Garnisons-Verwendungsfähig-Heimat, suitable for garrison duty at home.

2 The Volkssturm was a national militia established during the last months of the war. In *Wehrmacht und Waffen-SS im Partisanenkrieg* (2012) Carlo Gentile refers to criminal acts, the killing of civilians and partisans in Italy, committed mostly 'by young officers who had brought their methods of operating back from the war in the east'.

3 Merano was one of the main places in South Tyrol welcoming and offering a home to German soldiers, Nazi war criminals and high-ranking SS officials.

4 Ami – German slang for an American soldier.

5 'No identity card, 5 o'clock already, tomorrow again, 9 o'clock.'

6 Sterzing was a hub for Nazis escaping the Allies, imprisonment and prosecution, including Erich Priebke and Adolf Eichmann.

7 *Heimkehrer* – homecomer or returnee.

8 Peppele or Peppi is a common diminutive term for Joseph or Sepp.

9 *Sperrgebiet* – a prohibited area.

10 Tyrolean, unlike Hochdeutsch (High German), has a sweet, slightly childish tone which is rather endearing, charming the listener. High German can easily sound harsh and abrasive, especially to the ears of a Viennese Jew.

11 Sepp uses the term *landverschickt* not evacuated. *Kinderlandverschickung* (KLV) was intended above all to serve the purposeful and intensive ideological education of youth in National Socialism. The term *Evakuierung* (evacuation) was avoided and the term *Erweiterte* (extended) KLV was used instead.

Afterword

1 Sepp uses the word *Volkstum* translated here as 'nationhood', which was particular in its tenor to the National Socialists' language best described as the ethnic traditions of a people or ethnic minority – in marked opposition to the ideals of the French Revolution, such as universal human rights. This sense of the word is now criticised in academia, though it is still in use in the protection of ethnic minorities and is a legal standard in Austria.

2 This figure (which translates to 200,000) is misleading. The number of those who actually left was only 75,000. Firstly, the NS regime and its planning departments followed a complex resettlement plan making emigration impossible. Secondly, the clergy and religious families didn't want to leave, nor farmers owning land; women also opted to stay, though that didn't transpire in the applications as only men needed to sign these. Families didn't want to emigrate to a country where their sons would be drafted. By 1943 only some 73,000 had left, and thereafter emigration ceased altogether. (Michael Wedekind, *Breaking Point of the Axis*, 2015).

3 It might indeed not have been such a cheap argument but a well-founded one. The Option Agreement was entered into on 21 October 1939. At that point Germany was already at war. Furthermore, the South Tyroleans had until 31 December 1939 to decide. The possibility that young men moving to Germany would be drafted was therefore real.

4   Südtiroler Volkspartei – the South Tyrolean People's Party.
5   This book was initially published in German in 1984. Since then, the handing
    over of identical declarations by Austria and Italy to the UN Secretary-
    General in June 1992 marked the official settlement of the dispute on the
    implementation of the Paris Agreement. But Austria continues to exercise
    the protective function concerning South Tyrol's autonomy

    The Austrian government programme for 2017–22 envisages to grant,
    in the spirit of European integration and an ever closer union of citizens,
    members of the German- and Ladin-speaking ethnic groups in South Tyrol,
    for whom Austria exercises a protective function, the possibility to acquire
    Austrian citizenship in addition to their Italian citizenship.